IMAGES
of America

WEWAHITCHKA

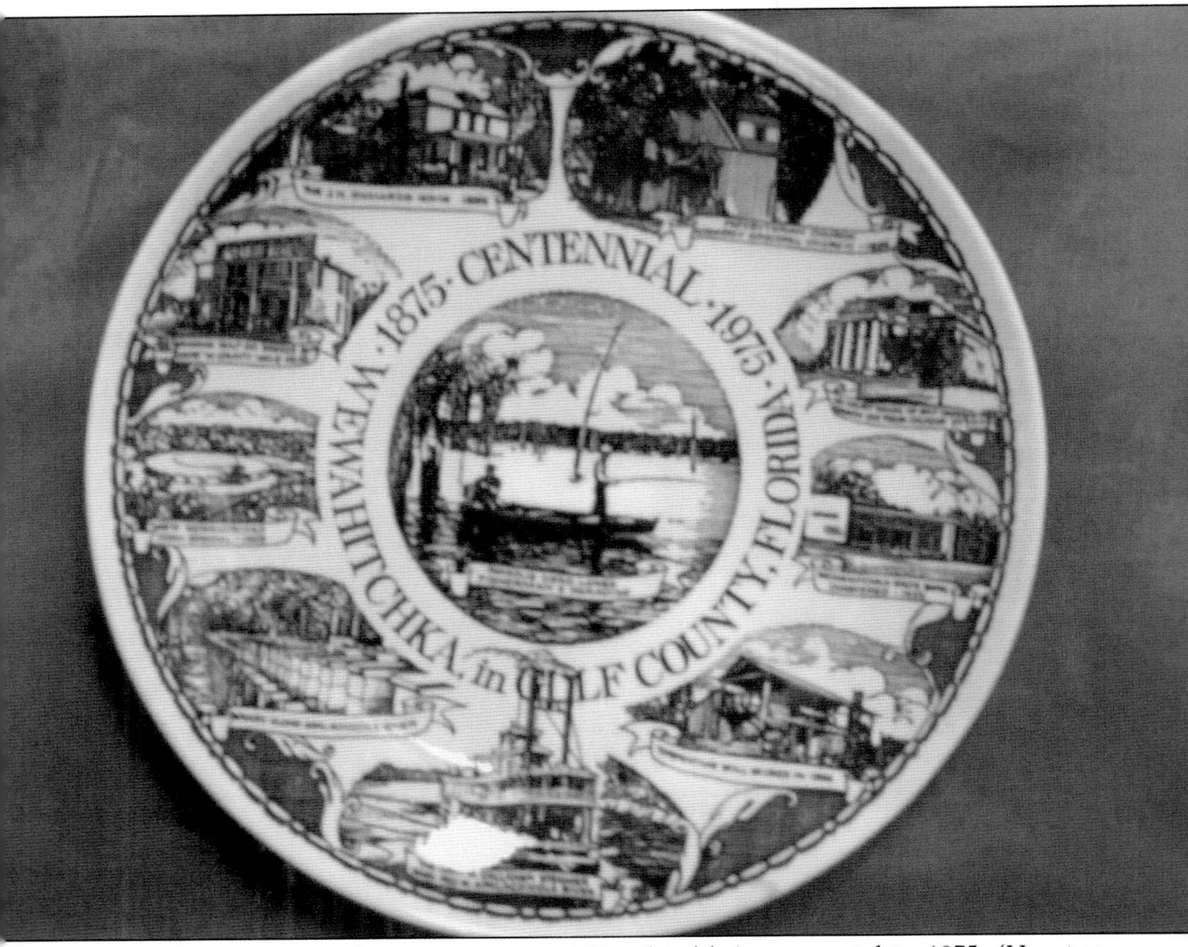

This plate was created to commemorate Wewahitchka's centennial in 1975. (Henrietta Darley Branch.)

On the Cover: Thomas McDaniel and his son Terry McDaniel are pictured fishing in the Dead Lakes around 1956. (Penny McDaniel McLemore.)

IMAGES
of America

WEWAHITCHKA

Beverly Mount-Douds

ARCADIA
PUBLISHING

ISBN 978-1-4671-1406-6

Published by Arcadia Publishing
Charleston, South Carolina

Printed in the United States of America

Library of Congress Control Number: 2014957935

For all general information, please contact Arcadia Publishing:
Telephone 843-853-2070
Fax 843-853-0044
E-mail sales@arcadiapublishing.com
For customer service and orders:
Toll-Free 1-888-313-2665

Visit us on the Internet at www.arcadiapublishing.com

In memory of my good friend George Core, with whose help and guidance my knowledge of Gulf County history has become my life's goal and more!

Also in memory of Betty Ann Gaskin Owens, who passed away April 17, 2015, just as this book was being completed. I love you and will miss you always!

Contents

ACKNOWLEDGMENTS

I want to thank the people of the northern part of Gulf County, the girls at the Wewahitchka Library, my friends on Facebook, and the families of Dalkeith, Overstreet, Kinard, and especially Wewa! Without you, this book would not be here today. A few others that I would like to acknowledge are my dear friends Angie and Alfred Whitfield, David Taunton, and all the stories from the *Gulf County Breeze* and from older newspapers' editors like Larry Evens, Ed Banjough, and Claude Hanlon. My very good friend Mr. George Core left to me papers and photographs. So many others provided photographs and stories that if I tried to name you, I would run out of word space. So, you know who you are, and I thank you from the bottom of my heart.

Photograph credits and courtesies are listed as follows: Angie Hires Dean (AHD), Barbara Redman Vickery (BRV), Betty Ann Glass Williams (BGW), Bobby King (BK), Henrietta Darley Branch (HDB), Bruce Husband (BH), Buck Rhames (BR), Bunny Bandjough (BB), Carol Ann Longshore Childress (CALC), Carolyn Britt Witten (CBW), Cedric Lenox (CL), Connie Whitfield (CW), Donna Dozier (DD), Doris Jean Rish Whitten (DJRW), Elaine Millergren Kennedy (EMK), Feraldine Hall Greer (FHG), Fran Forehand Walters (FFW), Gene Hanlon (GH), Grady Dean (GD), Iris Davis Corbett (IDC), James Ernest Rish (JER), James Jones (JasJ), Jerry and Joey Canning Turner (JJT), John Bishop (JB), June Nunery Causey (JNC), Kandi Ward Rollins (KWR), Kathay Gaskin Tillman (KGT), Kay Lister Whitfield (KLW), Linda Gale Borders and Gil Shealy (LGS), Marie Walters Wimbery (MWW), Martha Costin Spiva (MCS), Mary Giddens (MG), Mary Weeks Pitts Rollins (MWPR), Mary Ann Kilbourn Smith (MAKS), Mytrice Alford Dean (MAD), Norma Ramer Gibbs (NRG), Pam Gaskin Sumner (PGS), Penny McDaniel McLemore (PMM), Rhonda Murphy Pridgeon (RMP), Sandra Abreu Batson (SAB), Sandra Bass Joines (SBJ), Sandra McDaniel Causby (SMC), Scotty Brown (SB), Sherry Strength Whitson (SSW), Susan Carter (SC), Terry H. Linton (THL), Tom Godwin (TG), Tunnie Wade Miller (TWM), Tim Wade (TW), Weldon Davis (WD), Wewa Library Ladies (WLIB), Wilber and Mary Linda Butts (WMB), and George Core (GC).

INTRODUCTION

The Wewahitchka area is a very intriguing and beautiful place. To understand how Wewahitchka was born, it is necessary to go back in time about 150 years. In the early 1800s, there were no roads in West Florida; in fact, Florida was not a state, but a territory claimed by both France and Spain. Why would people want to settle here when they had the entirety of North America to select a place to build a community? The answer to that question is that the area around Wewahitchka had something that was attractive: the Apalachicola River system, which included the Chipola River. The river was a means of transportation. Sometime in the early 1800s, farmers began looking for a place to settle in the territory of Florida. Some came down the river on barges (called "float boats") and some came by mule and wagon. They were looking for farmland near the river.

The Iola area was the perfect place. A number of families settled in this area, and within a few years, there were several big farms and some of the first orange groves in North America. At the same time, the farm areas on both sides of the river in Alabama and Georgia were making great strides in planting cotton. That area of Alabama and Georgia had only one way to ship the cotton to market—it had to go down river to the seaport of Apalachicola. In the 1820s, steamboats were introduced to the cotton trade. All the cotton ended up in Apalachicola for shipment to textile mills around the world.

First, it is important to know that there were two Iolas. Here is a brief history of the first: Iola was located in the northeast corner of Section 4, T4s R9W, on what was then known as Tennessee Bluff. The only official map shows the railroad tracks of the Iola & St. Joseph Railroad Company running through the center of town, which had 10 blocks on the south side of the tracks and 11 blocks on the north side. The entire town covered about 35 acres. The railroad tracks ran down the street along the river where about 1,000 feet of dock area and warehouses stood. The railroad company operated about three years. Railways were constructed from Columbus, Georgia, to several port cities on the Atlantic coast. The cotton trade no longer went downriver by steamboat; it was shipped by train to ports on the East Coast. The Iola & St. Joseph Railroad Company filed for bankruptcy, and all of its property was sold at auction at the courthouse in Abe Springs. Everything was gone; even the brick streets went down in the mud.

But the Iola area was still attractive. Almost every hunter and fisherman in Alabama and Georgia wanted to go to the second Iola, located near the site of the first Iola on the Chipola River, later known as the Dead Lakes. It was easily accessible for people from Alabama and Georgia via the lake; the steamboats continued running the river but now carried all kinds of freight, passengers, mail, and livestock. The old dock area at the first Iola was used for a port of call for the new Iola on the lake. The difference was that a gangplank was now used for loading and unloading.

The H.A. Rish family owned a hotel there, and the R.T. Humbers from Greenville, Mississippi, owned a three-story hotel. There were several boardinghouses, one of them owned by J.W. Schuessler. This building was still standing in 1949—not only was it a boardinghouse, it was also the post office for the new Iola. Most of these residents were educated and owned businesses in their old hometowns. There were seven medical doctors in Iola. There were many high-class fishing and hunting clubs: La West Fishing Club, Barksdale Hunting & Fishing Club, Thronateeska Fishing Club, and Muscogee Club—with all but the Barksdale club active today. According to James Rish, who lived in the Rish Hotel as a small boy, the prime lifetime of Iola was between 1904 and 1922.

It seems that the two Iolas were first-class places. Some evidence of the area as a promising boomtown include the railroad providing transportation by land, the many steamboats that made Iola a regular port of call, the types of people who were moving there, and the region's soil. Col. Henry D. Stone, who first settled Iola, lived upriver a mile from the city. He was a landowner and farmer, served with Gen. Andrew Jackson, was later appointed president of the Territorial Council of West Florida, and was engaged in river activities.

Iola had several livery stables, five mercantile stores, and two gristmills. One could hire almost any type of help needed. Roads were now being built all over the United States, giving access to many areas such as Iola. Some of those living at Iola moved to the new settlement at what became Wewahitchka; it was not named at that time.

People were moving into the new town as early as 1874. The Stone family from Iola and the Richards families were the first to move to Wewahitchka. About the same time, Dr. John W. Keyes came here. According to John W. Richards, who preached the first sermon in a small log house built to serve as both a school and a church, he was requested to name the town. Keyes painted a sign with the name Wewahitchka on it and nailed it above the front door. People were now moving in from Alabama, Georgia, and Tennessee to Iola and to Fort Place, Mississippi. Amanda Richards, who was a longtime postmistress, said there were 10 families when her father, Norman, moved his family here in 1874, and there were about 30 families by 1876. Some of those following the Richards families were the Keyes, Stones, Maddoxes, Donaldsons, Stranges, McDaniels, Spencers, Smiths, Redds, Burgesses, and Bryants. Then, a little later, came the Shippy, Alderson, Mack, Higgins, Hollinger, Isabell, Whitfield, Taylor, Lanier, Rish, Meriwether, Hunter, Lister, and Gaskins families. Many residents today are direct descendants of these early settlers.

Wewahitchka had many outstanding men. Higgins, Hollinger, and Bryant were big in orange groves, lumber, and farming. George Gaskin was big in turpentine, farming, and cattle; later, his family owned the bank and was involved in real estate, sawmills, and lumber. John Griffin was big in cattle, with his specialty being milk cows. The Burgess family was big in timber and orange groves. Charlie Morgan was big in timber. The Lanier family was and continues to be involved in the honey business.

The first church in Wewahitchka was constructed by Frances Charles Rummel. The land description of the Episcopal church (later sold to the Presbyterian church), as recorded in the courthouse, states that the church was built facing the Marianna-Apalachicola Road, a two-rut roadway that is now State Road 71.

Wewahitchka has produced two medical doctors—Dr. John Washington Keyes and Dr. Thomas Meriwether. Dr. Keyes was the son of Gen. George Keyes and grandson of John Wade Keyes Sr., who fought in the Revolutionary War and was married to the niece of President Monroe. Dr. Keyes's brother Wade Keyes was assistant attorney general of the Confederate States of America throughout the Civil War. Dr. Keyes's name was at the top of any list in the state for outstanding medical doctors. The two lakes in town were named after Dr. Keyes's twin daughters, Alice and Julia.

One

Wewa Roots

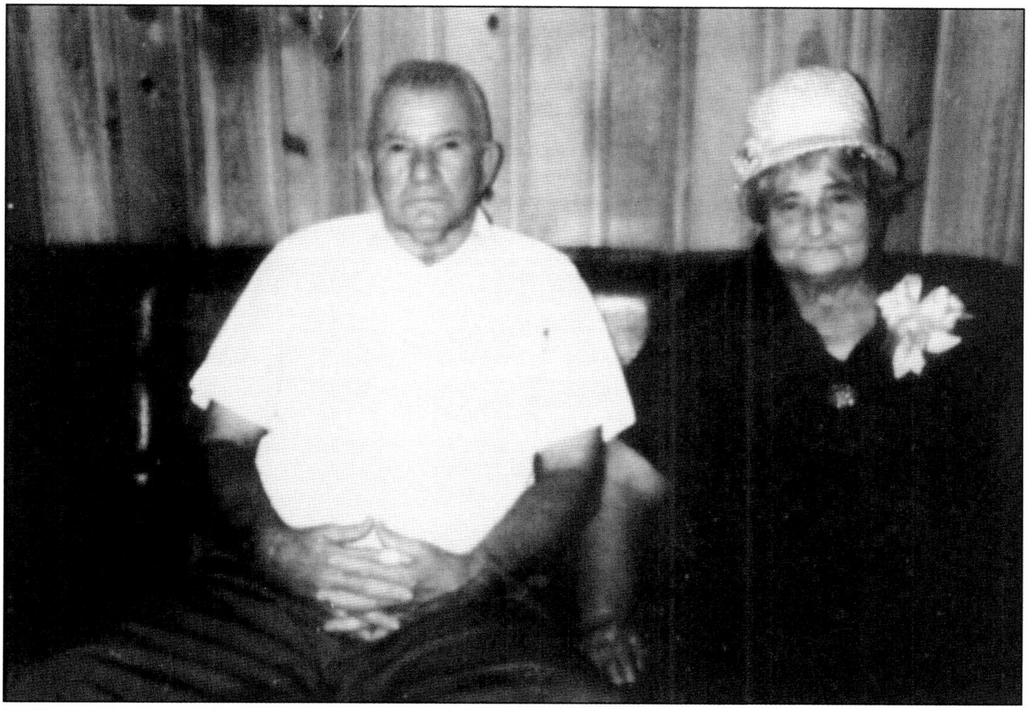

William Elias Branch Jr. came to Overstreet through his marriage to Lula Whitfield. While living in Calhoun County and after her death, he moved his family back to Overstreet to operate the ferry there on the canal. He married Lillie Hare and moved their family back to Wewahitchka. Branch worked in construction and farming, and both he and Lillie continued to live in town until their deaths. They are pictured here at a wedding in 1970. (HDB.)

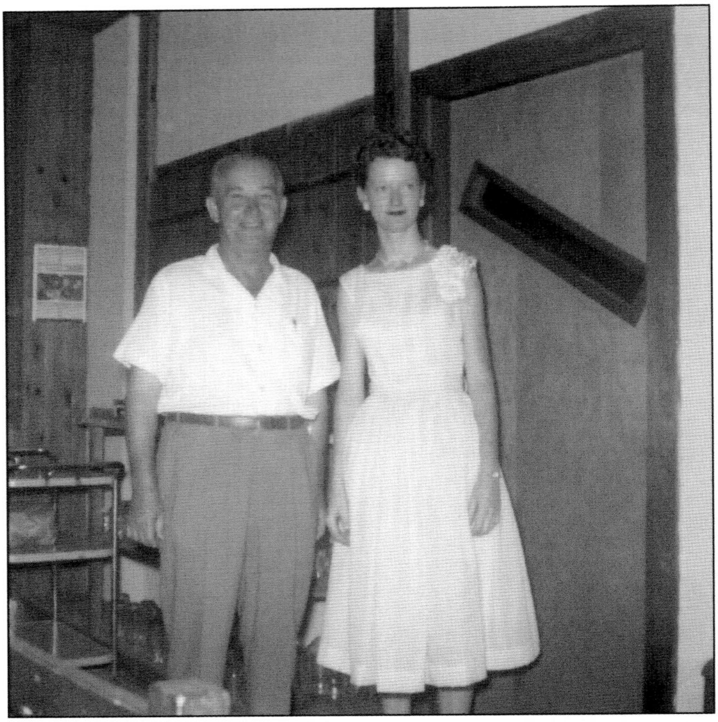

Family friend Sammy Patrick (left) performed the 1960 wedding of Betty Ruth Glass (right), daughter of Cecil and Sally Mae (Pitts) Glass, to Larry Williams. Patrick was Gulf County's veteran property appraiser for over 48 years and a resident of Wewahitchka since 1916. He also ran in 1940 for the position of tax assessor and was in office for another eight years. Patrick passed away in 1980. (BGW.)

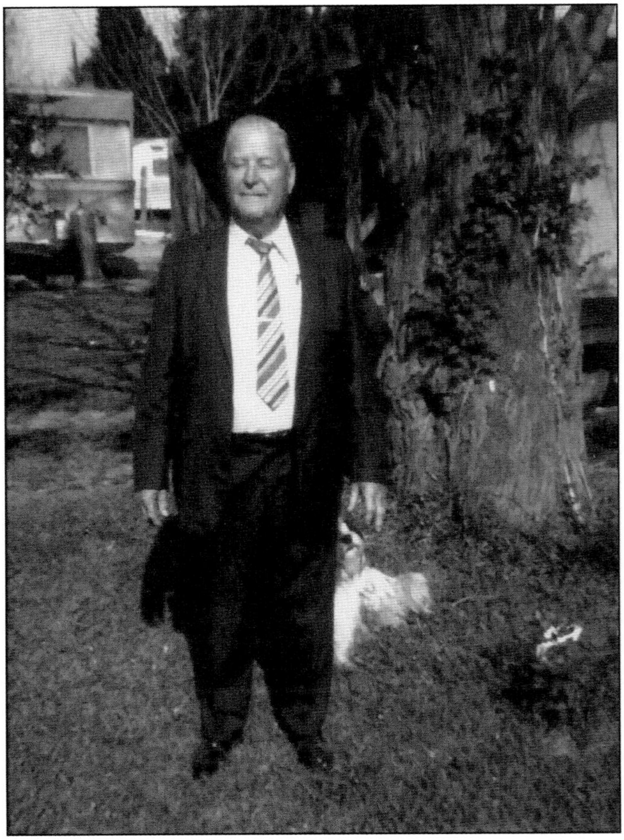

Cecil Glass, the owner of a local meat market, was a big, strong, and rugged-looking man. Everyone remembers him as the man who rode around town in an old car with a huge loudspeaker on top. Cecil would drive up and down the road telling people the price of his meats that day or what movie was playing at the Iona Theater. (BGW.)

Dave Gaskin, a member of a pioneer turpentine and timber family, was born in Kinard, Florida. The son of George and Kate B. Gaskin, Dave was the president of the Wewahitchka State Bank, and a leader in the Florida Bankers Association. His wife, Annie E. (née Traylor), started the Gaskin/Graddy Insurance Company. Dave also had one sister, Violet "Sis," who married Frank Graddy. Their children are still in Gulf County today. (FFW.)

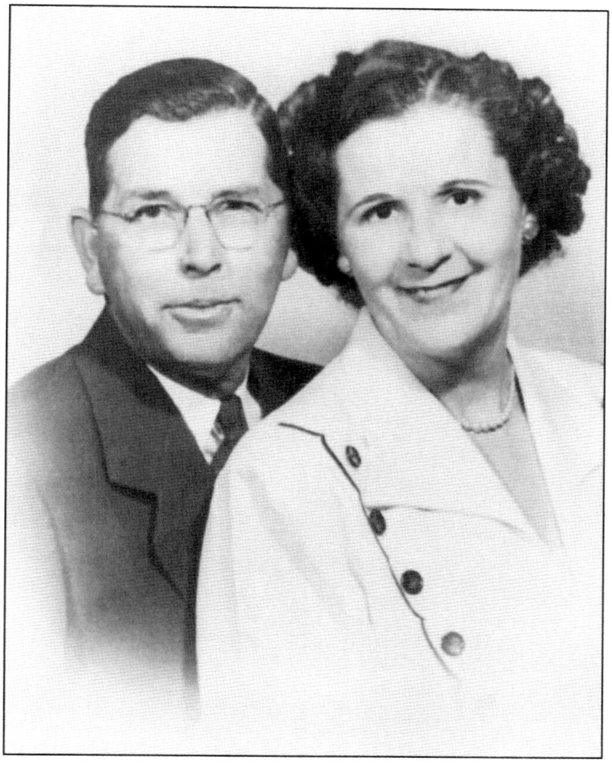

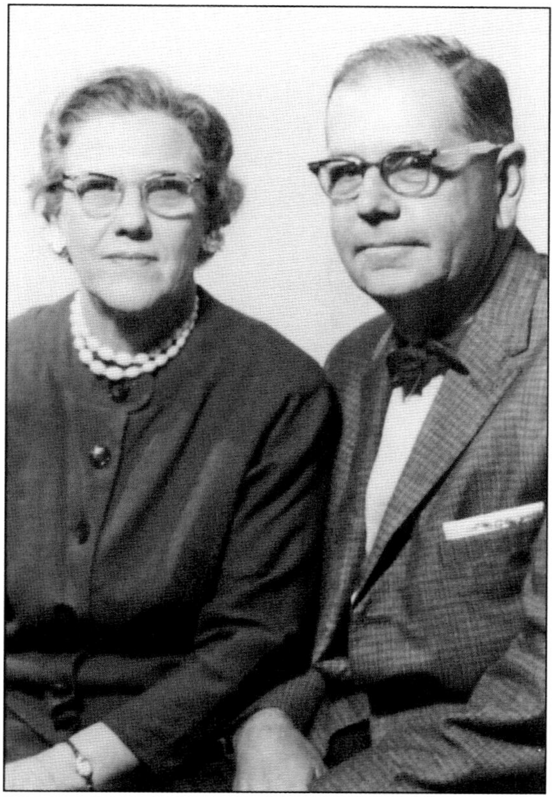

Rudy Sr. and Anna Belle Gaskin were the parents of Betty Ann Gaskins Owens and Rudy Jr. and former owners of the Iona Theater in Wewahitchka. Anna Belle attended Florida State College and taught school for over 35 years. Rudy Sr. was in the turpentine business, and he had stills in and around Marysville and Indian Bayou until the 1940s. After the war, the timber industry took off, and Rudy Sr. and his brother Charles went into the sawmill business. (FFW.)

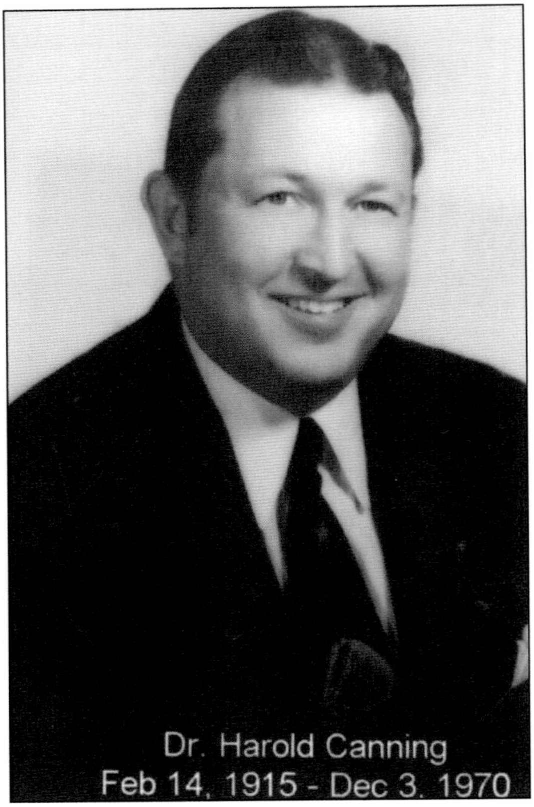

Dr. Harold B. Canning is a man who believes in turning the other cheek. He has been mayor of Wewahitchka longer than any man or woman in history and has devoted a lifetime to "community projects" of one sort of another. Dr. Canning graduated from Emory Medical School, then spent several years in Africa. He settled in Wewahitchka nearly two decades ago and served as the city's physician. (JJT.)

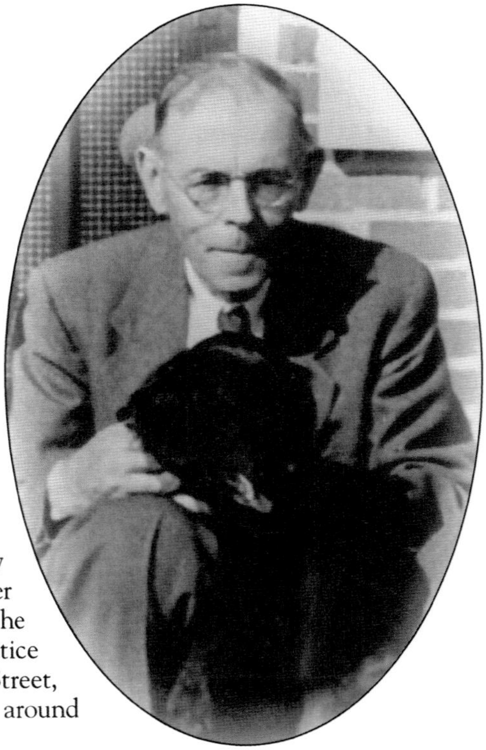

Thomas Meriwether was a doctor in Montgomery when he was hired to come to Wewahitchka to deliver Emmie Millergren. He fell in love with the hunting, the fishing, and the people in the area, moved his practice and family to town, and built a house on Main Street, which had his office in the back. Meriwether died around 1949. (MAKS.)

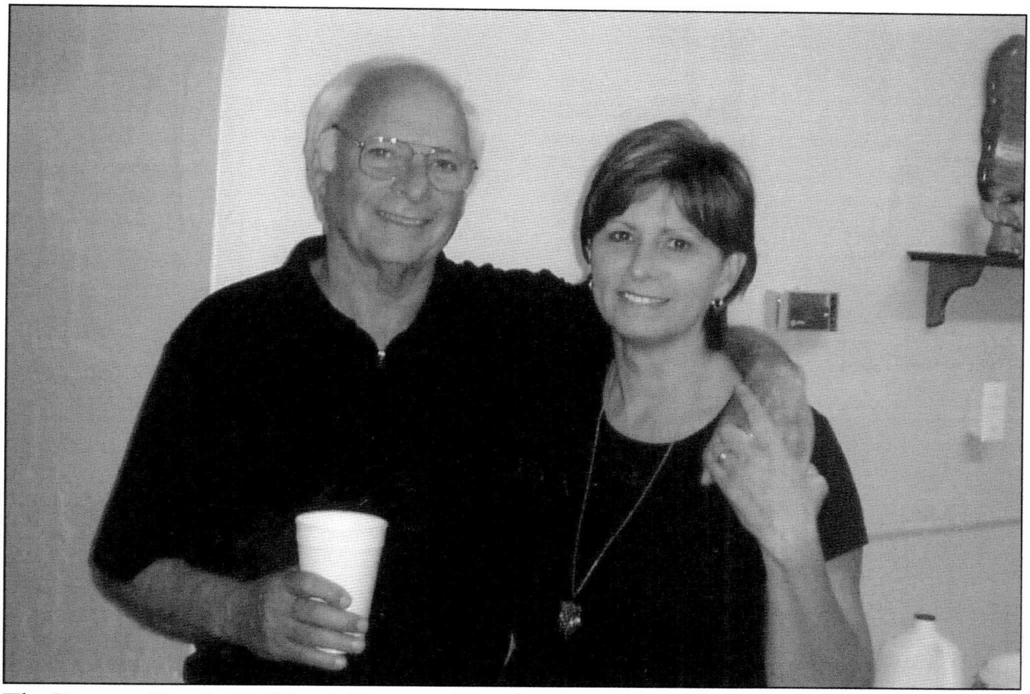

The Taunton Family Children's Home in Wewahitchka is a privately funded home operated by David and Abigail Taunton (pictured), who began caring for children in 1979 and have adopted many children and provided a home for more than 150 youngsters. David, a former high school principal and Methodist lay minister, was also the county judge for several years in Gulf County. Daughter Diana is now taking over as a caregiver. (HDB.)

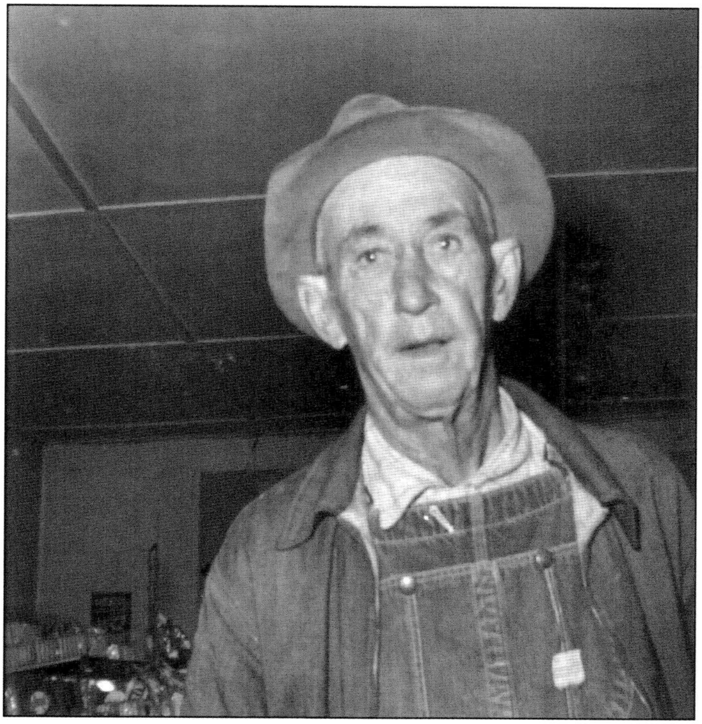

Malachi C. "Mallie" Skipper, a citizen of Wewahitchka and friend to many, was the spouse of Lavonia Ola (Jackson) and the father to Inez, Montez, Otis, and Billie. The Skippers, who were from Alabama, married in 1925 and moved to Gulf County between 1935 and 1940. Both are buried here, in Jehu Cemetery. (PMM.)

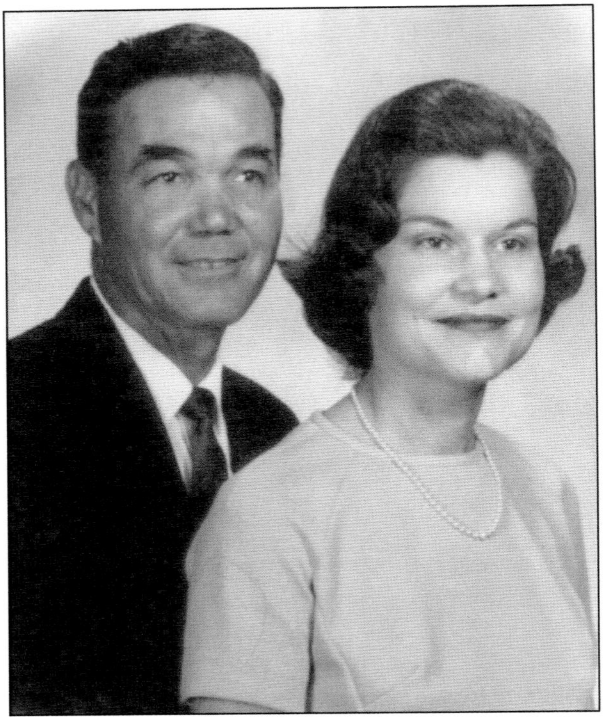

Alfred and Angeline (Santo) Whitfield are typical Wewahitchka folks. Born in Gulf County, Alfred got his first view of the outside world when he joined the Army and went overseas. After the Army, he returned home to join his family in the beekeeping business. In 1949, Angeline Santo answered an advertisement for a home economics teacher and moved to the area to teach. She later met and married Alfred, and they raised their family here. (CW.)

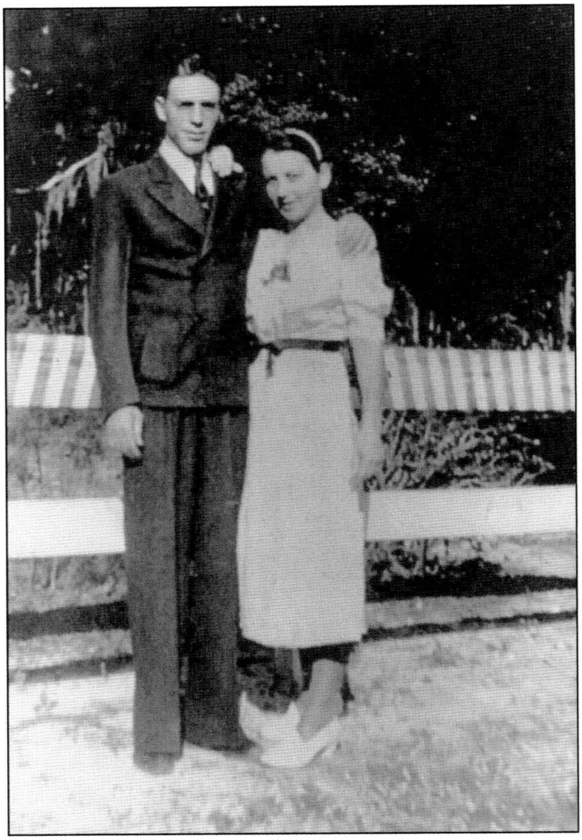

Cecile June (Melton) and John Milton Whitfield married here in Gulf County in July 1935. Married for over 68 years, they were lifelong residents of Wewahitchka and served as officers for the Glad Tidings Assembly of God Ministries. Cecile and John had five children. Cecile passed away in 2003, and John, shortly afterwards. (CD.)

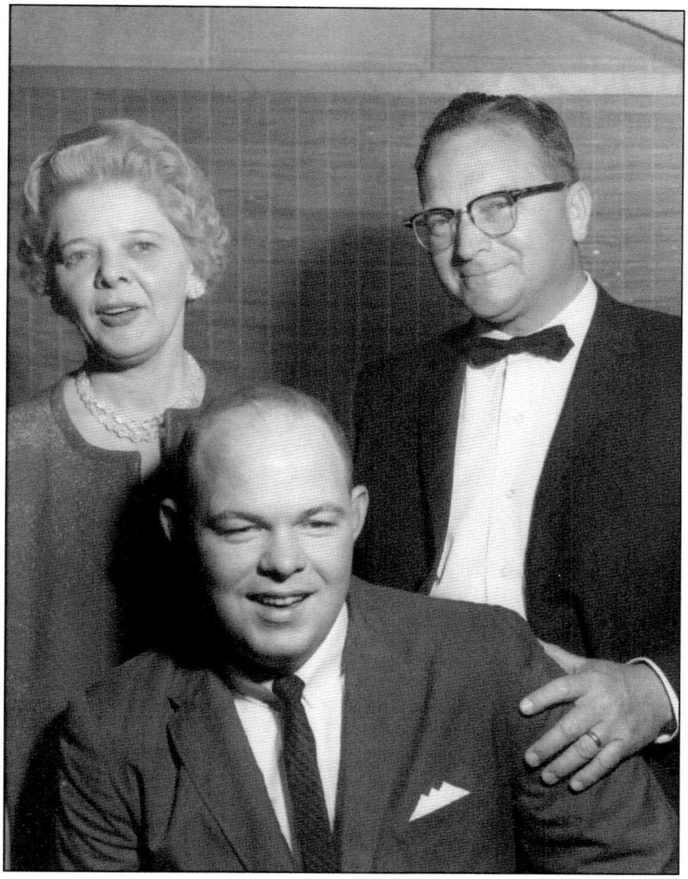

Eddie Belle White, the youngest of eight children, grew up in the Lister Still commissary owned by her father, Henry C. Lister. From 1932 to 1938, White resided in Lynn Haven, where her father ran a second turpentine still. White was the oldest licensed hairdresser in the state of Florida, lived into her 80s, and worked up until her death. She is pictured here with her son Clay Cox (center) and her husband, Larry White (right). (KLW.)

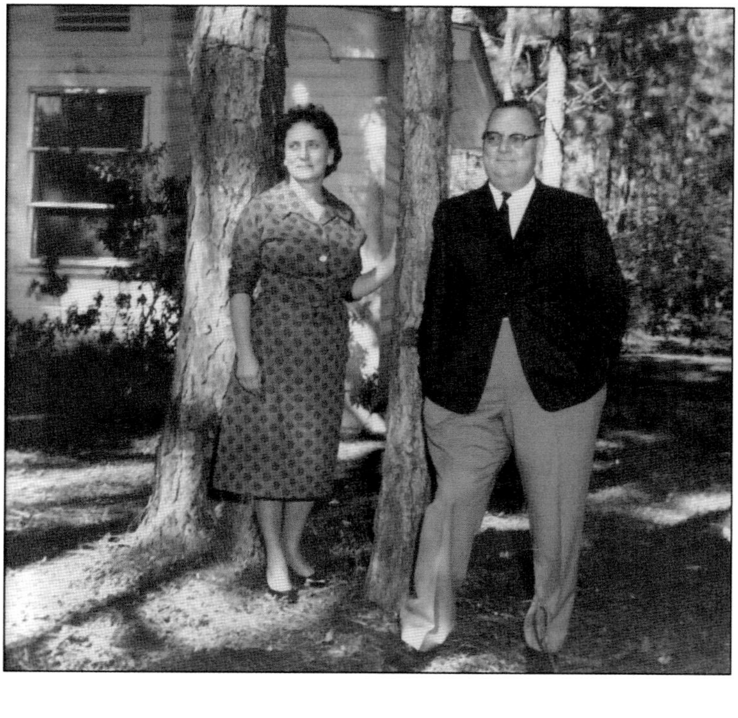

Floyd and Doris Lister met in grammar school and were married in 1946. Floyd was a building contractor who constructed homes. In later years, he became a pulpwood dealer. Floyd was a generous community leader and businessman. Folks looked up to him. Doris worked with him in his office. They had three children—Bodie, Kay, and Debbie. Doris was a sweet, kind, and devoted Christian who practiced her faith. (KGT.)

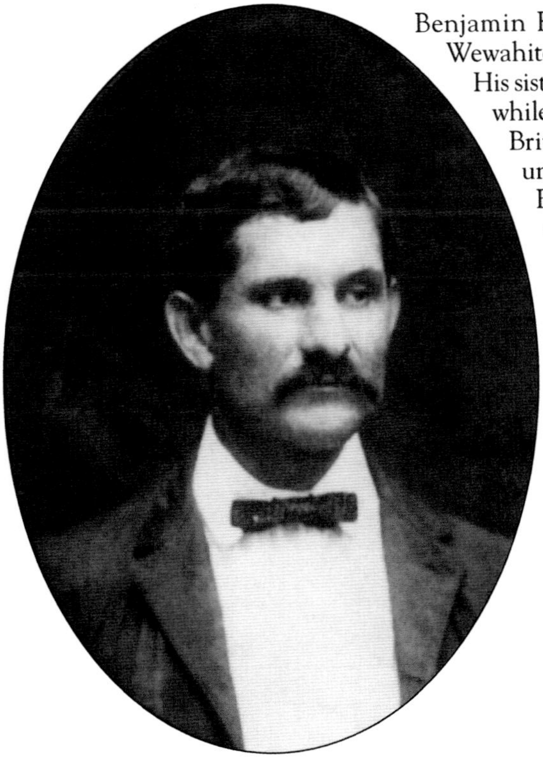

Benjamin Franklin Britt followed his two sisters to Wewahitchka from North Carolina in the late 1800s. His sisters—one was named Smithy—ran two hotels, while Benjamin worked in the turpentine industry. Britt married Hettie McDaniel in 1903. Their union produced four sons and a daughter before Benjamin's untimely death in 1921 at the age of 51. (CBW.)

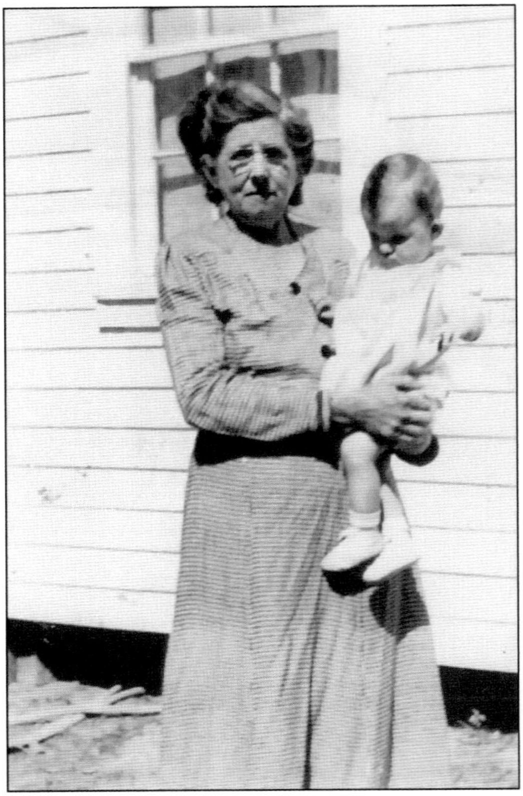

Hettie McDaniel Britt is shown here holding Carolyn Britt Witten, one of her three granddaughters. This photograph was taken in 1946 during Carolyn's first trip to visit her grandmother in Wewahitchka, after her father's discharge from the Army following World War II. Hettie was a wonderful cook and operated Britt's Cafe in downtown Wewahitchka. The café was later operated by her son and daughter-in-law, Sam and Irene Britt. (CBW.)

Burice Vivian (Davis) Gaskin was the wife of Jesse Gaskin. Soft-spoken and with a gentle nature, she was the mother of two beloved daughters, Kathay (left) and Betty Jo Gaskin. This photograph was taken around 1945 in Wewahitchka, where they grew up and developed great love for their families, friends, and community. (KGT.)

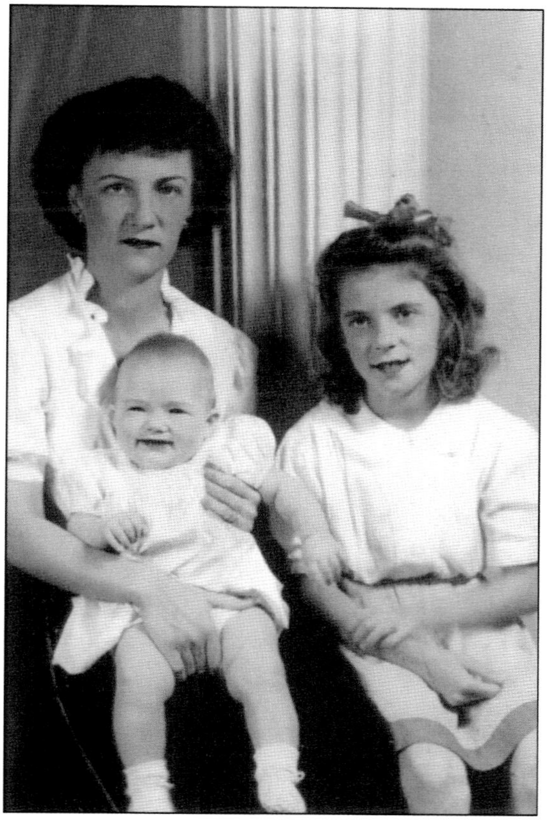

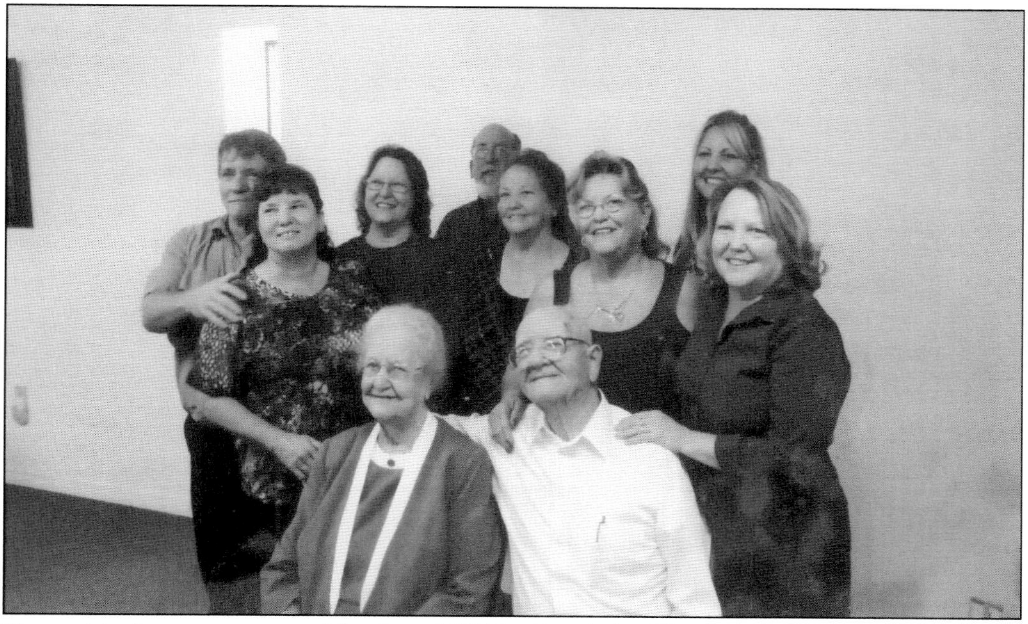

Pictured in front are parents Claude and Wilda Grinslade. Claude was a Pentecostal preacher and the eldest son of Herman and Lillie (Connell) Grinslade. Lillie was the sister of William Roy Connell, steamboat captain of the *John W. Callahan*. Their children are, from left to right, Clark, Paula, Wanda, Calvin, Lydia, Irene, Larena, and Nola. (BB.)

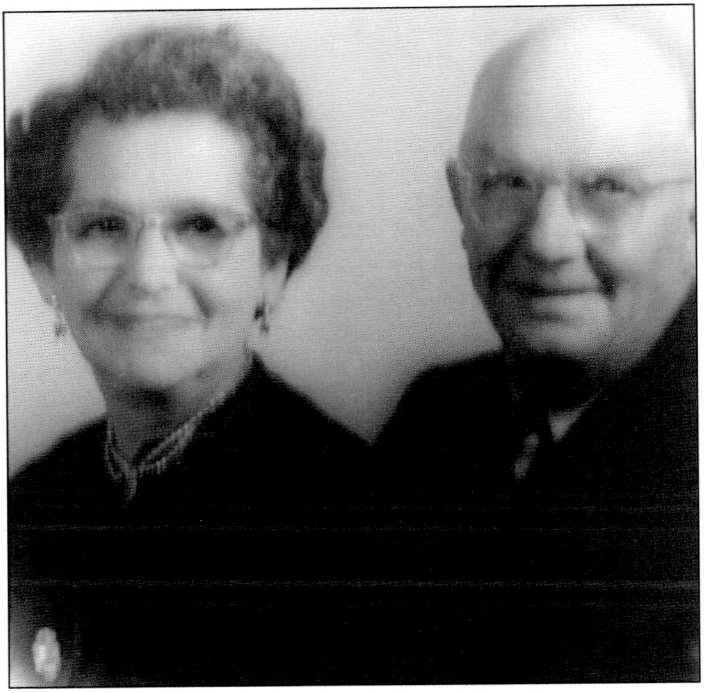

Capt. William Roy Connell was born and reared in the Dead Lakes country. For many years, he was a pilot and steamboat captain on the *John W. Callahan*; after leaving the river, Captain Roy was manager of the local water, ice, and power plants. In 1940, he sold the electric plant to the Rural Electrification Association. He and Annie Mae (McMurria) Connell were married for over 46 years. (BB.)

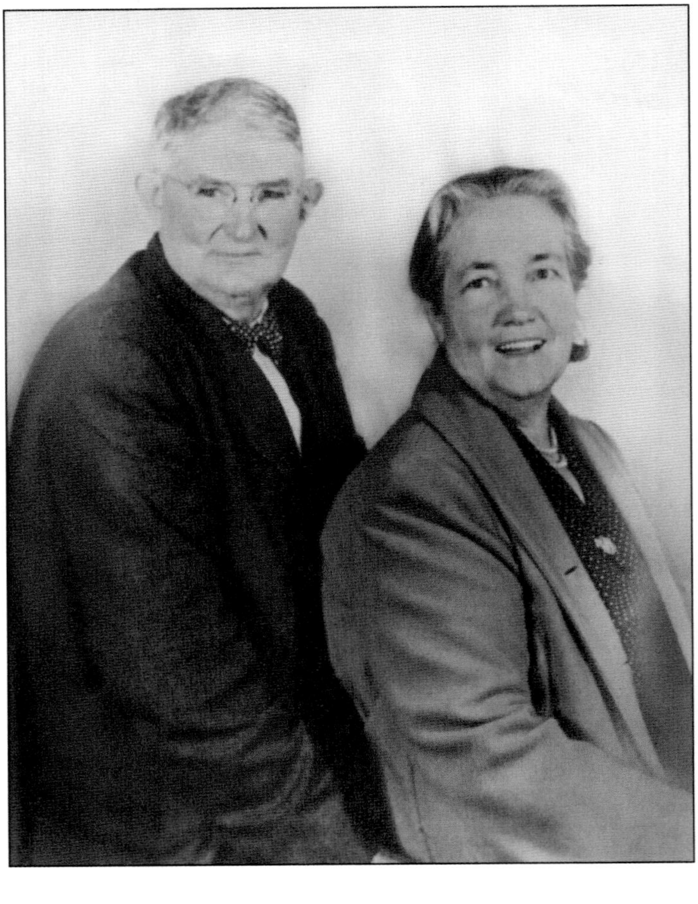

Edward C. and Emily J. (Linton) Pridgeon were tax collectors. Ed was the first tax collector in Gulf County, Florida, and he died while in office. The governor appointed his wife, Emily, to serve out his term. When that term ended, their son Harland Pridgeon ran for office and was elected to serve. (PMM.)

Lula Whitfield Branch, daughter of Frank and Laura Whitfield, was born and raised in the Overstreet area. She married William Elias Branch Jr., and they moved to Calhoun County and lived there until her death during a 1937 flu epidemic. She was the mother of seven children, with five surviving to adulthood and living in Wewahitchka and Port St. Joe. This photograph was taken in the early 1930s. (HDB.)

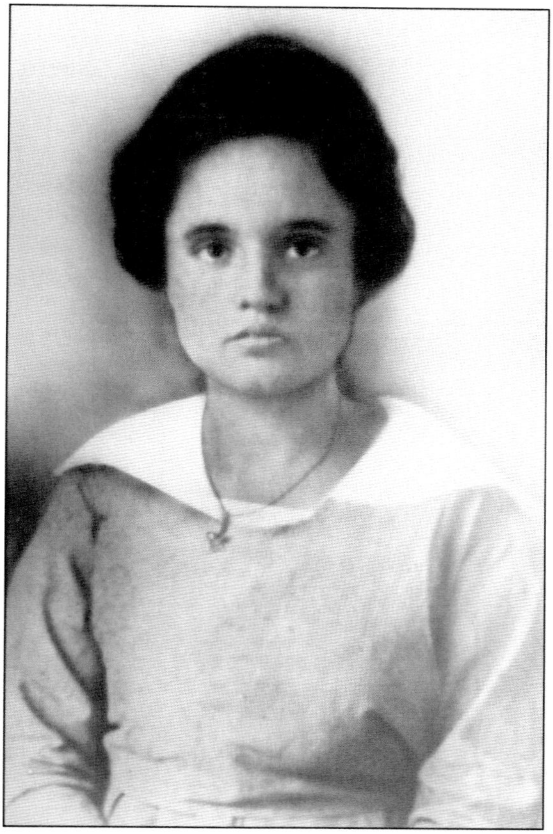

The turpentine industry is what brought Henry Clay Lister to the Wewahitchka area in 1921, around the time of this photograph. He bought the Bob Jones College in 1933, where he and his family lived until moving back to Wewahitchka in 1938—later selling the college buildings and land. Here, he is standing with his family. Pictured, from left to right, are Henry, Dutchie, Floyd, Claude, R.D., Minnie and "Mama" Mary Lister. (KLW.)

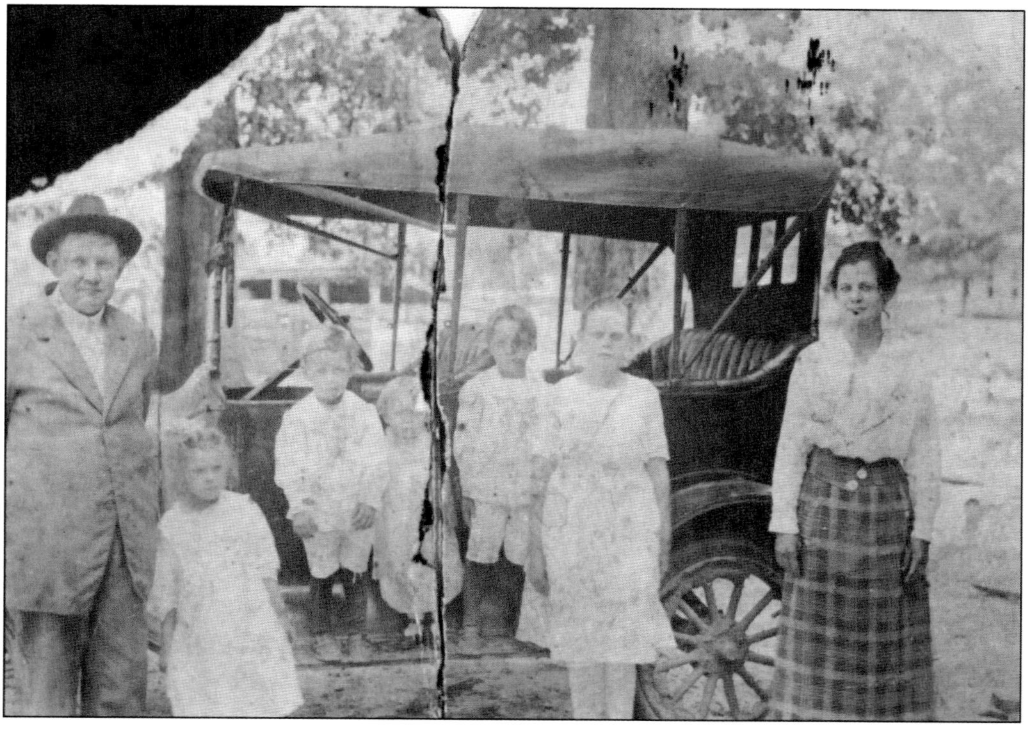

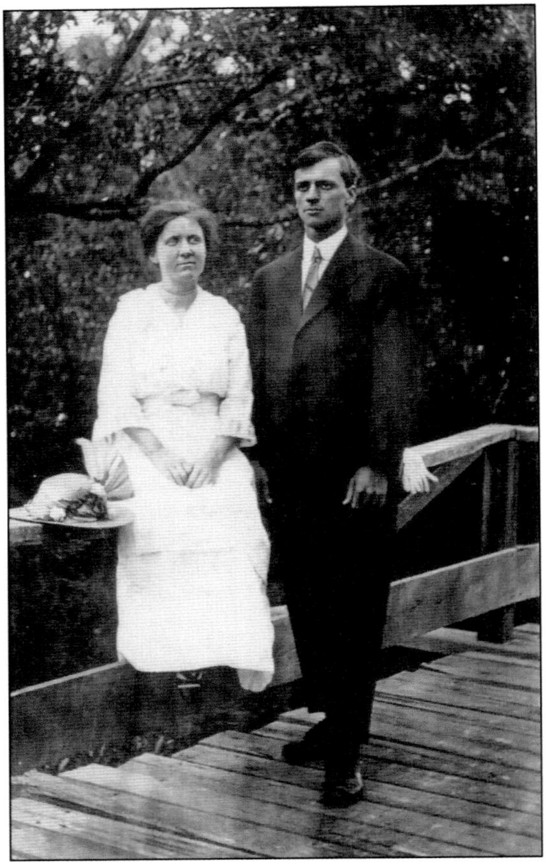

Ralph R. Davis and Clemmie (Ford) Davis married in 1915 in De Funiak Springs and moved to Wewahitchka in 1920. They owned a general store next to their home, which was located at the corner of Highways 71 and 22. Ralph was a Gulf County commissioner in 1936. The Davises also produced and sold pure tupelo honey. They raised two daughters, Burice Gaskin Pridgeon and Doris Davis Lister. (KGT.)

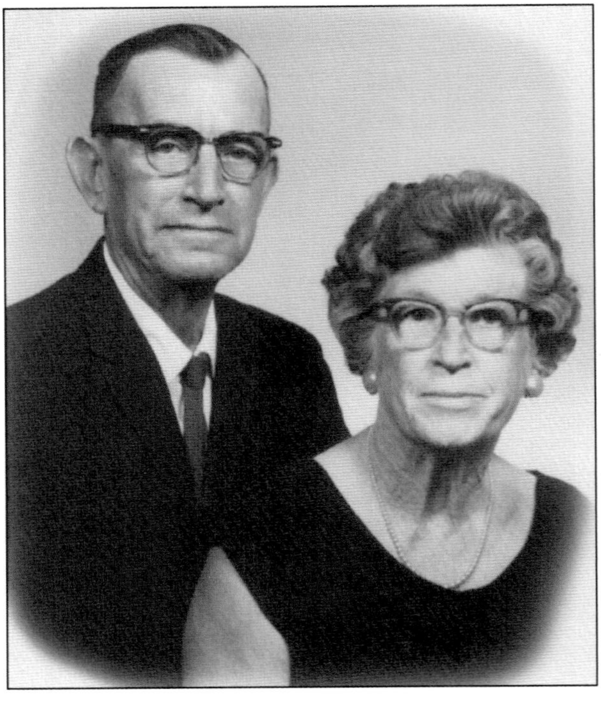

Shelby "S.B." and Lemmie (Slay) Brown moved to Wewahitchka many years ago from Mississippi and raised six wonderful Christian children—Mary Louise Smith, Robert Brown, Betty Millergren, Buddy Brown, and twins Ned and Ted Brown—who in turn raised 17 grandchildren for them. S.B. Brown was also one of Wewa's city commissioners in 1941. (EMK.)

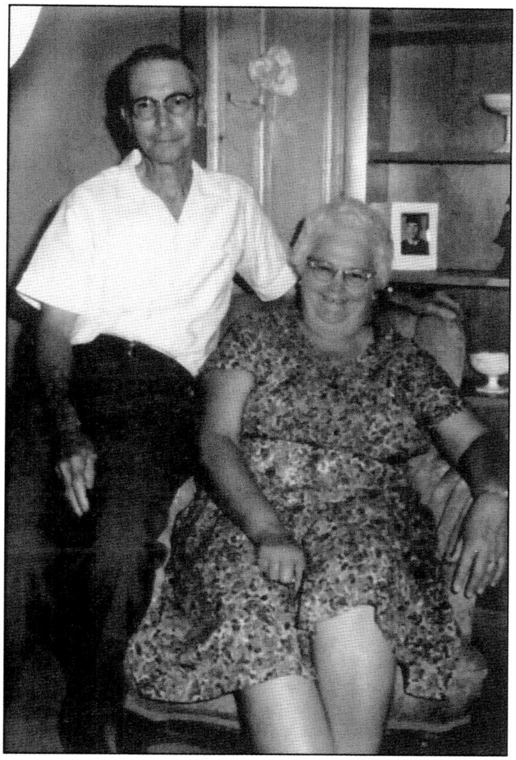

James Ander Glenn was the son of Charles F. and Luella (Harper) Rish. James was married to Ester Lee (Meredith). Like his father and grandfather—James A. Glenn, born in 1823 in Georgia—before him, he was in the farming and beekeeping business. The family had apiaries in Iola way back in the 1800s. There is also a landing named for them, Glenn Landing, located on the Dead Lakes and near the Apalachicola River. (BH.)

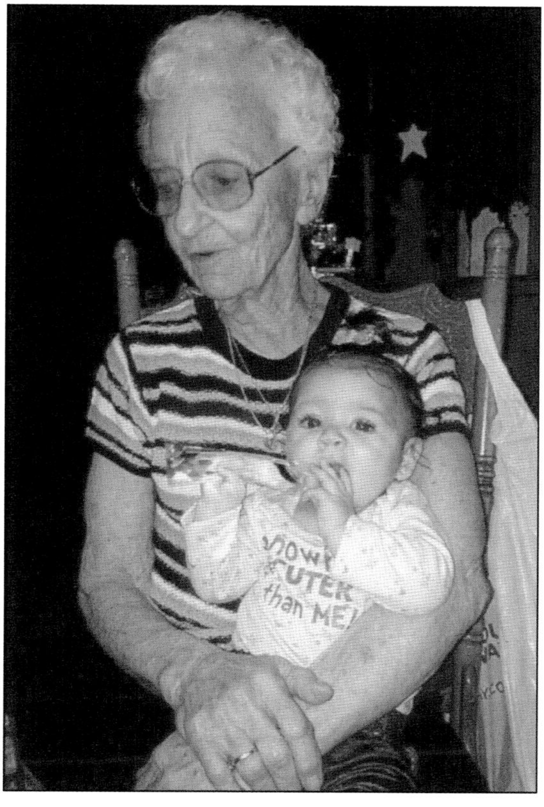

Nellie Wade came to Florida after World War II and settled in Wewahitchka. She worked as a nurse for Dr. Anderson, Dr. Canning, Dr. Muina, St. Joe Paper Mill, and Dr. Barnes. Nellie is the oldest registered nurse in Florida. In addition, during the 1970s and 1980s, she worked as a midwife, delivering more than 1,000 babies. She is still working at the age of 90. Here, she is pictured with one of her great-grandchildren. (TWM.)

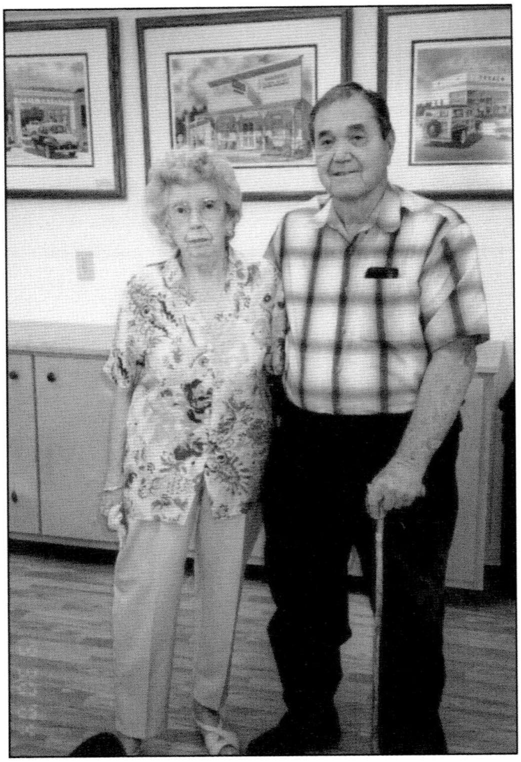

In 1924, Lorraine Norton, daughter of John Frazier and Florence (Yates) Williams, moved to Wewahitchka, where her father had a turpentine operation. Lorraine married Charles Wesley Norton, a bookkeeper, in 1932 and had two children. She taught school during the war years and later opened a dress shop. Lorraine was also the first florist in town. Here, she is standing with Alfred Whitfield during an Oldtimers meeting at the Wewahitchka Library. (CW.)

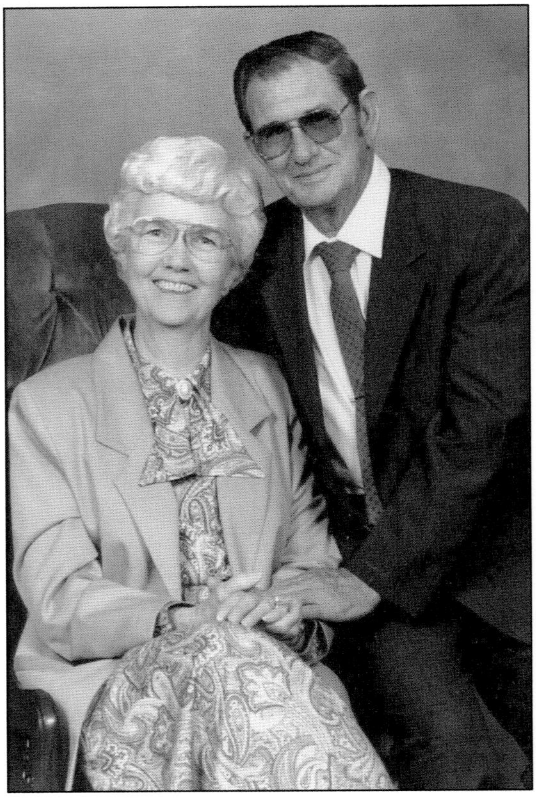

Betty and Bobby Rish married in August 1950. The Rishes were married for 60 years and raised two daughters, Ann and Doris Jean, in Wewahitchka, where they always resided. Bobby was the son of Roy and Lucy Rish. Generations of the Rish family have been in Calhoun and Gulf Counties since Iola was a bustling community. This photograph was taken in 1989. (DJRW.)

Ada Dozier, a native of Wewahitchka, was the eldest of 10 children born to Rev. Robert T. and Cora (Rouse) Keith. Ada lived most of her life here, working for several families in town. She was a marvelous mother to her own children and known as the world's greatest nanny to others. Ada's life has been fraught with joys as well as heartaches and hardships, but she has truly come through it all like a queen. (DD.)

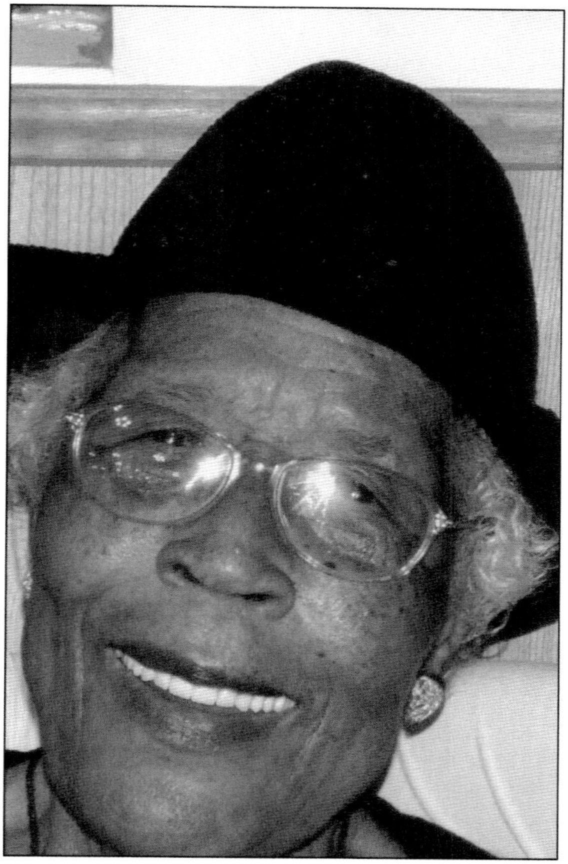

In 1918, Luther and Leitha (Meredith) Joines settled in Wewahitchka, where they raised four children. They are identified from left to right as follows: Amelia married a serviceman and lived most of her life away from home. Alfred, after serving in the Coast Guard, and his wife made their home in St. Joe, where he was employed by St. Joe Paper Company. Nita married William Linton and lived in town, and Marie married Chauncey Costin and resided in St. Joe. (MCS and SBJ.)

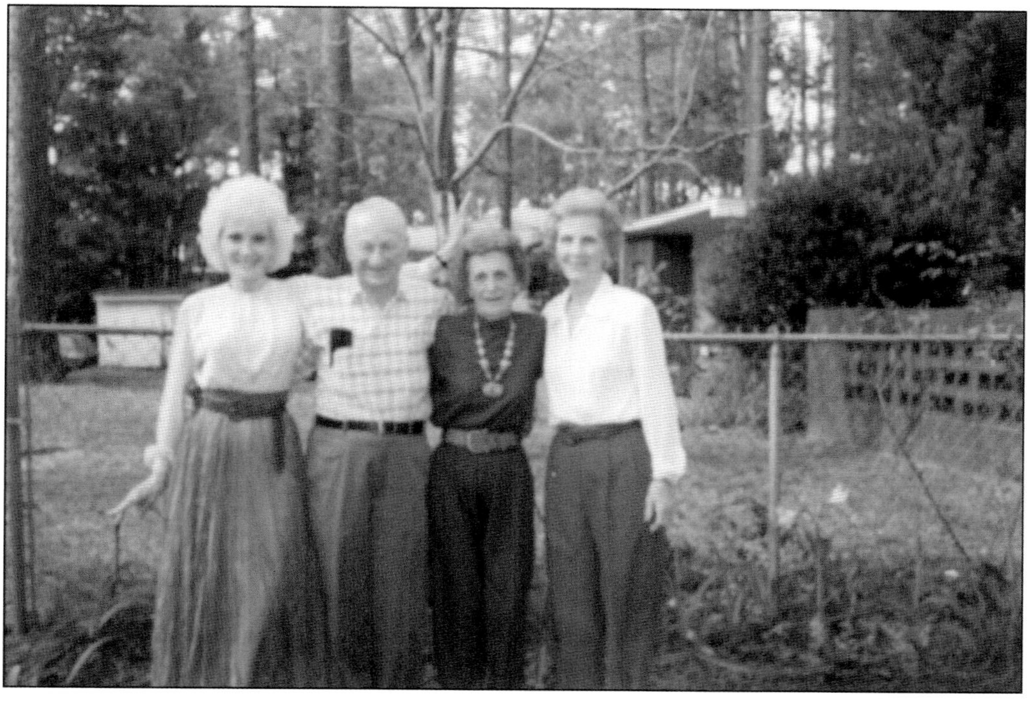

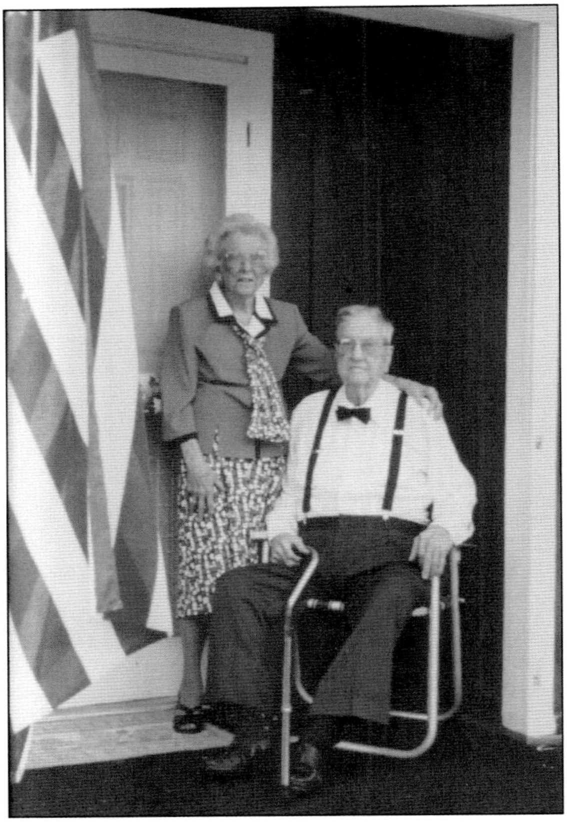

Max and Rosenia (Meriwether) Kilbourn moved to Wewahitchka in 1949. He was a civil engineer, and she, an elementary teacher. They were both very interested in the community and invested much of their time in many projects. Rosenia helped restart the Episcopal church, of which they were both very active members. Rosenia graduated from Florida State University when it was a women's college, and Max went to college at the University of Florida. (MAKS.)

Alvin and Beatrice McGlon ran the gas station at the corner of Highways 22 and 71. In those days, attendants pumped customers' gas, checked their oil, and cleaned their windshields. Alvin had a wrecker service as well. Before coming to Wewahitchka, he built engines for NASCAR and worked on Edward Glenn "Fireball" Roberts's pit crew at Daytona. (BH.)

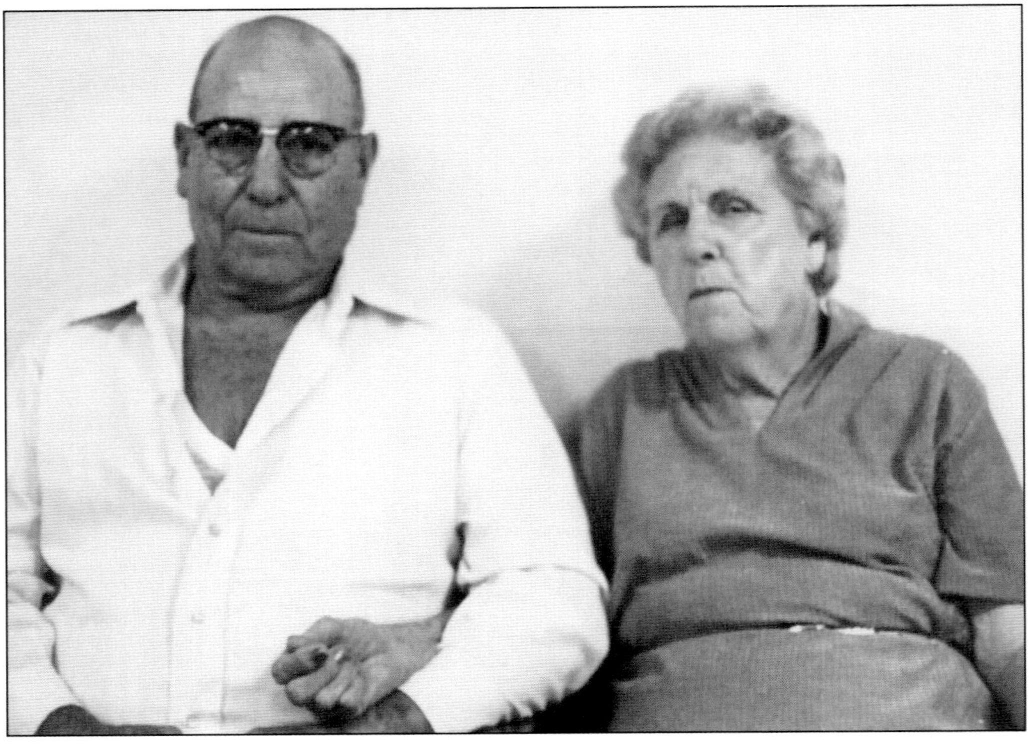

Two

Logging, Forestry, and Beekeeping

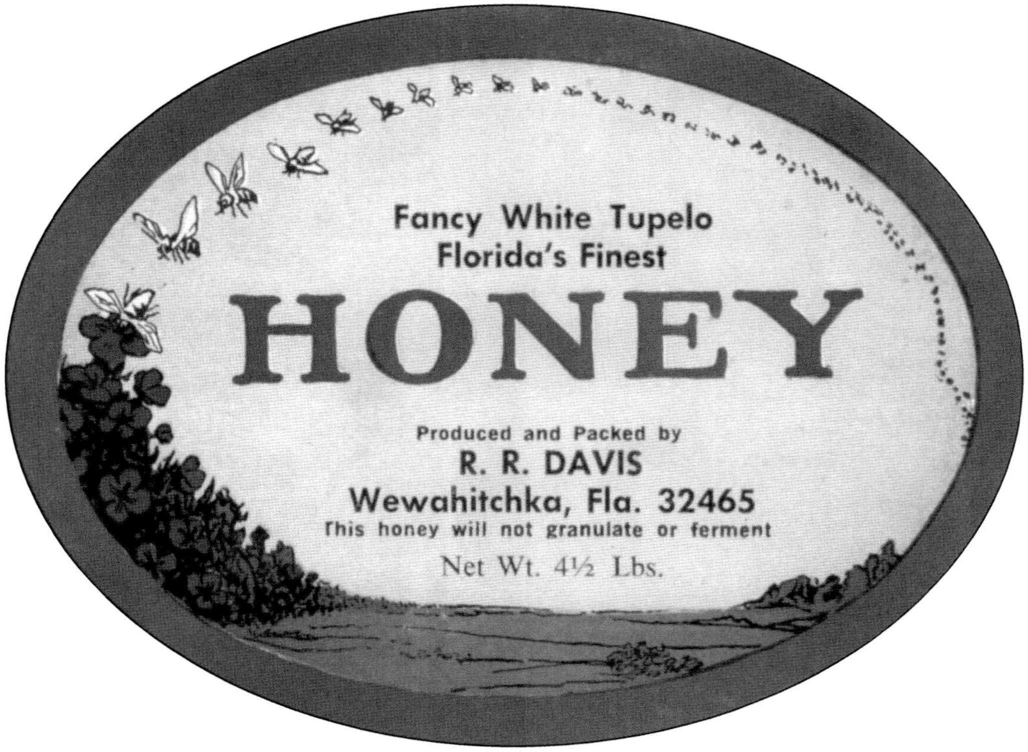

This is one of the many labels found for Wewahitchka's delicious pure tupelo honey. This one is produced by Ralph Raymond Davis and his family. A clear, golden color, the honey is a top grade and is shipped to customers all over the world. (KGT.)

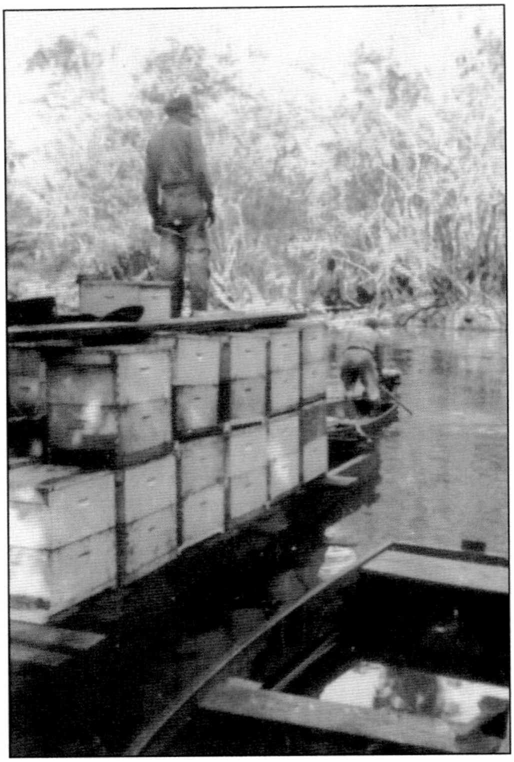

Ralph R. Davis and his unidentified helper move bees on a barge to his apiary, located below Bryant's Landing on the west side of the Chipola River, in about 1948–1950. Here, tupelo trees were found for miles in any direction, ensuring that there were ample blooms to produce pure tupelo honey. Everything in those day was done by hand, with no modern machinery—just hard, heavy work. (KGT.)

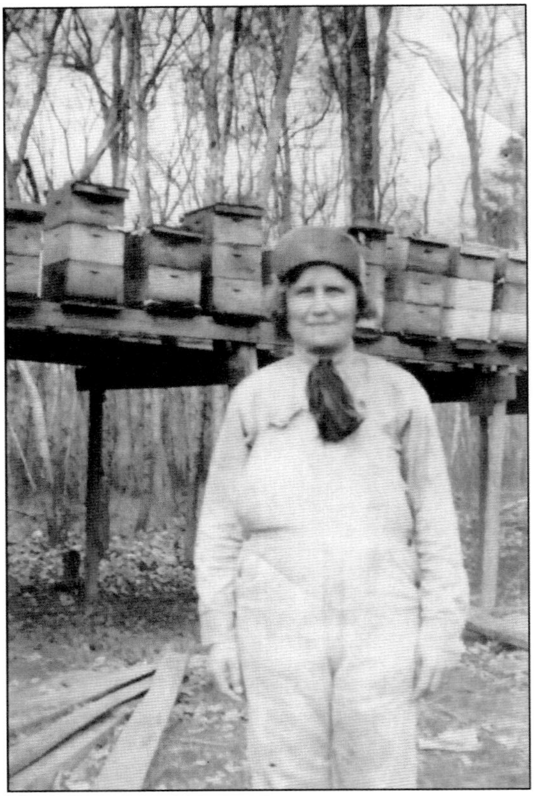

Phoebe McDaniel was a beekeeper and the wife of Jim B. McDaniel, who also ran a drugstore in town. Phoebe was born in 1902 and lived her whole life in Wewahitchka before dying in 1956 from a heart ailment at the age of 55. (EMK.)

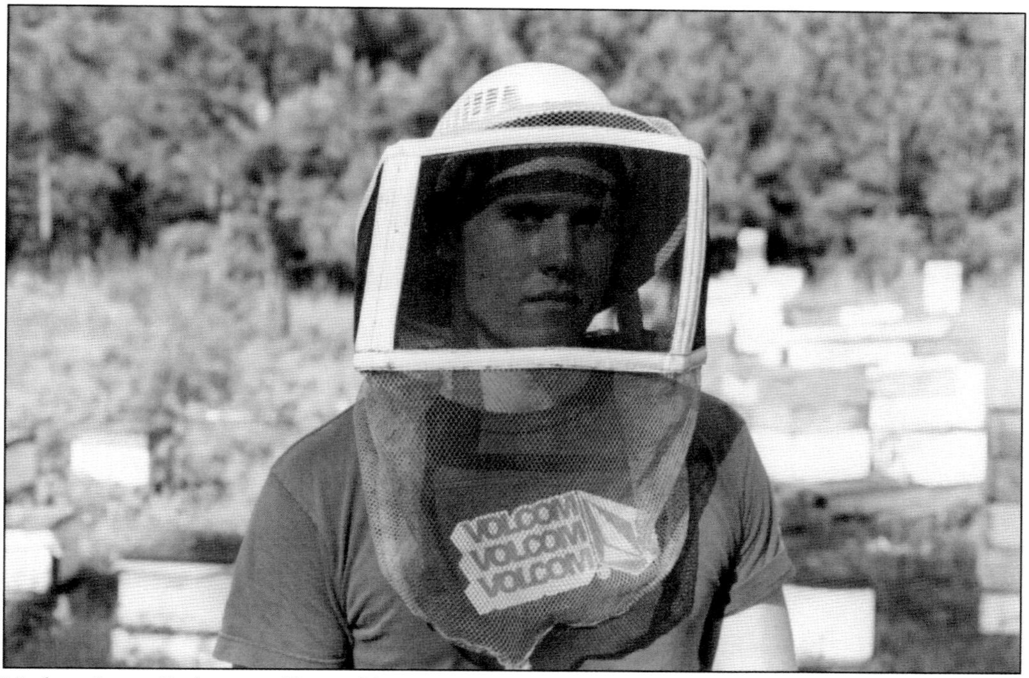

Nathan James Rish, son of James E. Rish, is the fifth generation of his family in the honey-making business. Iola-Wewa resident James Franklin Rish Sr. and son James F. Rish Jr. had been raising bees and making honey most of their lives. They inherited these traditions from James Sr.'s father, Henry A. Rish, who ran a hotel and was mail carrier in Iola, where he started the tupelo honey apiaries in the late 1800s. (JER.)

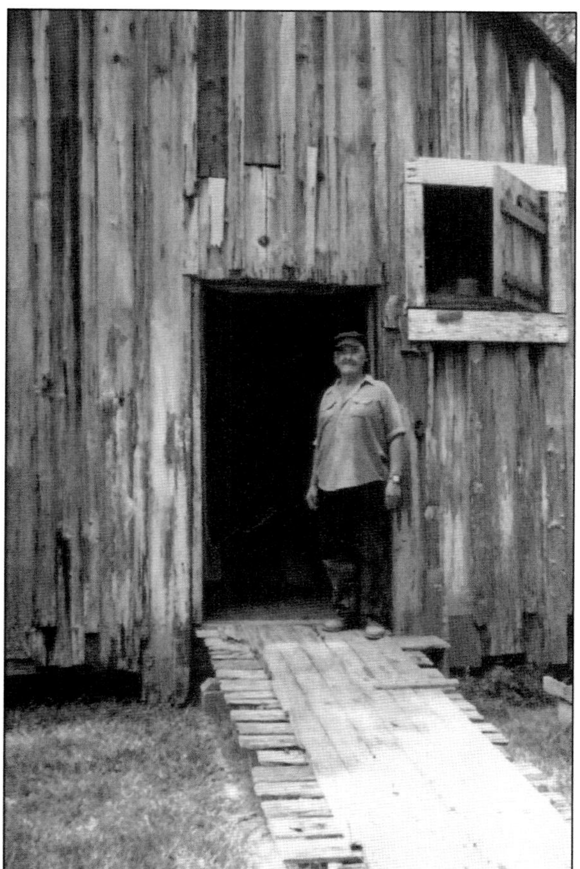

Here, James F. Rish Jr. stands in front of the family's old honey house at Iola. The structure has now been moved to the Pioneer Settlement at Sam Atkins Park in Blountstown. It is currently being restored for historical purposes to show the way the honey-making business was back in its earlier days when everything was done by hard work and by hand. (JER.)

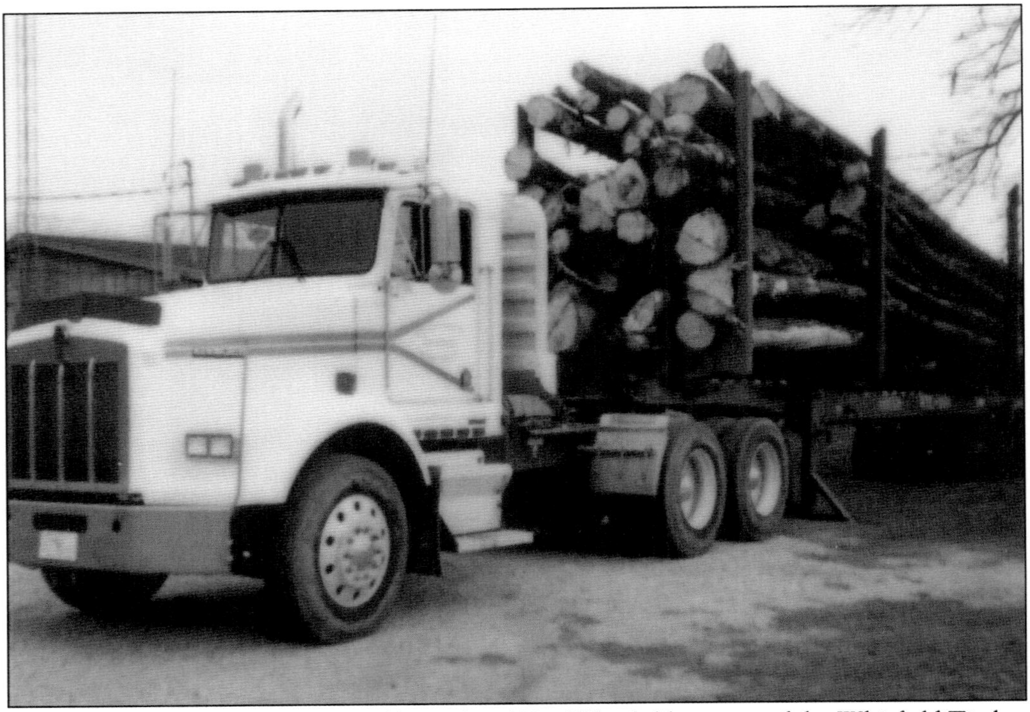

Here is a truckload of logs produced by Ted and Kay Whitfield, owners of the Whitfield Timber Company. Kay is a third-generation descendant of Henry C. Lister and is the daughter of Floyd Lister. (KLW.)

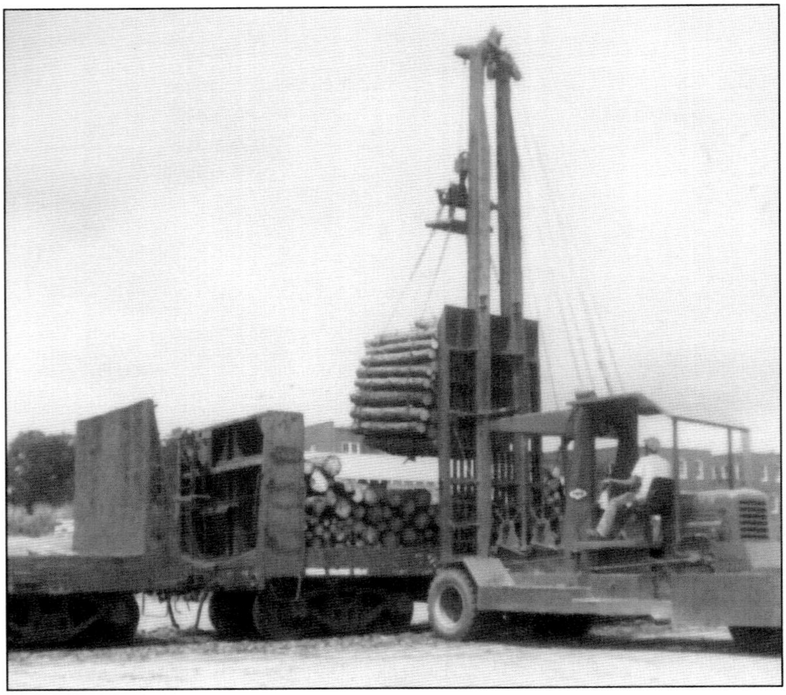

This is one of the logging yards of the Lister Timber and Pulpwood Company. Owner Floyd Clay Lister was one of the sons of Henry C. Lister, who had many sawmills in the area and was one of the region's large landowners before Gulf County was created. (KLW.)

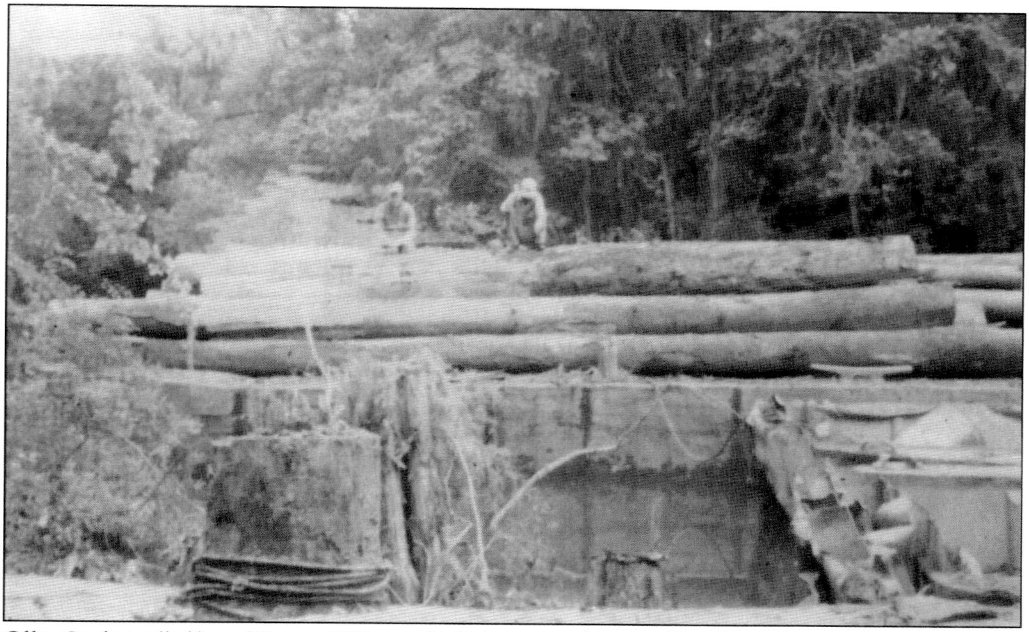

Ollie Godwin (left) and Buster Tillman (right) are on a barge of logs being loaded at Florida River above Wewahitchka. These logs were cut down and skidded to the riverbank with a loader on a separate barge, then stacked onto a transport barge for Owl Creek. Some logs were so large they had to be cut into three sections. (KGT.)

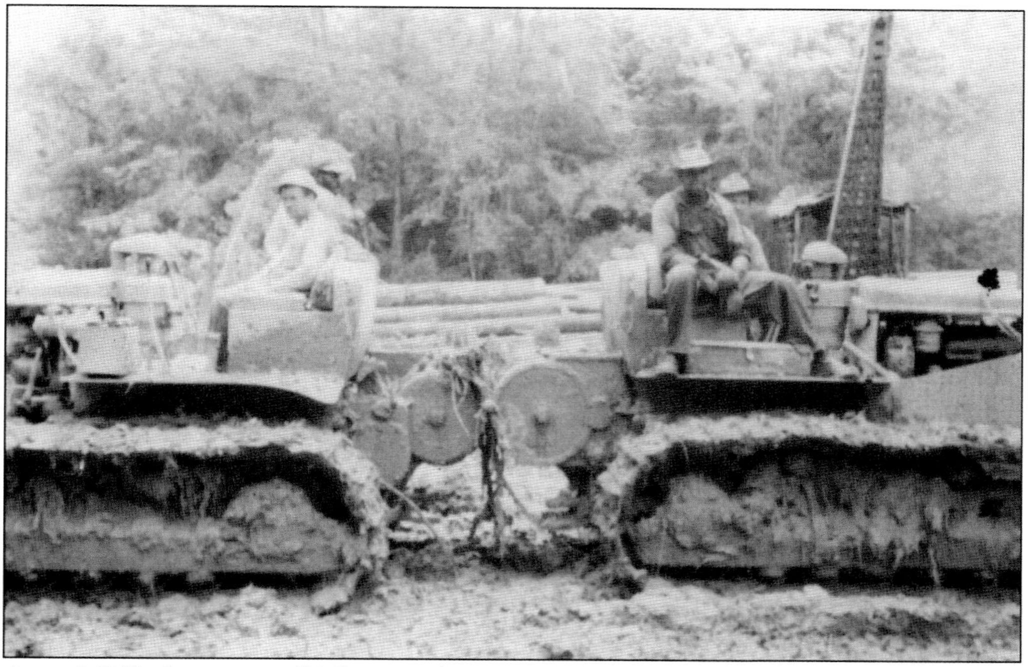

Around 1957, the owners of Tillman and Son Logging Contractors were Thomas "Buster" and son Billy Tillman. These men seen logging trees on the Florida River are Oscar Holms (left front), Dolly Fisher (left back), Donnie Martin (right front), and Harvey Thomas (right back). They pulled timber and loaded barges to carry to Owl Creek at Right Landing. There, it was loaded and sent to Elberta Crate & Box Company in Tallahassee. (KGT.)

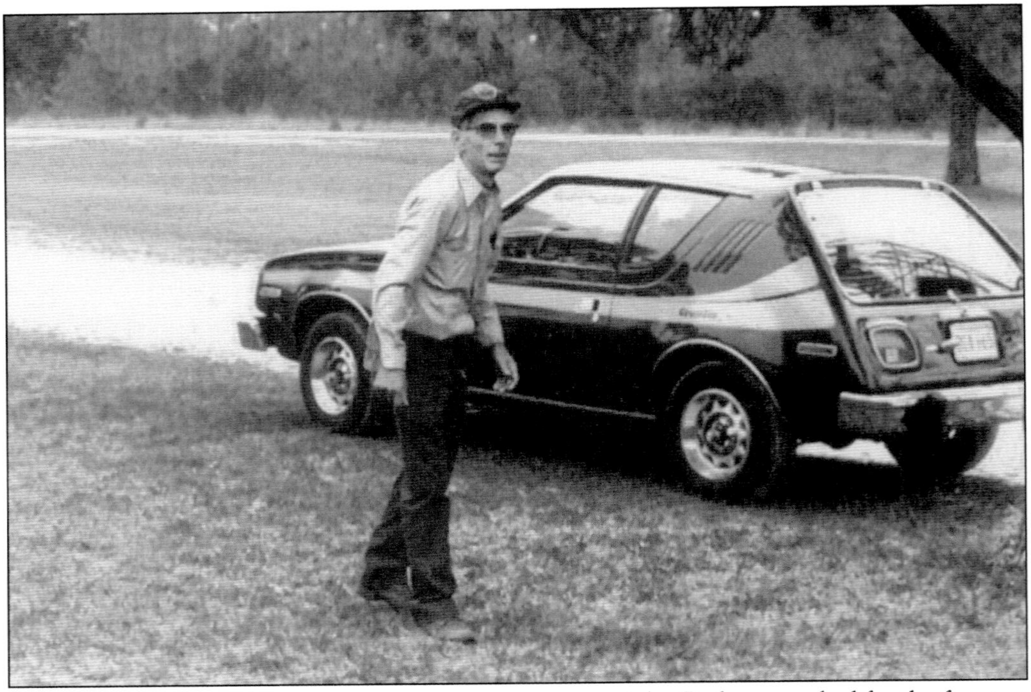

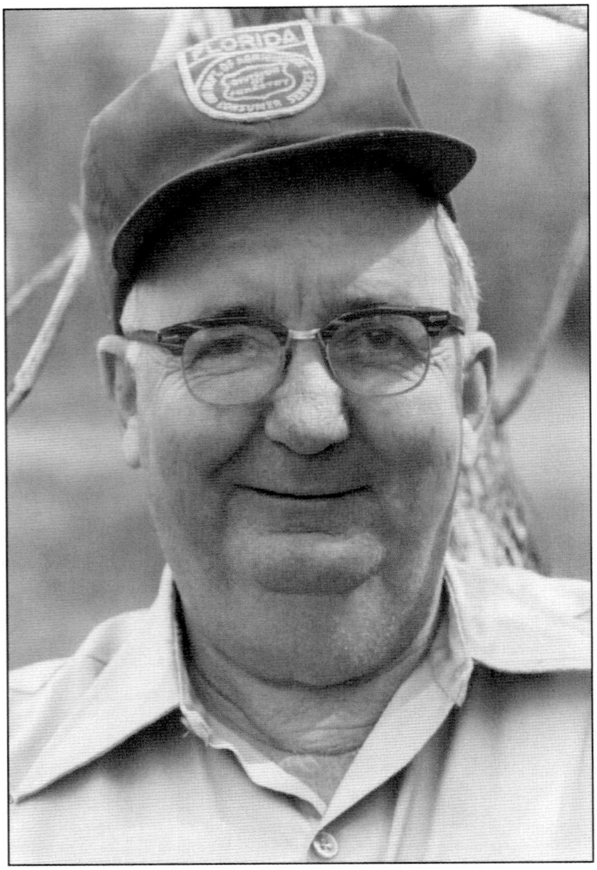

John Redman worked for the forestry service in Gulf County from around 1956 to 1975. He was hardly ever seen not wearing his uniform; he was even buried in it. The forestry industry was a big deal for many years in the panhandle. It was the reason for the Port St. Joe Paper Mill and the primary source of income for many families in Gulf County. (BRV.)

Milton Strength lived and breathed the Florida Forest Service and teaching others about forestry. He would come home with a face covered in soot and smelling of smoke. Milton began his career at the White City Forest Service tower site in January 1, 1950, and retired in August 1979. One of the things that Milton enjoyed most was teaching children about fire prevention. (BB.)

Three

School Days

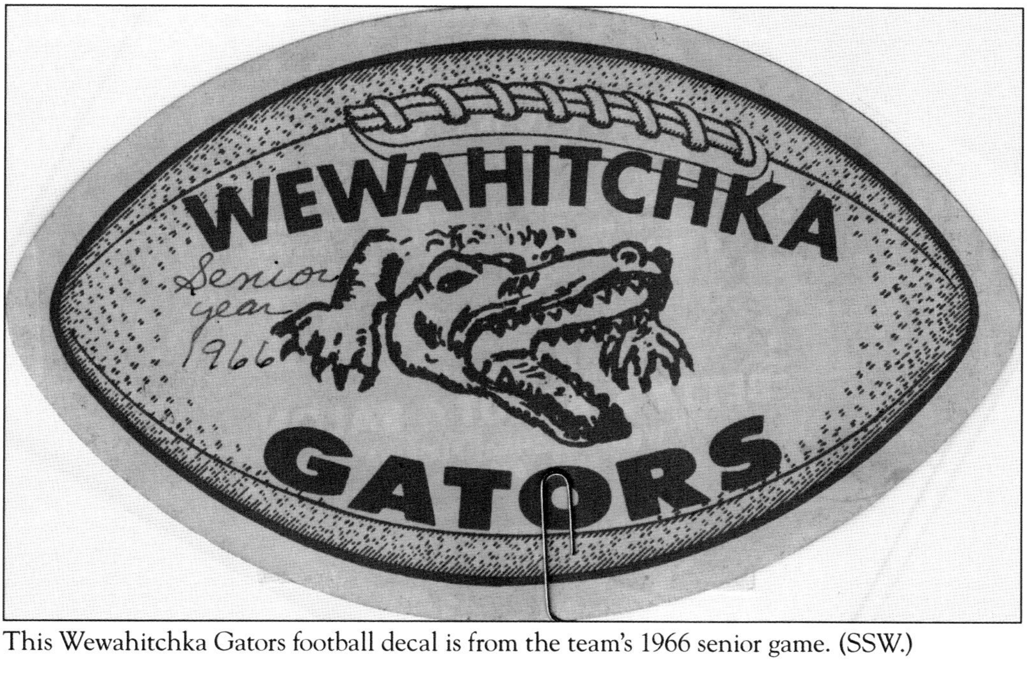

This Wewahitchka Gators football decal is from the team's 1966 senior game. (SSW.)

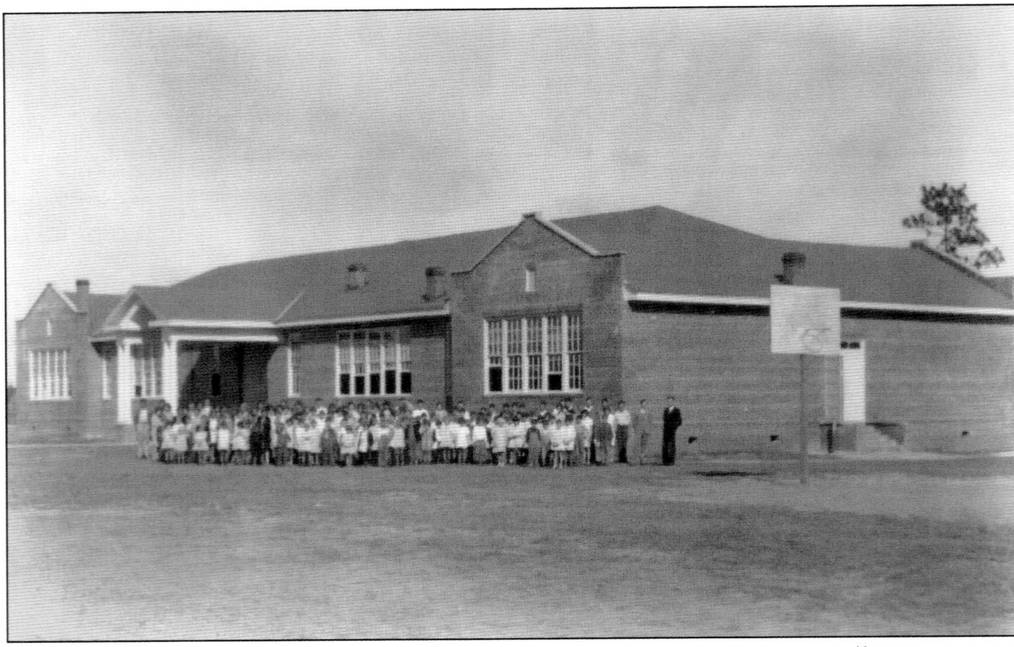

Before 1920, as many as 30 district schools accommodated the pupils in small communities. When Gulf County was carved out of Calhoun County in 1925, a newly appointed school board began making plans for a new schoolhouse in Wewahitchka. The result was the beautiful redbrick Wewahitchka School that was located for many years just off Main Street south of town. (BB.)

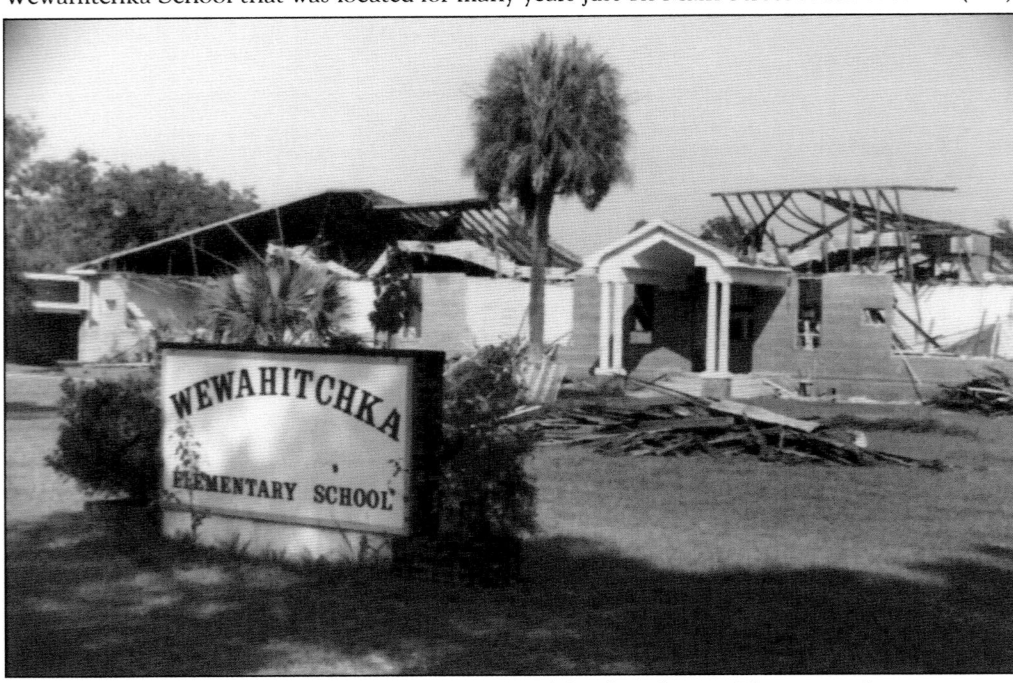

The old school building in Wewahitchka is slated for demolition. The original structure was erected in 1925. Over the years, it has been added to, remodeled, and revamped to the point of no return. It was used every school year from fall 1926 through spring 1986—a total of 61 years. It is finally at the point that it is more economical to build a new facility. (BB.)

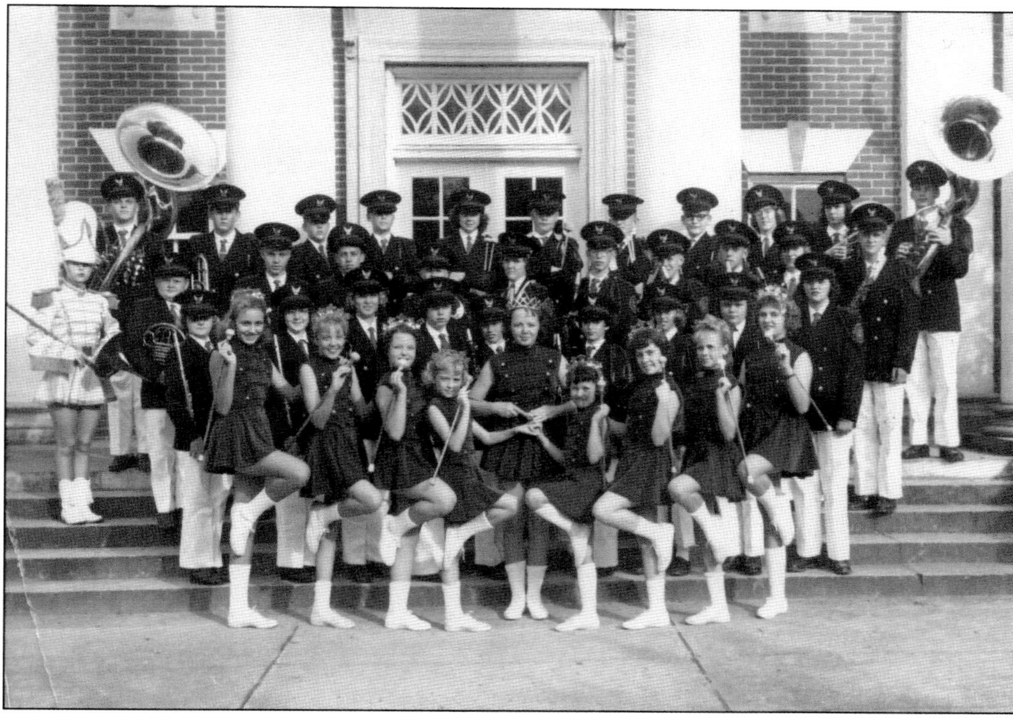

The Wewahitchka High School band was organized in early 1952–1953 by director Robert A. Wol. It has, in these years, attained the reputation of being one of the best bands in its class. The group has attended the District Band Festival for five years, Band Day for four years, and also attended the State Band Festival, receiving high ratings. In 1955, the band attended the Gator Growl. (IDC.)

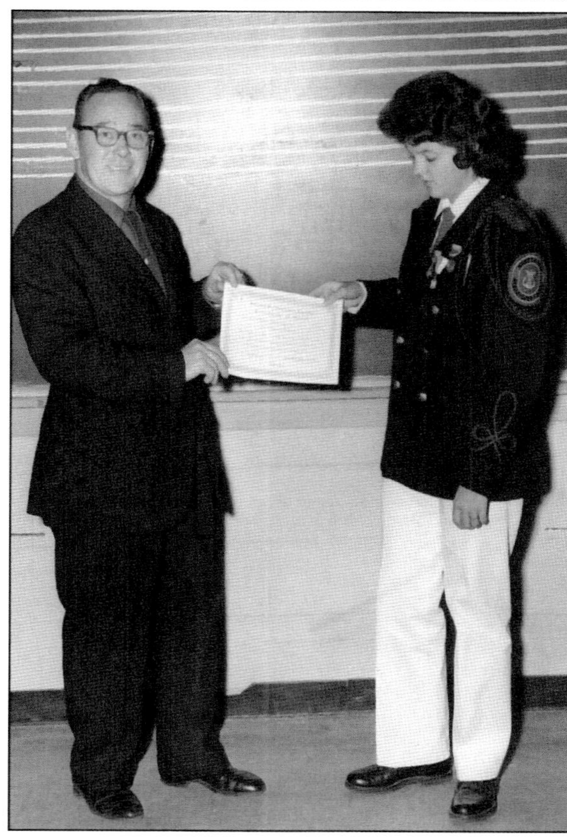

Band director Anthony McCarty is shown here with 14-year-old student Carolyn Britt (Witten) in 1959. (BH.)

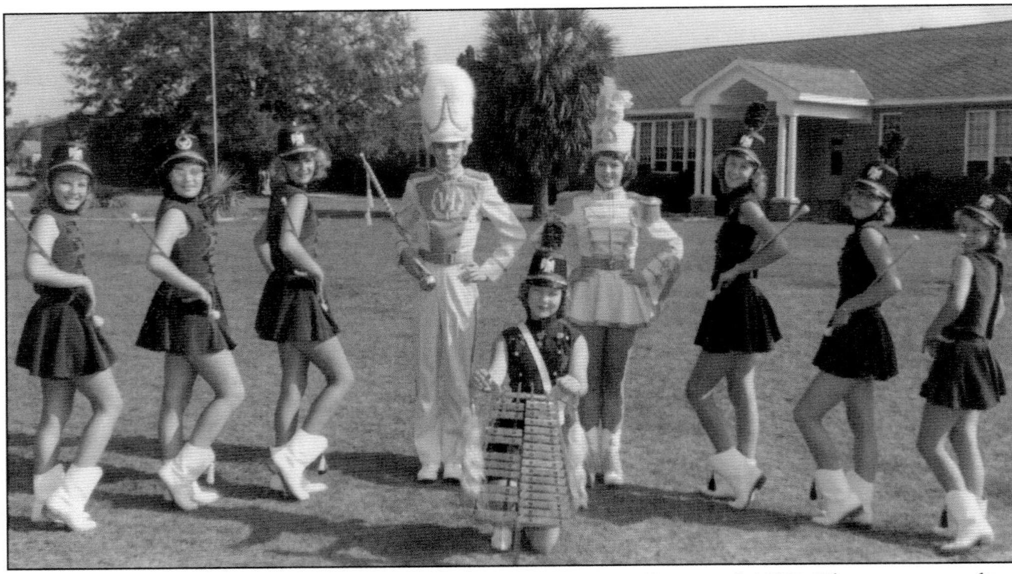

The Wewahitchka drum major and majorettes are pictured around 1957. They are, standing, from left to right, Mary Anne Kilbourn, Mary Ann Pitts, Sandra Whol, Benny Lester, Carol Sue Holman, Bunny Bandjough, Lamar Bateman, and Carol Ann Longshore. Kneeling down in front is Jeanie Longshore. (CALC.)

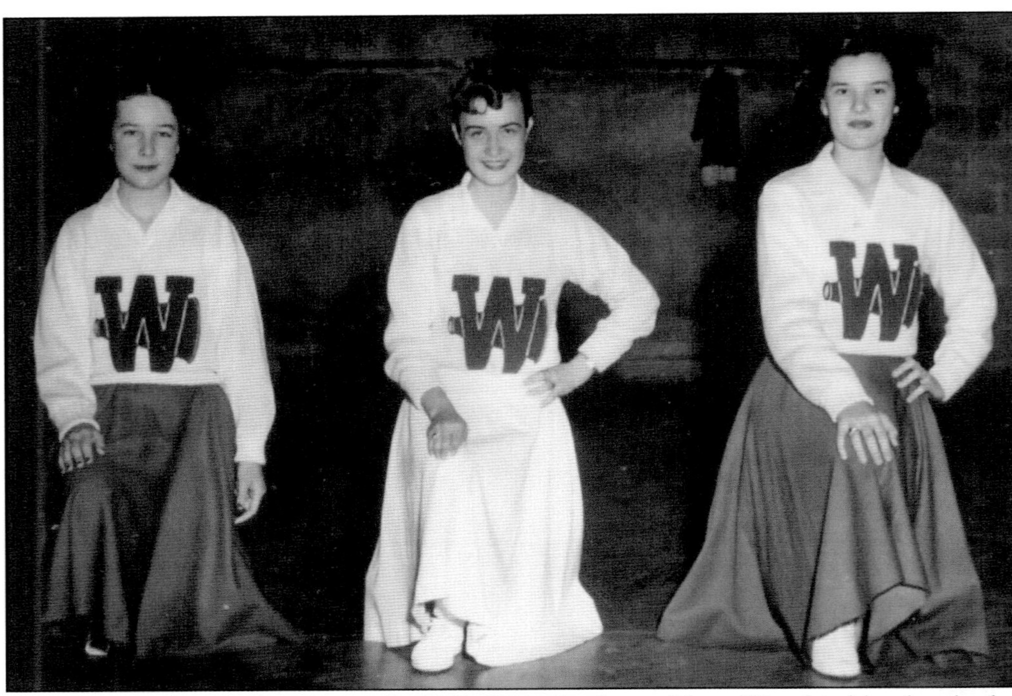

This photograph was taken during the 1953–1954 school year. These Wewahitchka cheerleaders are, from left to right, Jerrie Nations, Ann Mayfield, and Hazel Lamp (Millergren). Born in 1936, Millergren died in 2011. (GD.)

During her 39 years at Wewahitchka High School, Angeline "Angie" Whitfield held numerous extracurricular responsibilities, including girls' basketball coach, Future Homemakers of America advisor, senior sponsor, and student council advisor. Ultimately, she became the school's librarian, which is how she finished out her career. (CW.)

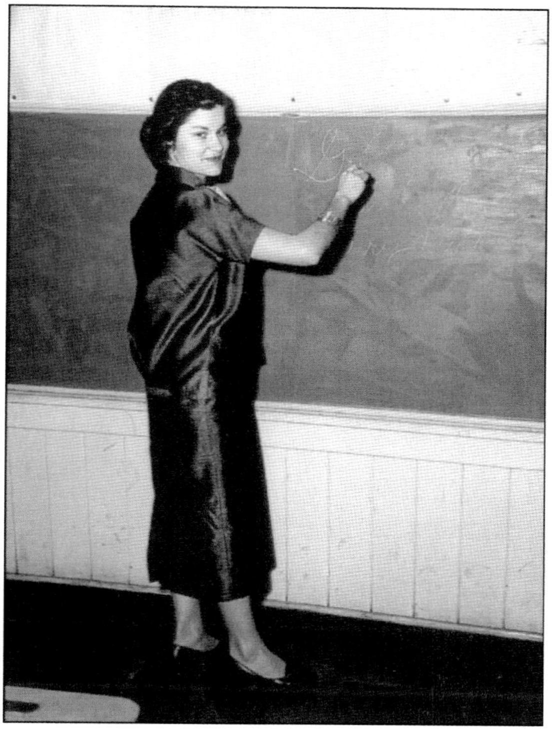

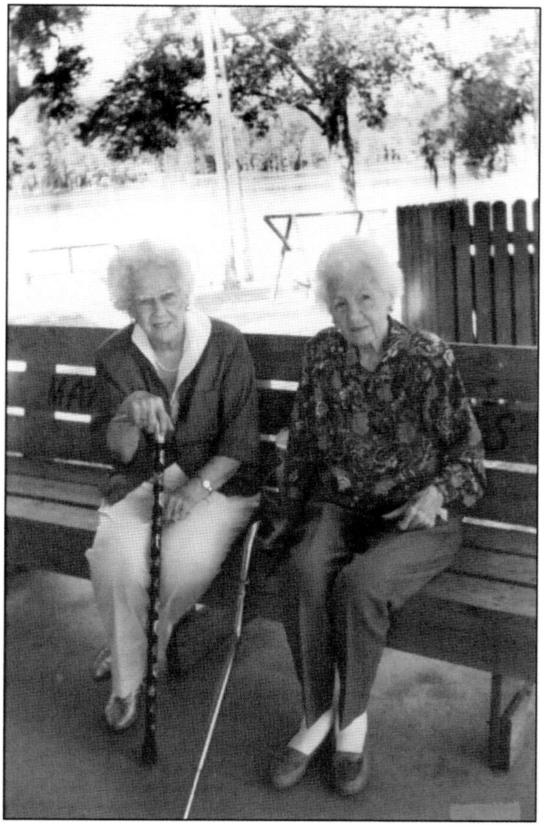

Anna Belle Gaskin and Irene Connell were schoolteachers. Gaskin came to Wewahitchka from Jackson County. She taught school in Calhoun, Bay, and Gulf Counties for over 35 years. Irene Mays was born in Monticello and she graduated from Florida Southern College for Women in 1929. She met and married Jack Connell, and she also taught at Wewahitchka for 35 to 40 years. She and Anna Belle were very good friends. (CT.)

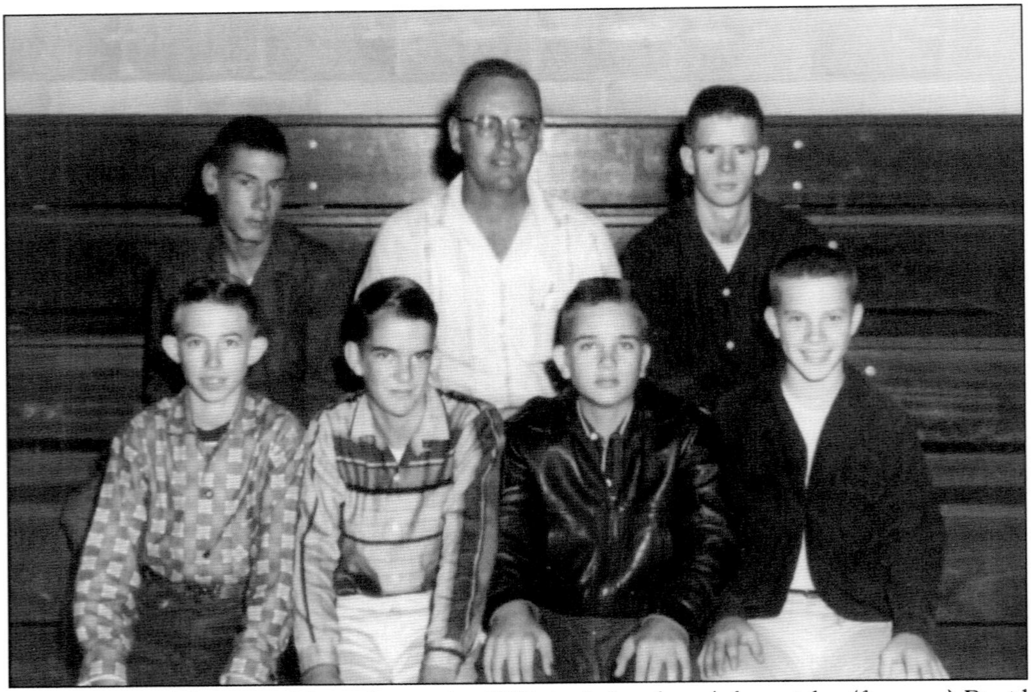

The Electric Club pictured here during the 1950s includes, from left to right, (first row) David Roach, Ricky Faile, Pete Smith, and Terry Linton; (second row) Ellis Brogdon, teacher Hugh Semmes, and unidentified. (THL.)

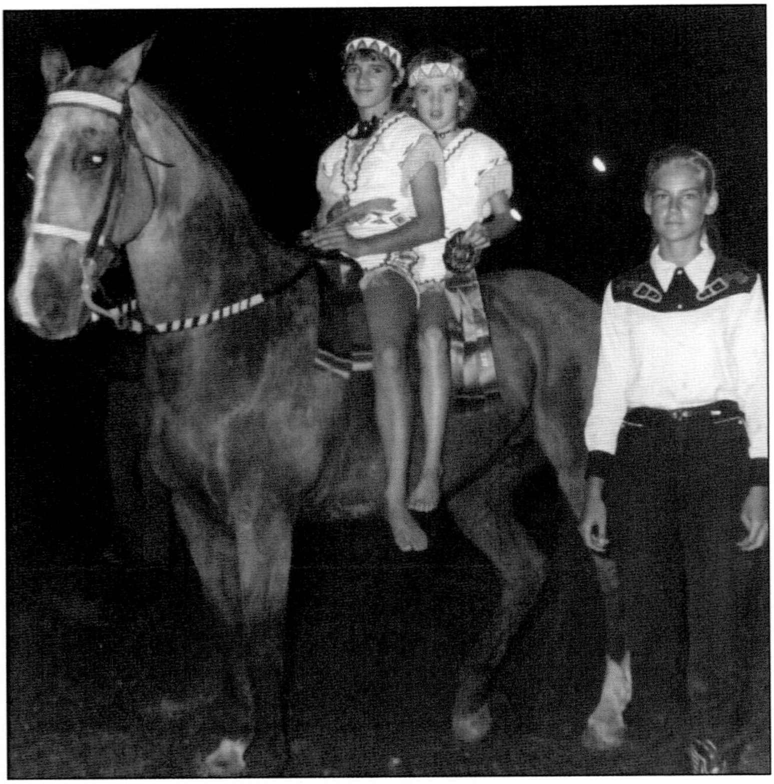

This photograph was taken in Jacksonville, Florida, in October 1961, at one of the horse shows that the Saddlin' Seminoles from Wewahitchka were attending. Biscuit is the horse's name and Joey (front) and Judy Canning are the girls on horseback. The unidentified young judge standing to their right was handing out the ribbons for showmanship. (JJT.)

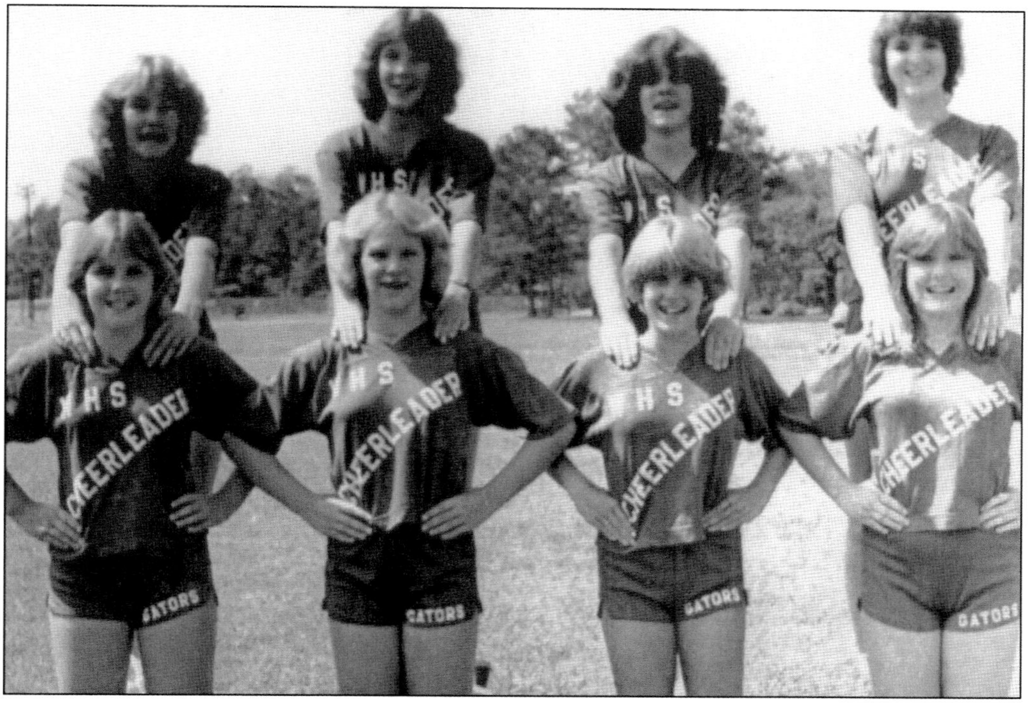

The junior varsity cheerleading squad is pictured here during the 1980–1981 school year. The members are, from left to right, (first row) Tracy Hodges, Kelli Pridgeon, Monica Redmon, and Tammy Melton; (second row) Micah Peak, Angel Rogers, Rene Gortemoller, and Melody Marsh. (BH.)

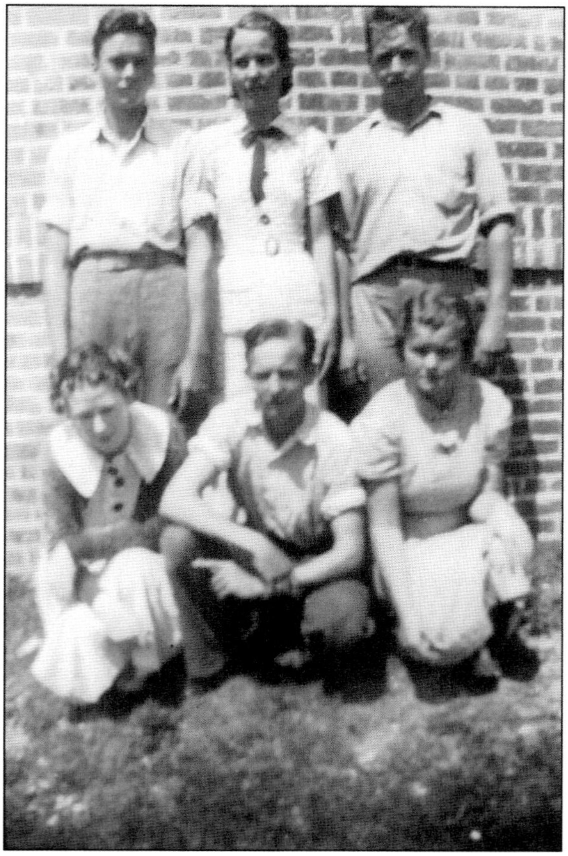

The Wewahitchka High School graduating class of 1937, one of the first to graduate from the new school, posed for this group photograph. Pictured are, from left to right, (first row) Nell Connell, Benjamin Dickens, and Maggie Kemp; (second row) Eric Anderson, Cosetta Darley, and James F. Rish Jr. (JER.)

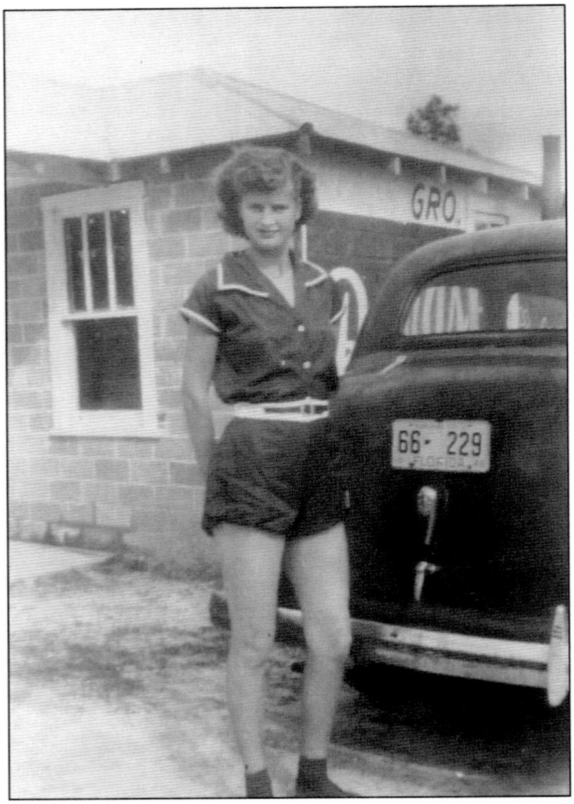

Carolyn Jean Crutchfield Strange, the daughter of Walter and Carmi Crutchfield, was friendly as well as beautiful. In high school, she was part of the girls' basketball team, the Wewahitchka Lady Gators. This photograph was taken around 1950. She loved to dance, go fishing, and sew. Carolyn died in an automobile accident in 2000. She had married her high school sweetheart, Tommy Strange, and was a loving mother to four children. (MG.)

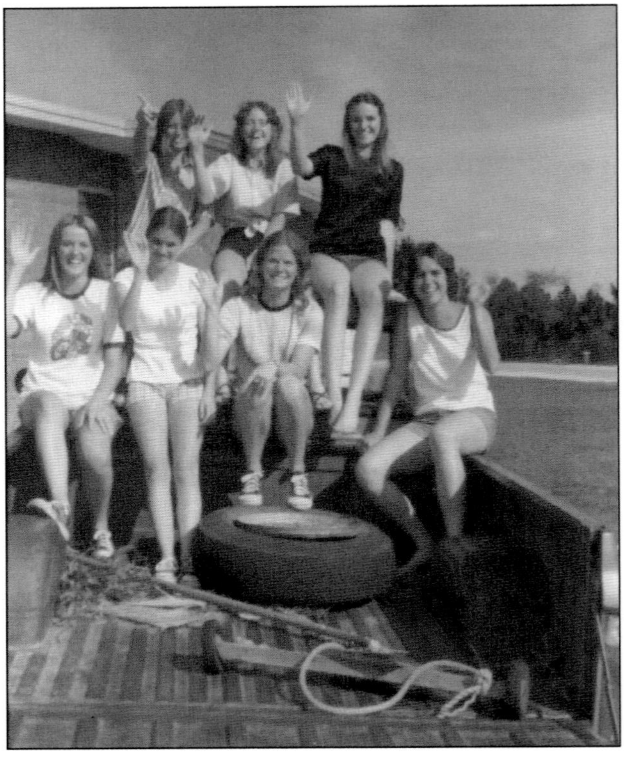

Pictured on the back of this truck, from left to right, are (first row) Carolyn McGill, Nickie Smith, Becky Cleckley, and Tina Harbuck; (second row) Cindy Stripling, Brenda Eubanks, and Doris Jean Rish. Known as "the Group," the young women pictured here in 1975–1976 are still friends and get together regularly. (DJRW.)

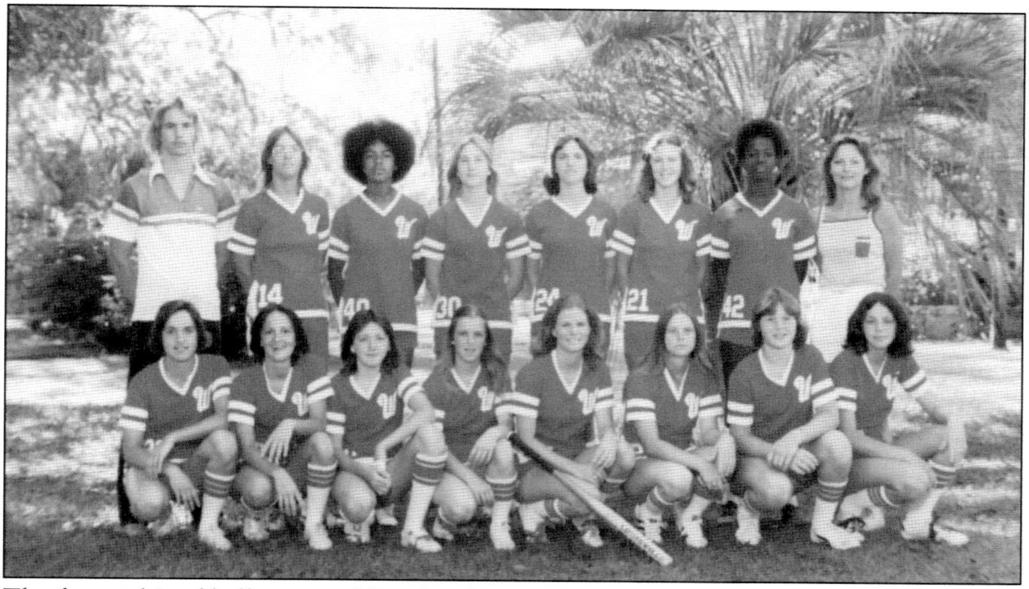

The first girls' softball team at Wewahitchka High School, seen here, was formed in 1977. Pictured are, from left to right, (first row) Tina Harbuck, Sherry Baxley, Dinah Stewart, Margaret Stripling, Becky Cleckley, Cindy Stripling, Valerie McNamara, and Jane Eubanks; (second row) assistant coach Cory Nelson, Teresa Huddleston, Sylvia Ranie, Ann Graddy, Doris Jean Rish, Brenda Eubanks, Mary Ann Bass, and Sharon Gaskin. The team won the Apalachicola Big Bend Conference Championship that year. In coach Charles Fortner's final season in 2007, the Lady Gators won their first softball state championship—in their fifth consecutive Florida Final Four appearance. At that time, Fortner had taught school for more than 38 years. (DJRW.)

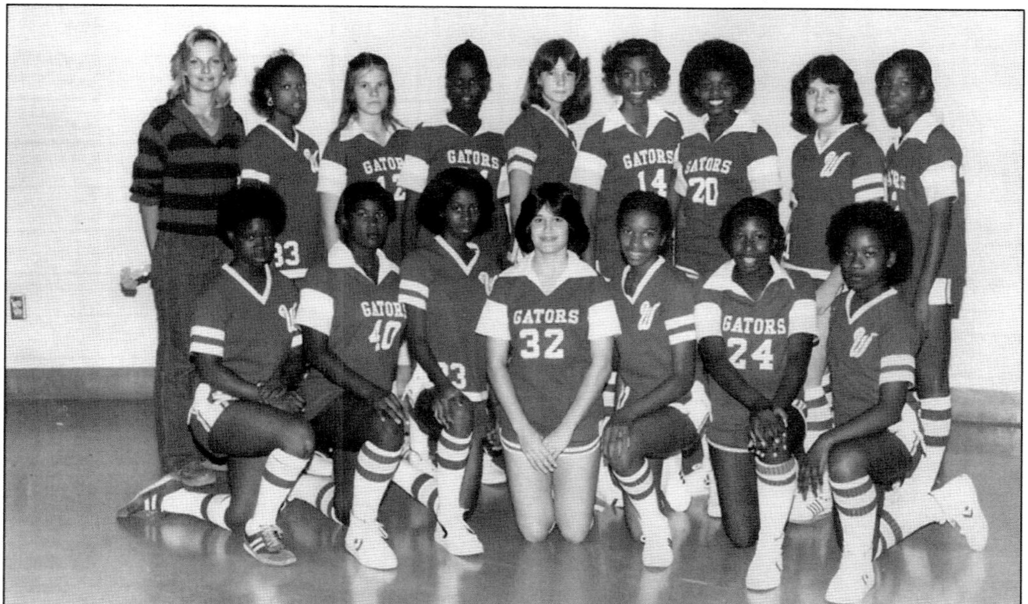

In this image of the girls' basketball team from around 1980–1981 are, from left to right, (first row) Georgia Finley, Marietta Fisher, Frieda Williams, Kim Mathes, Fern Williams, "Little Jackie" Myers, and Valerie Gainer; (second row) coach Sharon Gaskin, Cynthia Hill, Shelia Tucker, Kim Myers, Micah Revell, "Big Jackie" Myers, Barbara Castor, Sherry Hartley, and Malinda Hill. (BH.)

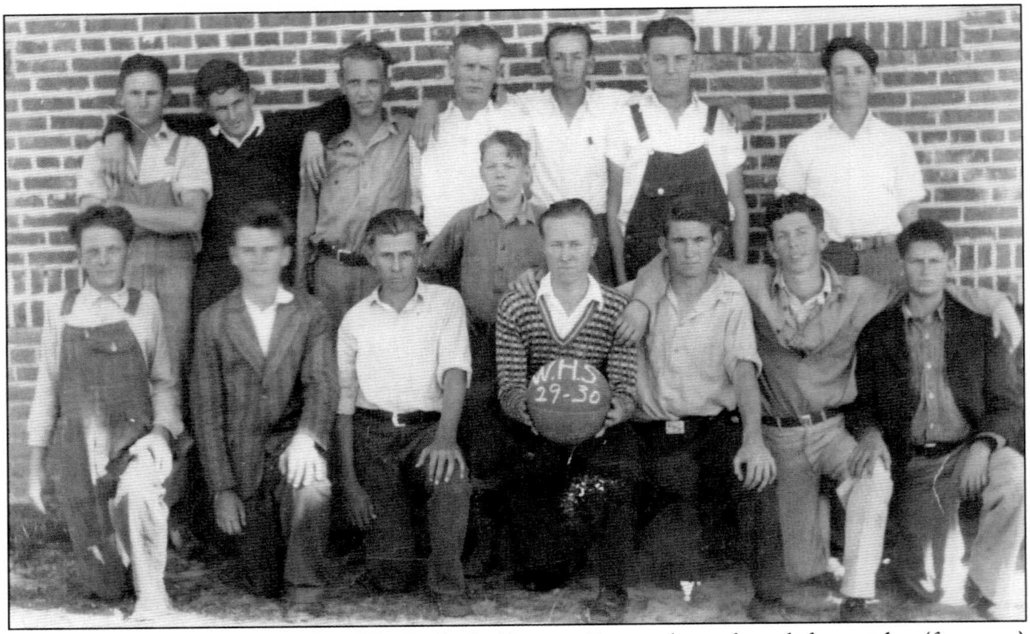

This is the 1929–1930 Wewahitchka basketball team. Pictured are, from left to right, (first row) R.D. Lister, Roy Morrow, C.L. Land, Earl T. Pridgeon, Jerry ?, Woodrow Stokes, George Gaskin, and Gaston Dickens; (second row) Frank Britt, Harland Pridgeon, Ralph Cumbie, Hubert Chafin, Jack Connell, J.P. Smith, and Charlie Gaskin. (BB.)

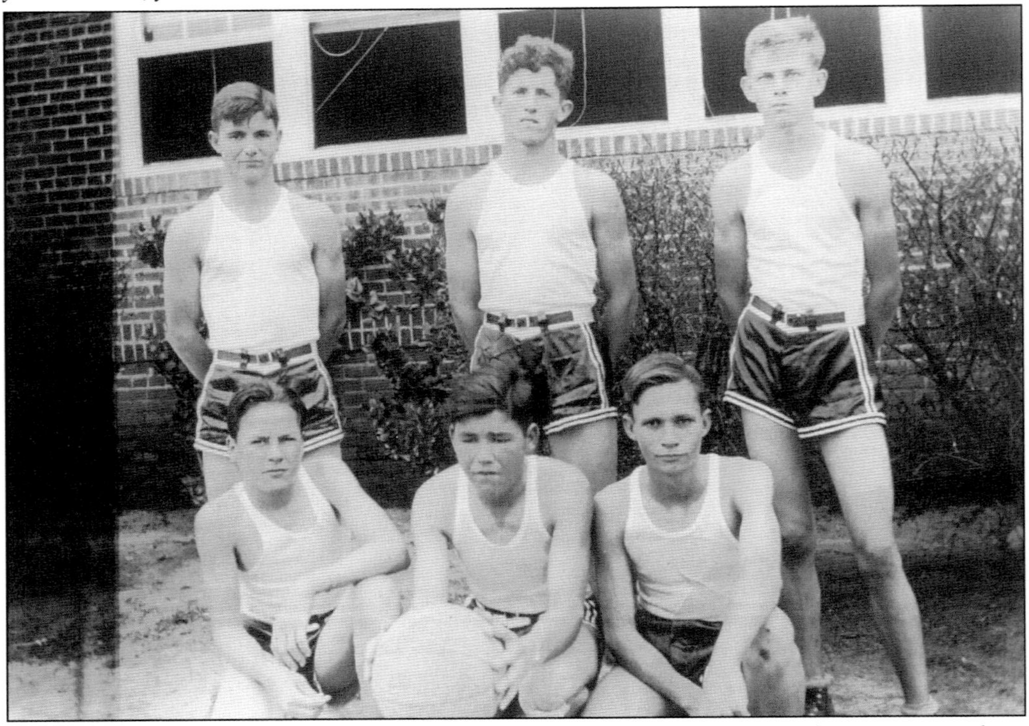

Wewahitchka's six-man basketball team is seen here back in the 1940s. In the picture are, from left to right, (first row) Jiggs Gainer, Kenneth Whitfield, and Tommy Roberts; (second row) Ernest Whitfield, Chap Millergren, and Roy Rish. (EMK.)

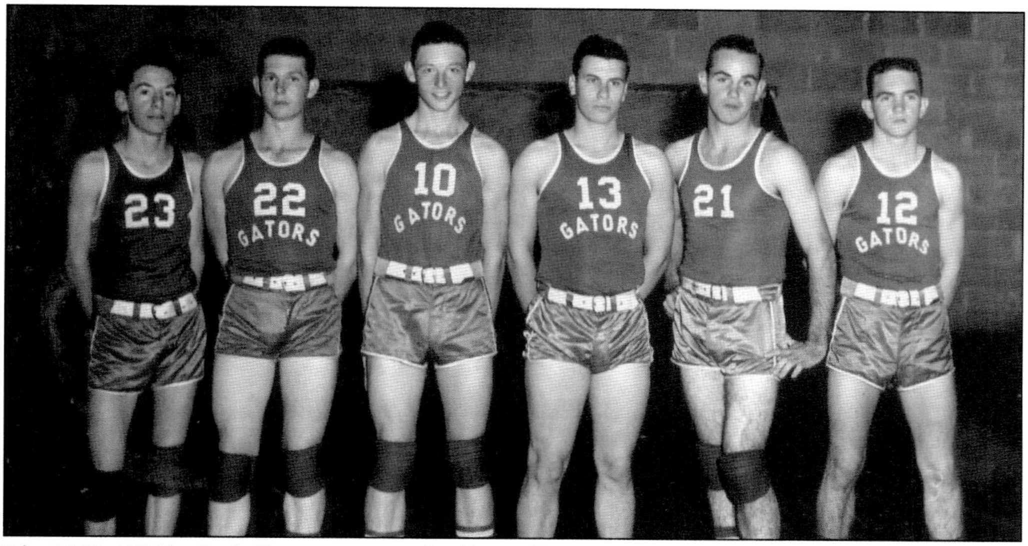

The 1953–1954 basketball team was coached by William Linton, known as a brilliant math teacher and a basketball genius. From 1952 through 1956, the Wewahitchka Gators went to the state finals five consecutive times. They were state champions three of those five years. The players pictured are, from left to right. Jackie Connell (23), Grady Dean (22), Ray Stripling (10), Billy Tillman (13), Bobby Lester (21), and Don Lanier (12). (GD.)

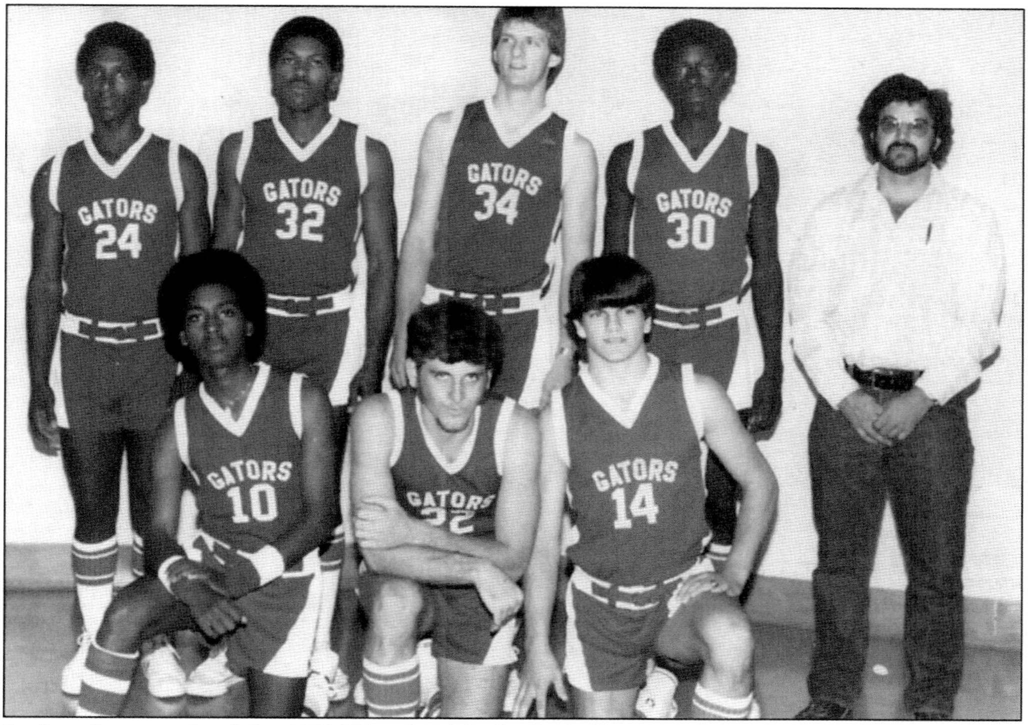

In this photograph of the 1981 Wewahitchka basketball team are, from left to right, (first row) Chris Rouse, Tim Taunton, and Charles Grice; (second row) Vincent Jones, Willie Owens Jr., Darwin Borntrager, Clifford McFann, and coach Charles "Scootsie" Fortner. (BH.)

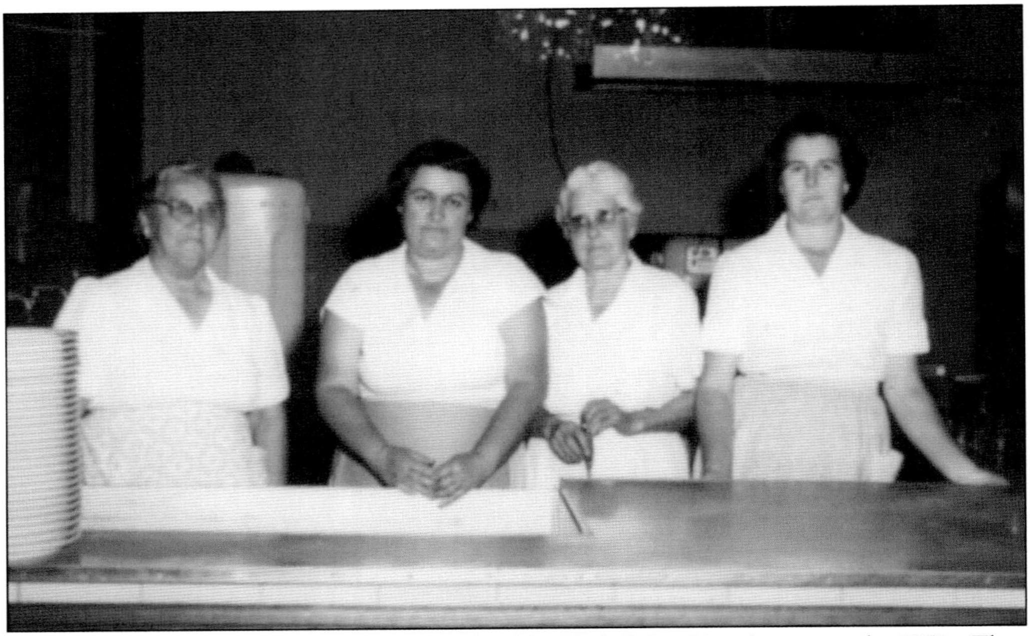

These wonderful ladies served in the Wewahitchka High School lunchroom in the 1950s. They are, from left to right, Lola Hanlon (retired in 1963), Edna Alford (who began in 1946 and became manager after Hanlon's retirement), Leitha Joines, and Gausie Griffin. (THL.)

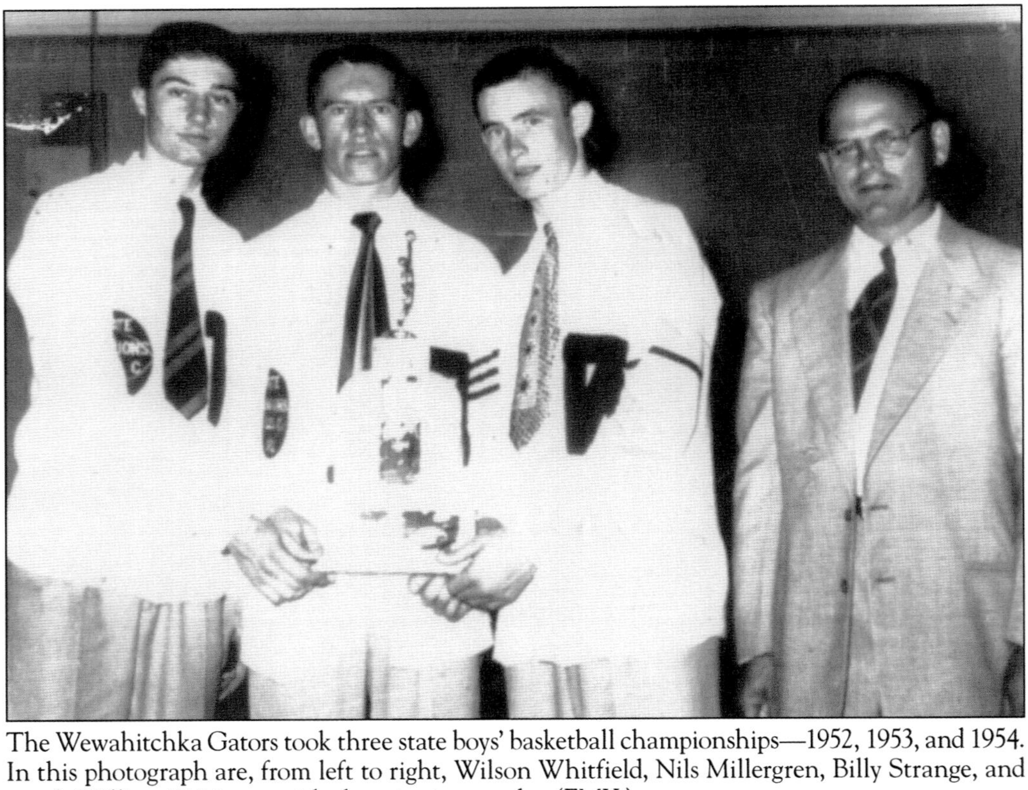

The Wewahitchka Gators took three state boys' basketball championships—1952, 1953, and 1954. In this photograph are, from left to right, Wilson Whitfield, Nils Millergren, Billy Strange, and coach William T. Linton with the winning trophy. (EMK.)

Four

Around Town

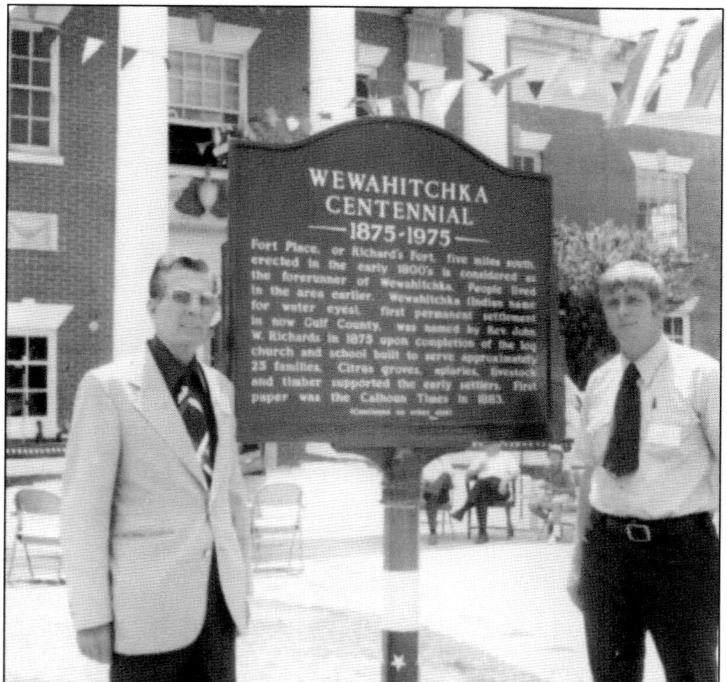

At the time of Wewahitchka's centennial, Gulf County's Golden Anniversary Celebration was planned to promote a new love and pride for this nation and a sense of hope for the future. Here, celebration chairman Jesse Stone (left) and county commissioner Otis Davis Jr. (right) are dedicating a marker to place in front of the courthouse, designating it the "New Courthouse" in Gulf County and the second official seat of government. (BB.)

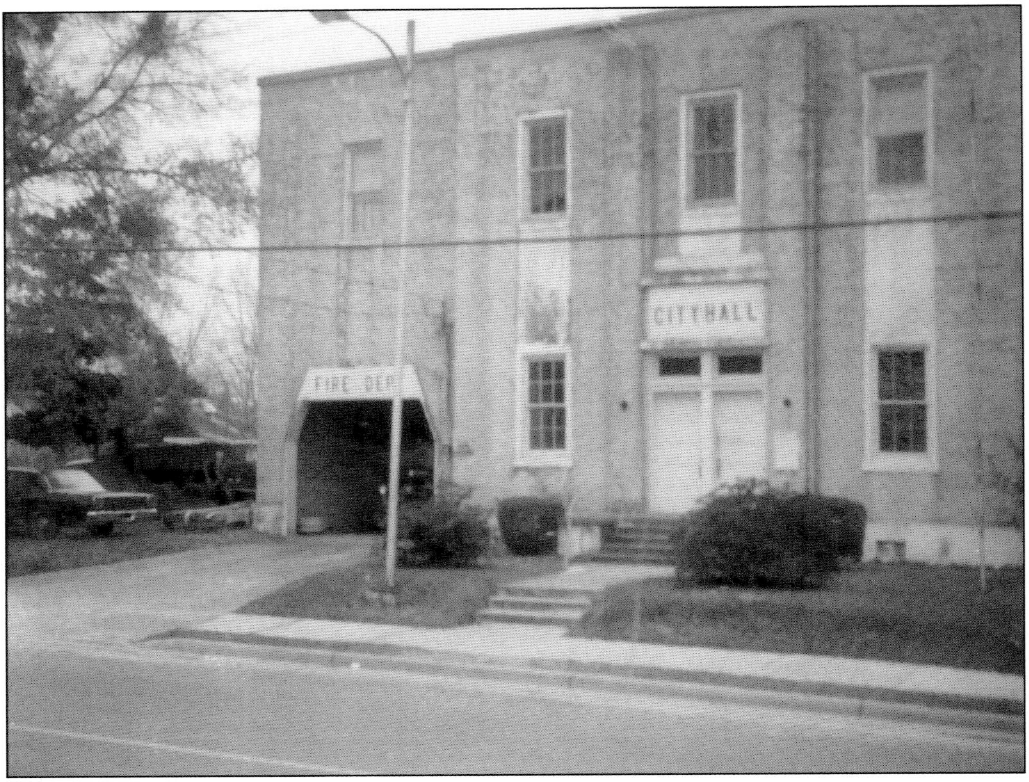

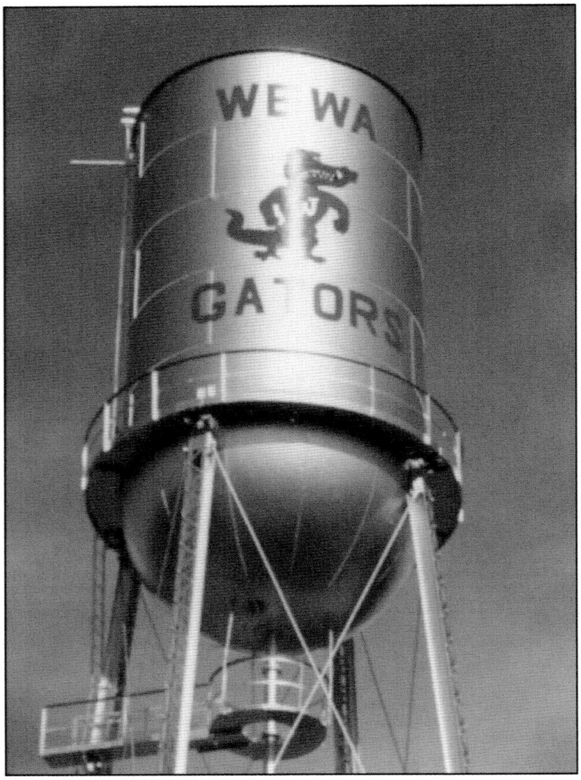

The Old Wewahitchka City Hall was first built in 1941 using Work Projects Administration money and labor. City officials at this time were mayor and city commissioner Charles L. Morgan; city commissioners George D. Campbell, Dave Gaskin, Larry Evans, and Shelby B. Brown; city attorney Fanel M. Campbell; and city clerk Joseph A. Whitfield. (BB.)

The Gators' team name is painted on the town's water tank in this 1986 view. During the years before the City of Wewahitchka had the responsibilities of managing its own utilities, the city's water was handled by the Connell Water Works, managed by Jack Connell Sr. After Captain Roy Connell died in 1957, the Connell family sold the waterworks to the city. (BB.)

Edward Bandjough, born and raised in the small mining town of Masontown, Pennsylvania, had nine brother and sisters. During his high school and college years, he played clarinet in a band he helped organize. This, plus working as a soda jerk, allowed him to put himself through college. Ed was elected Wewahitchka's mayor and served for more than five years. He stepped down in 1980 because of health problems. (BB.)

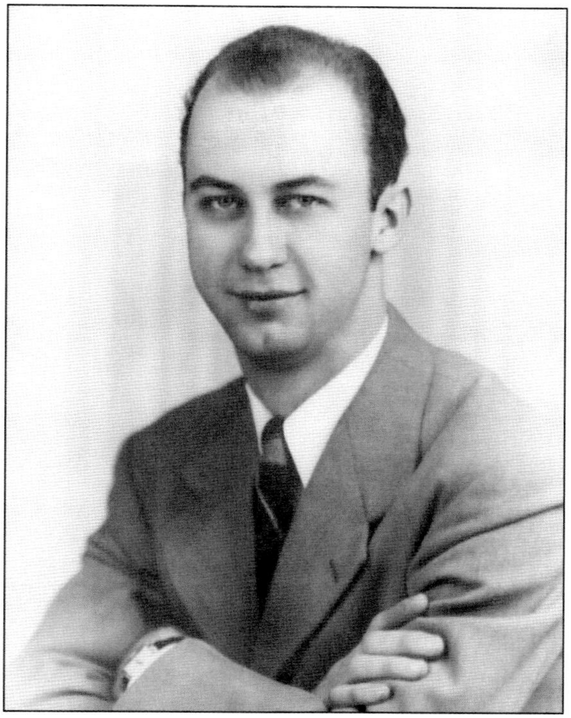

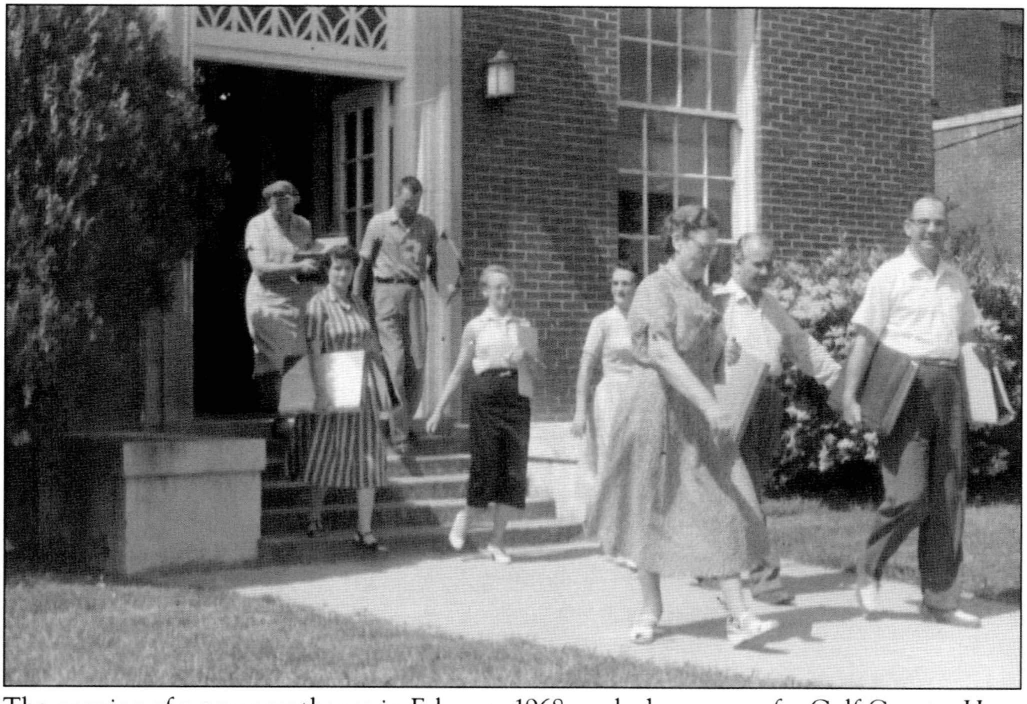

The opening of a new courthouse in February 1968 marked a new era for Gulf County. Here, employees are moving files out of the old Wewahitchka Courthouse and into the new courthouse in Port St. Joe. From left to right are an unidentified lady (in the doorway), Rosie Gaskin, Roy Taylor, Donna Jean (Lister) Tillman, Margaret Lanier, Ella Chafin Smithy, Sammy Patrick, and George Core. (GC.)

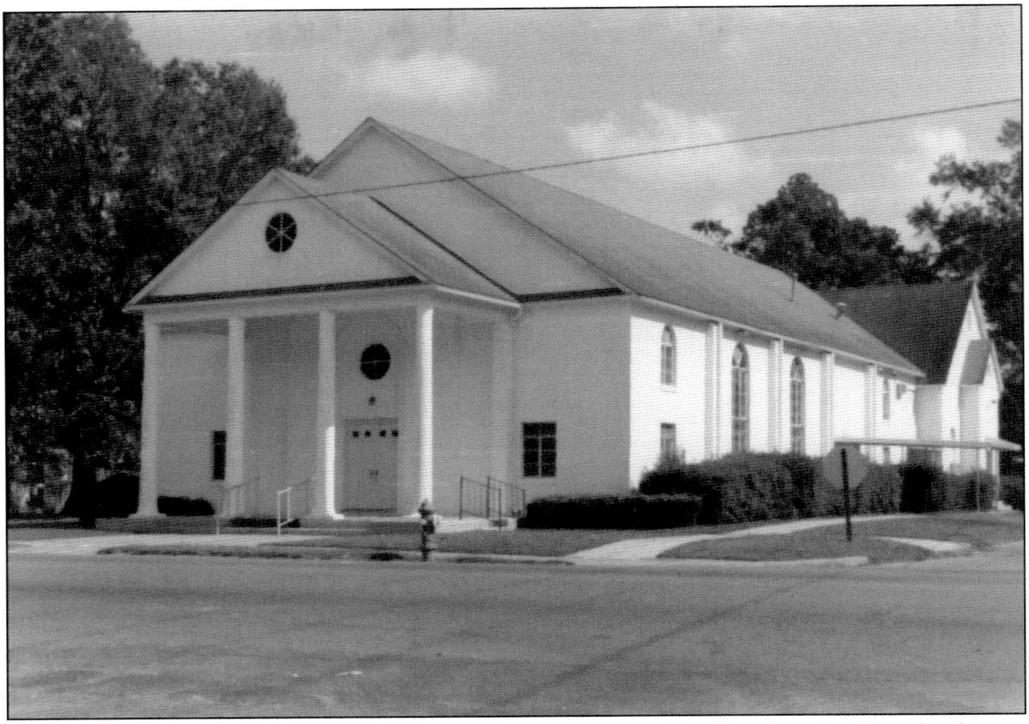

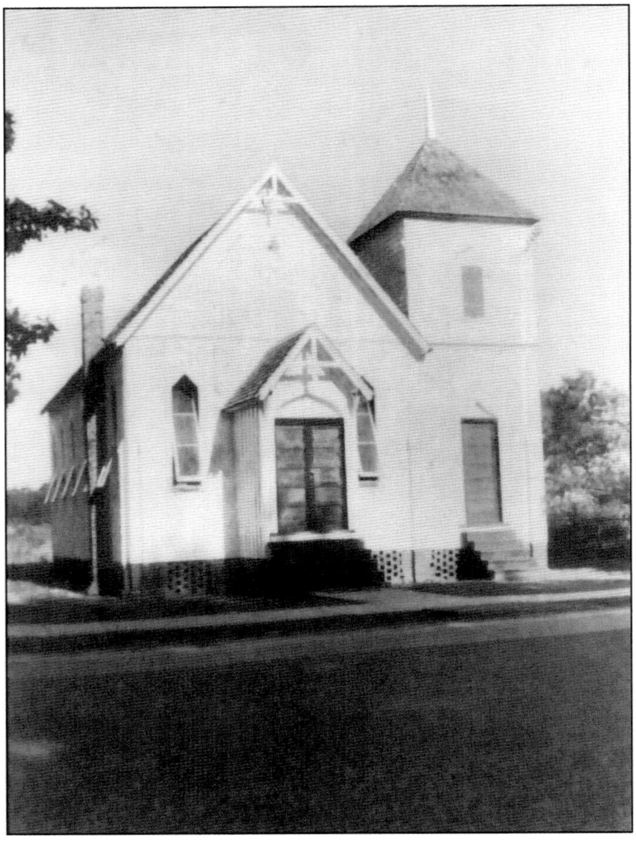

The First Baptist Church of Wewahitchka (built about 1840) is one of the oldest in the state. The church was first located in the vicinity of the Jehu Cemetery, about one mile north of town, which was the site of the first settlement. In 1891, it was moved on logs drawn by oxen from Jehu to its present site in Wewahitchka. It was during the 1940s that the first parsonage was built. (BB.)

The Presbyterian church was the first church actually in Wewahitchka. St. John's Church was built by Francis C. Rummel, a carpenter and skilled craftsman who was born in Bohemia. Rummel was persuaded by Dr. John W. Keyes to move to town from Augusta, Georgia. Dr. Keyes was one of the early settlers of Wewahitchka. It must have been about 1942 that the church was sold to the Presbyterians for a token sum of $500. (EMK.)

Carol Ann Longshore and best friend Carolyn Britt spent much of their childhood and youth playing together around Lake Alice or at Idlewood Fishing Lodge. This photograph, from 1953, was taken on a Sunday afternoon at Idlewood. Carol (left) and Carolyn are standing in front of a car belonging to David and Tweeta Gaskin, Carol's uncle and aunt. (CALC.)

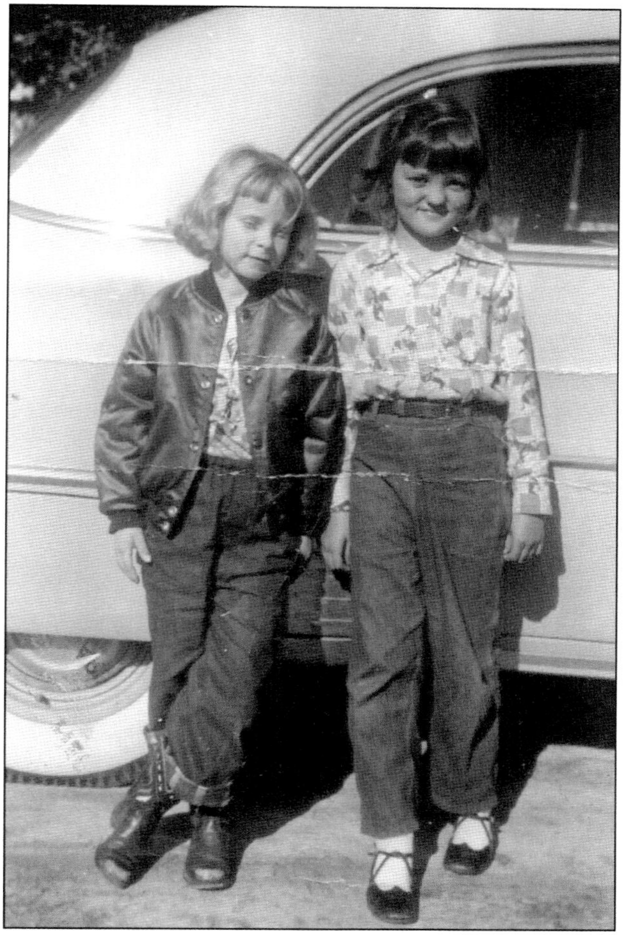

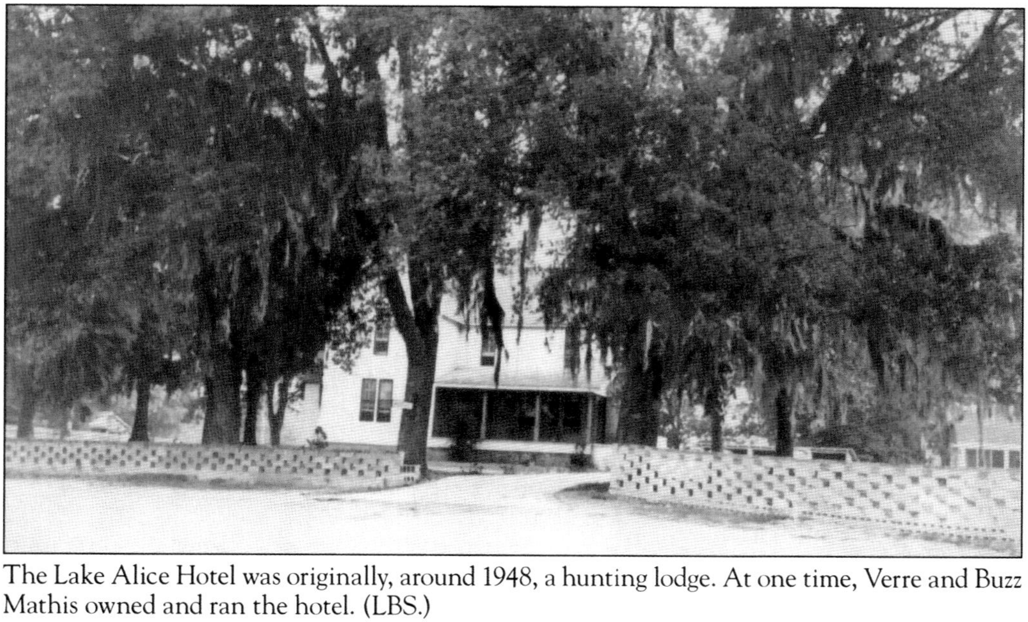

The Lake Alice Hotel was originally, around 1948, a hunting lodge. At one time, Verre and Buzz Mathis owned and ran the hotel. (LBS.)

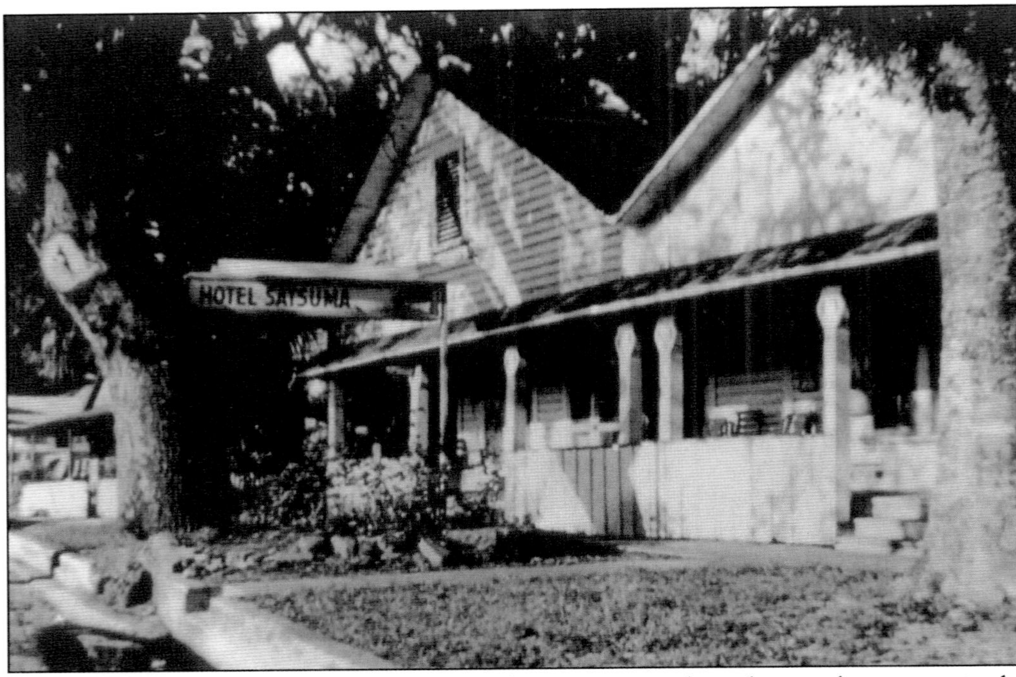

Satsuma Hotel, built in the early days, about the 1920s, went through several managers in the 1940s and 1950s, ending with Forrest and Peggy Revell. Revell bought the hotel in September 1958, and it burned down on the cold night of January 31, 1960. It was located on Main Street in town where the bank is today. (BH.)

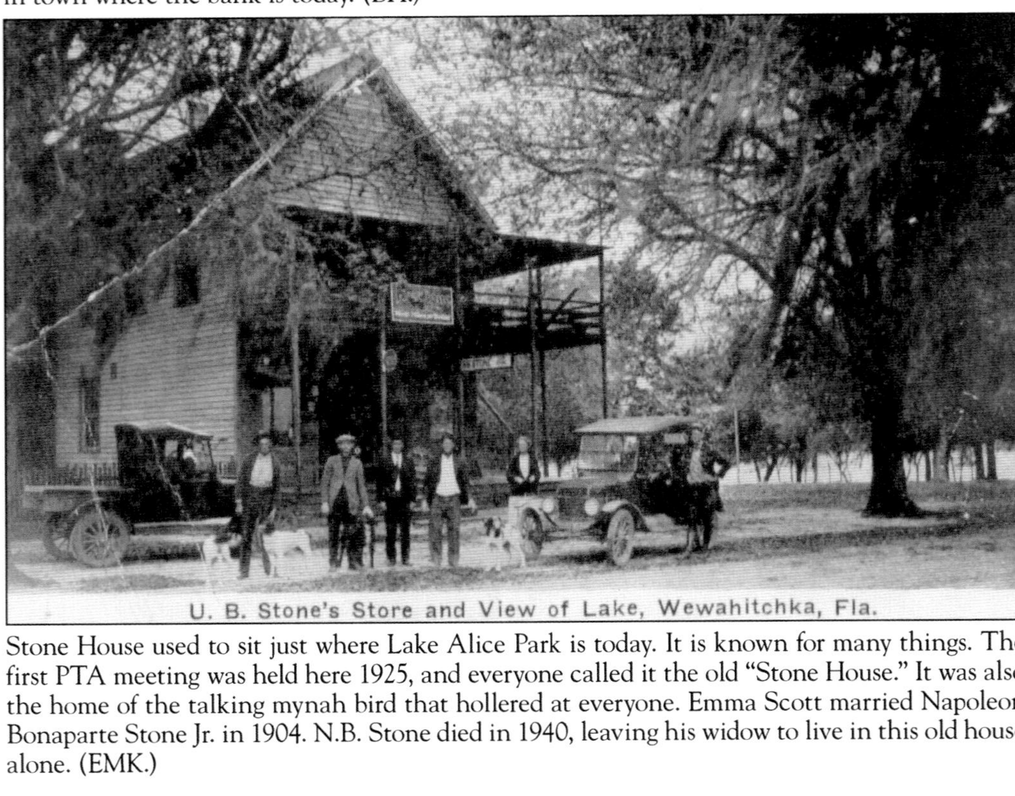

Stone House used to sit just where Lake Alice Park is today. It is known for many things. The first PTA meeting was held here 1925, and everyone called it the old "Stone House." It was also the home of the talking mynah bird that hollered at everyone. Emma Scott married Napoleon Bonaparte Stone Jr. in 1904. N.B. Stone died in 1940, leaving his widow to live in this old house alone. (EMK.)

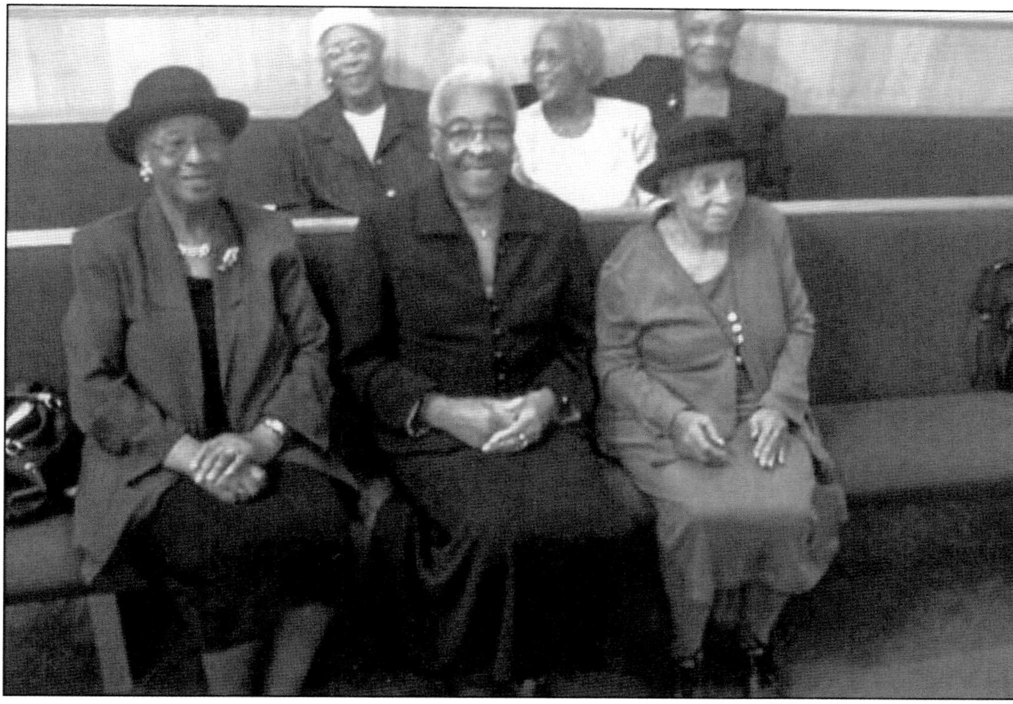

Carter Temple, First Born Church, ladies pictured are, from left to right, (first row) Nevene Colvin, Stella Scott, and Lillian Russ; (second row) Ada Dozier, Gracie Ranie, and Annie Lee Granberry. Gracie was a loving neighbor, always looking after others, and the pound cakes she made caused people to say, "Oh, my goodness!" They are all remembered as good, sweet ladies. (DD and CL.)

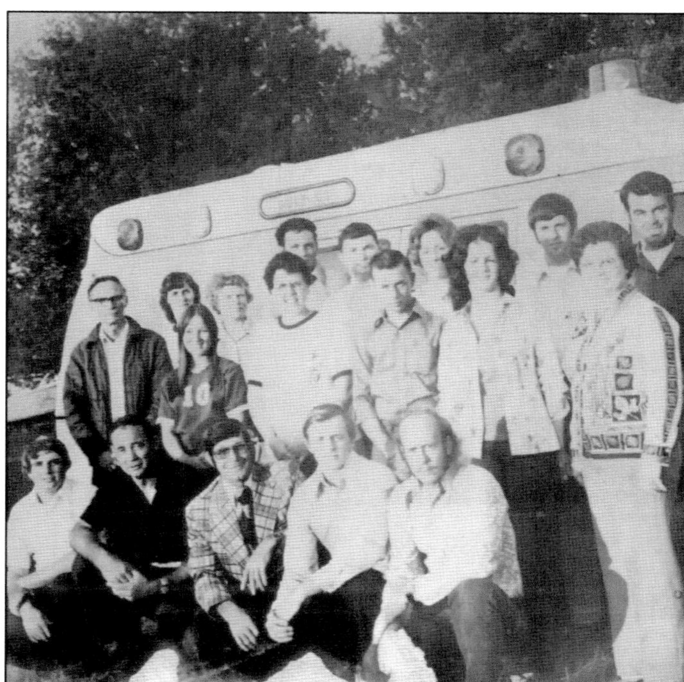

The first Emergency Medical Treatment (EMT) class in Wewahitchka was taught by Mytrice Dean. Charter members here are, from left to right, (first row) Perry Flowers, Skeet Jones, Carl Dean, Arlan Guffey, and Gary Roberts; (second row) Ann Rish Mitchell, Elsie Cauley, Oscar Redd, Doris Herring Pybus, and teacher Mytrice Dean; (third row) Jim Roberts, Betty Cleckley, Tweeta Gaskin, Ward McDaniel, Donald Gilmore, Donna Jones Gilmore Drew, Houston Whitfield, and Sherrill Hartley. (BB.)

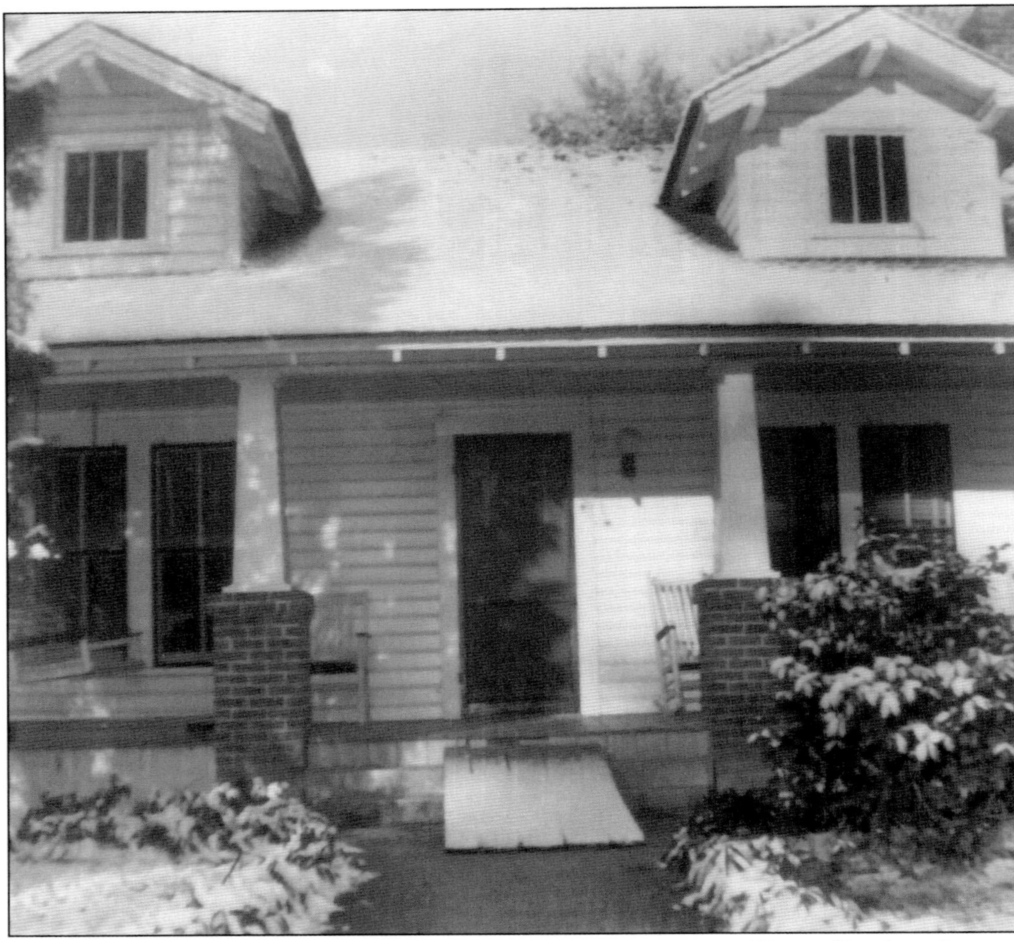

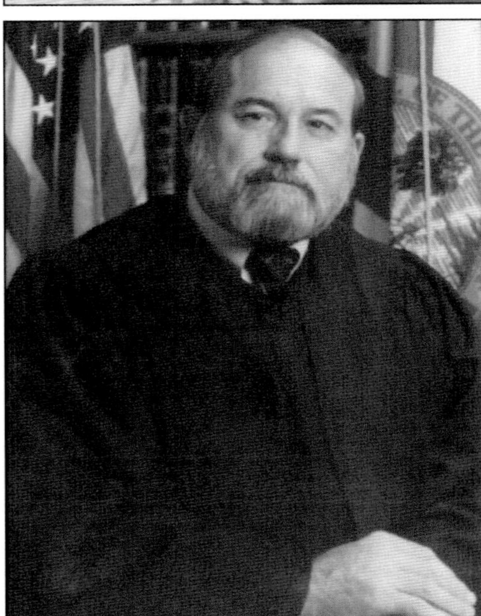

Here, snow is seen on Henry Clay Lister's home in 1958. Lister moved his family from Mississippi to Wewahitchka in 1924. At auction in 1932, Lister bought the Bob Jones College in Bay County, and the family lived there until 1939. The same year, he moved his family back to town and built this house from wood taken from the college buildings. Today, this is David Lister's dental office. (KLW.)

Judge Robert Moore graduated in 1967 from the University of Florida with a juris doctor degree. After graduating, Moore and his family moved to Gulf County, where he began his life's work. He first worked for attorney David Carl Gaskin and as an associate for attorney Cecil G. Costin Jr. In 1970, Moore began his own law practice and served as county attorney and public defender for Gulf County. He served Gulf County for over 30 years. (Phyllis Moore.)

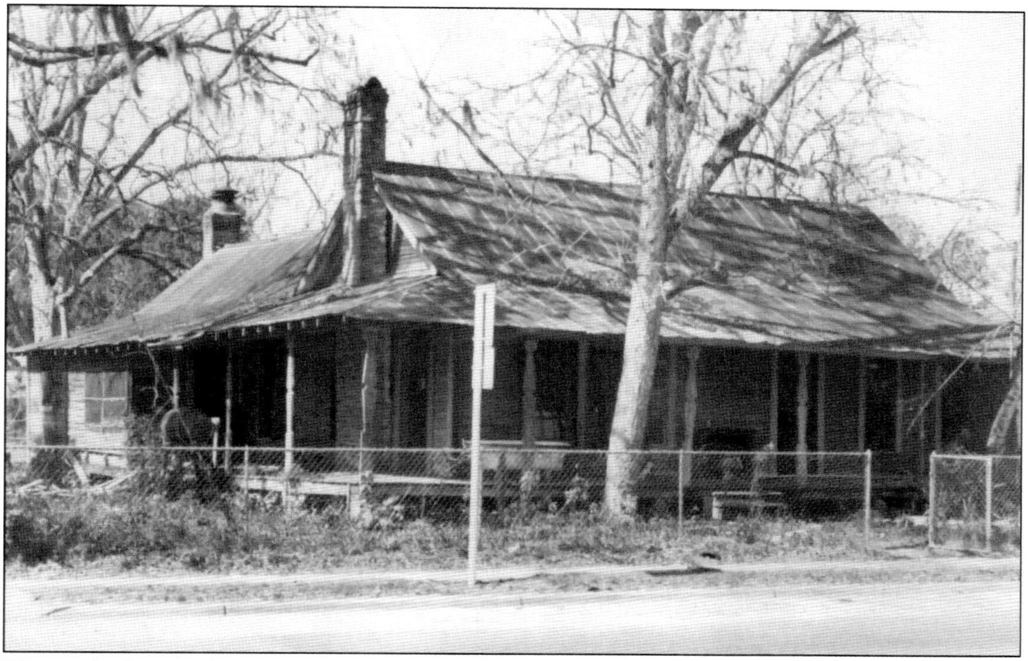

This is the home of Ralph R. Davis and his wife, Clemmie; they came here in 1920. This house has stood at the corner of Highways 71 and 22 for the past 60 years. In 1980, the landmark house was sold and moved. (KGT.)

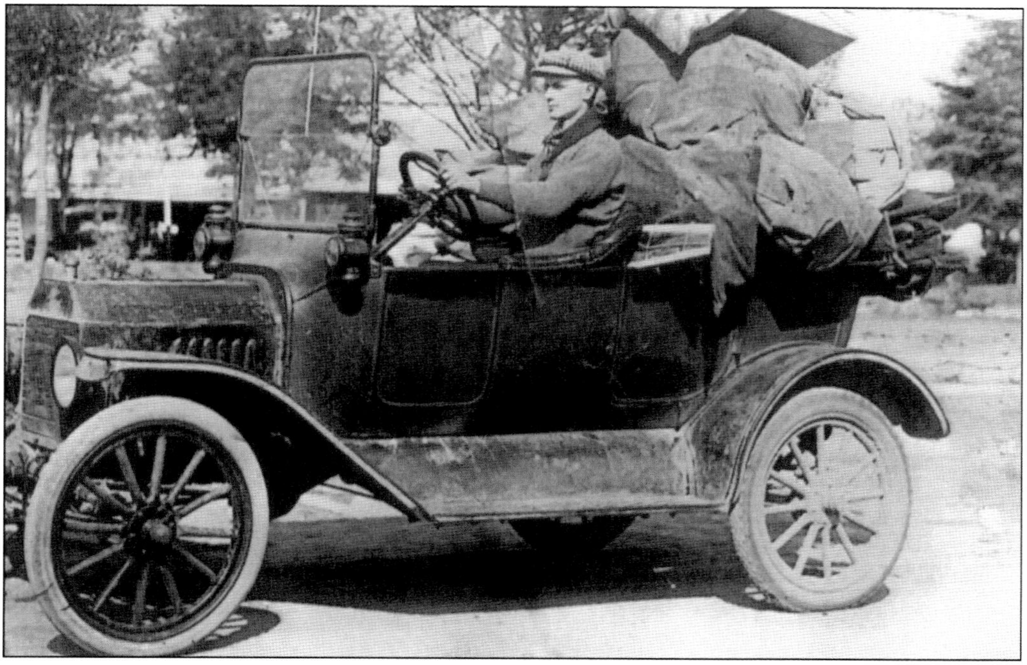

Ralph R. Davis was transferred here as a mail carrier in 1920; his route took him from Wewahitchka to Clarksville to Marianna. Davis said that, in the beginning, he had to go by horse and wagon. It would take him up to two days to do his route, and he would sleep under his wagon. After buying a car, however, it only took a couple of hours to make his run. (KGT.)

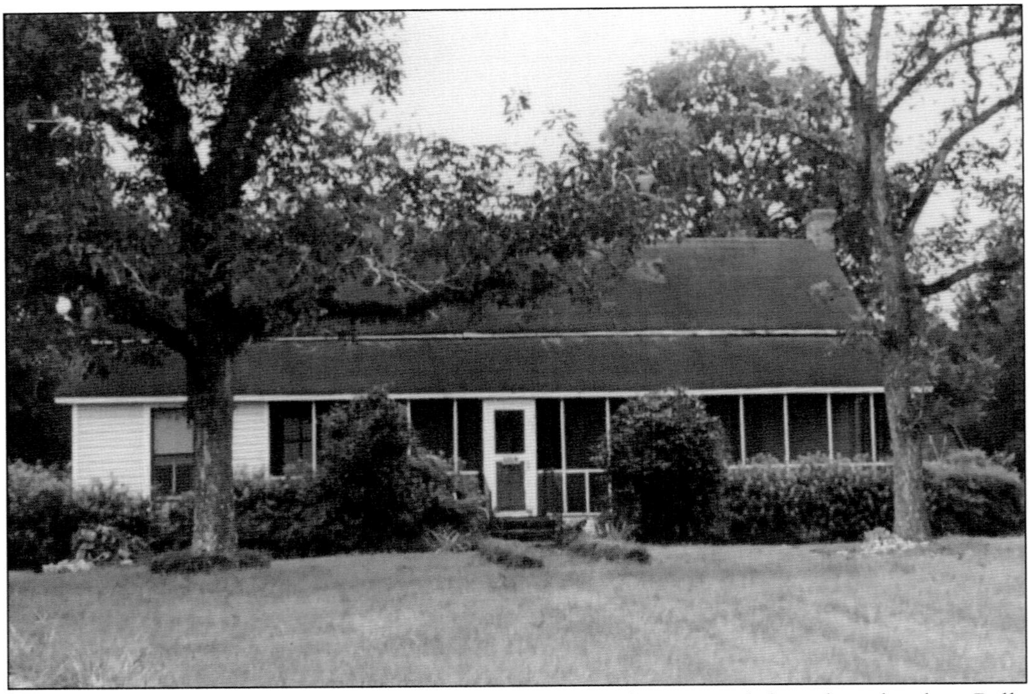

The Gaskin home place was built by George and Kate Gaskin. It was left to their daughter Belle Gaskin McDaniel Cumbie, and she lived there until her death. After her passing, it became part of the estate of Charlie Gaskin, her youngest brother, and it remains in that part of the family. The house is in Dalkeith, about six miles from Wewahitchka. It was built very early in the 20th century. (SMC.)

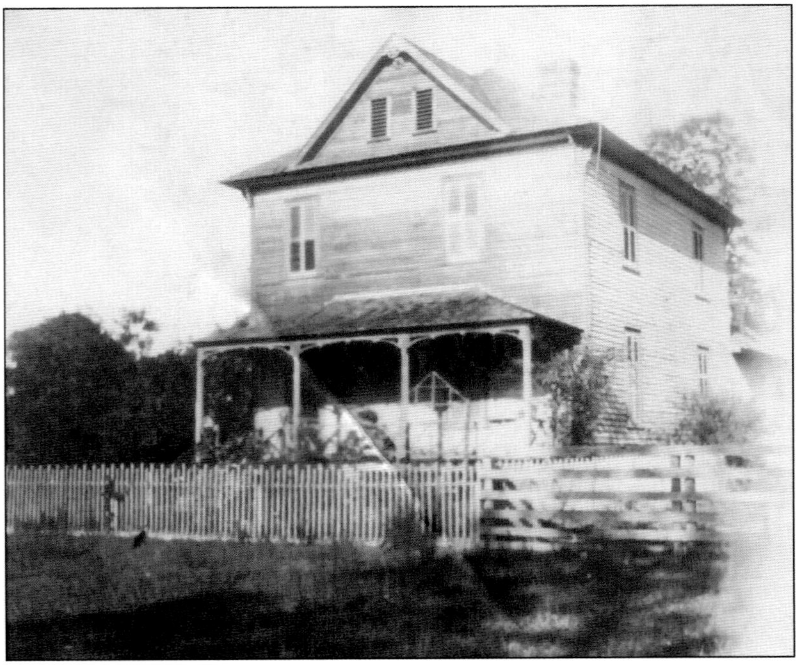

The old Isabell place is the home of James K. and Emma S. Isabell, the family that took in Alf Millergren when he jumped ship in the Panama City area, which was still Washington County in those days. Millergren was Swedish and could not speak English. (EMK.)

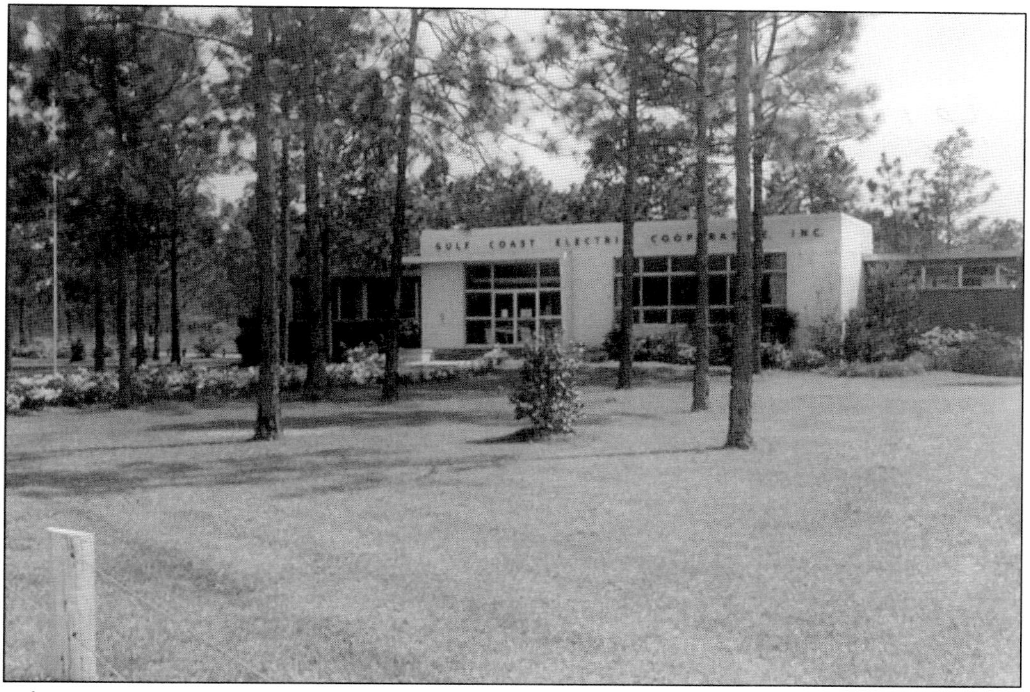

When Pres. Franklin D. Roosevelt created the Rural Electrification Administration (REA) on May 11, 1935, a new day dawned for rural America. Today, more than 900 electric cooperatives are growing strong, bringing more and more conveniences to their consumers. Gulf Coast Electric Cooperative, headquartered in Wewahitchka, Florida, is no exception. This photograph was taken in the 1970s. (REA.)

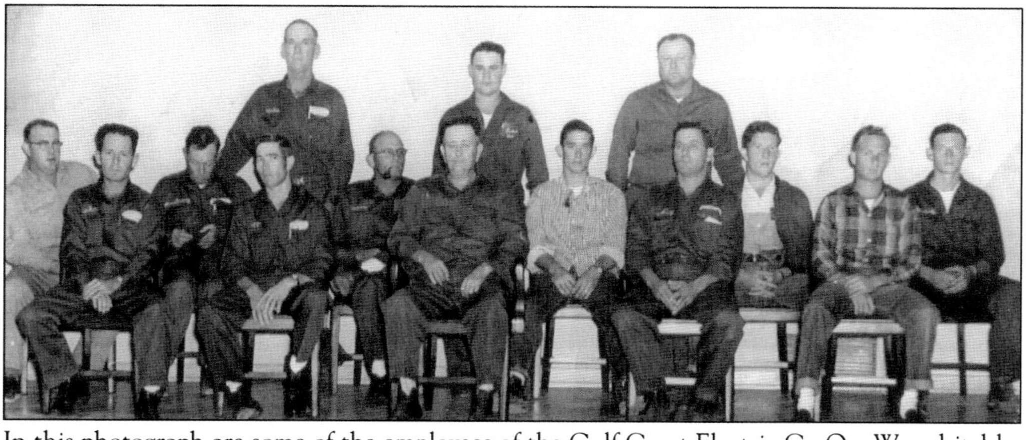

In this photograph are some of the employees of the Gulf Coast Electric Co-Op, Wewahitchka branch. This picture was taken in the late 1950s or early 1960s, and the men are, from left to right, (first row) Tommy Turner, Martin Rocher, Harold Armstrong, Charles Sapp, unidentified, Milton Paramore, Charlie Strange, unidentified, Jimmy Gortman, Burl Grinslade, and Ray Stripling Sr.; (second row) Joe Weeks, and Ray and Perry Ludlum. (Jerry Turner.)

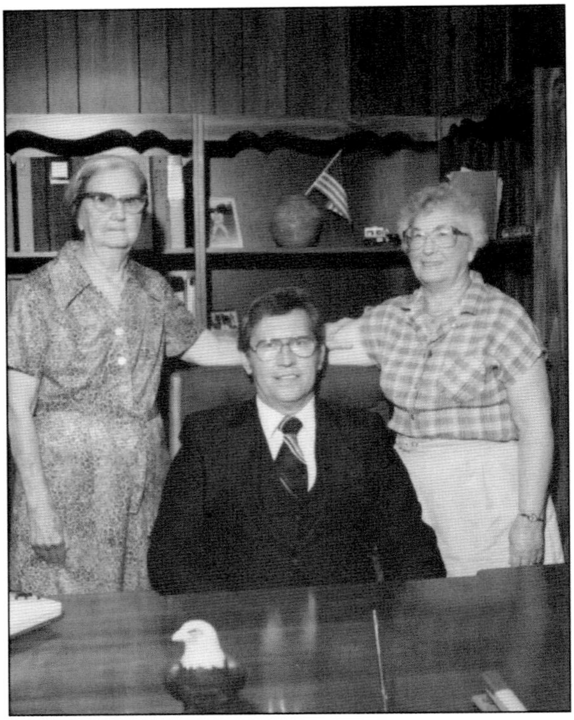

Seen in this c. 1962 photograph, the staff at the Wewahitchka Post Office includes, from left to right, Lucy P. Rish, clerk; Nils Millergren, postmaster; and Emmie Bateman, clerk. Nils took over as postmaster after his father, Alf, retired. (DJRW.)

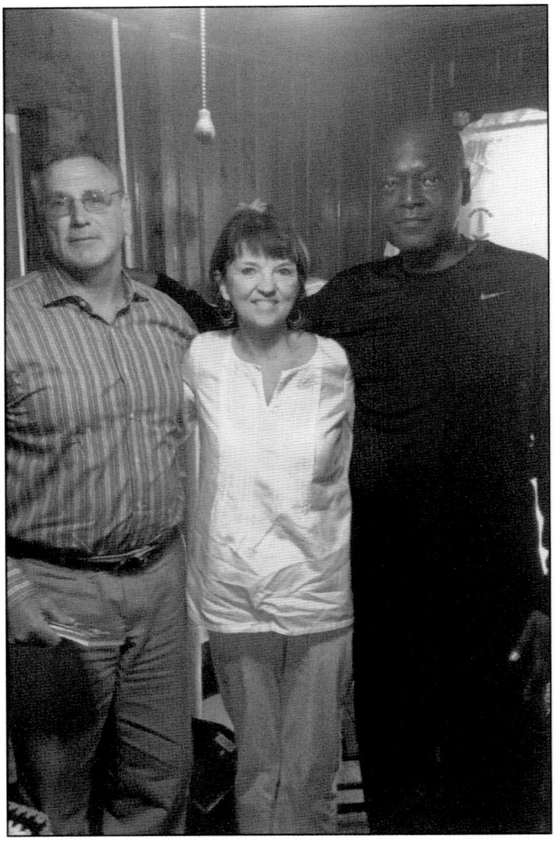

James E. Hurd Jr. (right) was raised in Wewahitchka, Florida, and began his theater work at Florida State University and Florida A&M. He became a playwright and director, coauthoring civil rights–themed dramas. A 1974 graduate of Wewahitchka High School, he authored *Turpentine Jake*. Here, he is pictured at his book signing in the summer of 2013 with classmate Harold Branch and history/government teacher Carolyn Britt Witten. Following his July 2014 death, a memorial service for James was held on July 26 that year. (CBW.)

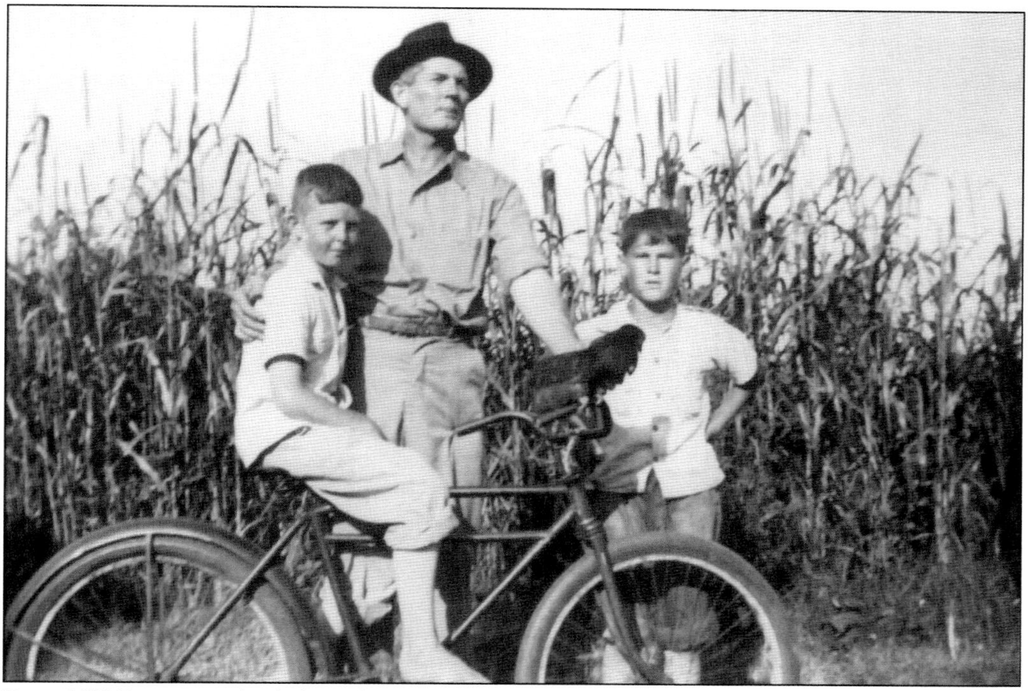

Daniel W. Dean was the father of Grady, Carl, and William Dean and husband to Eula Mae (Ramsey) Dean. Here, he is standing with son Grady (sitting on bike) and his friend Raymond Stephens; Grady's pet chicken can be seen riding on the handlebars of his bike. This picture was taken around 1946. (GD.)

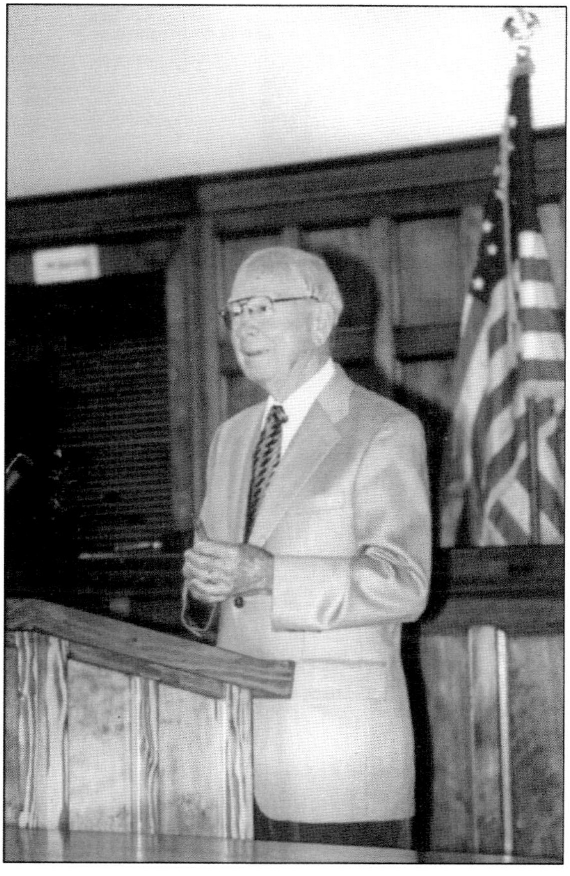

George Core was born in Apalachicola and entered the Army in 1942. He lived in Wewahitchka for over 17 years and was appointed clerk of the circuit court by Joe Hunter in 1948. George retired in 1980. He loved and knew all the history of this area. Of all types of local hunting, George loved to turkey hunt the most. (Author.)

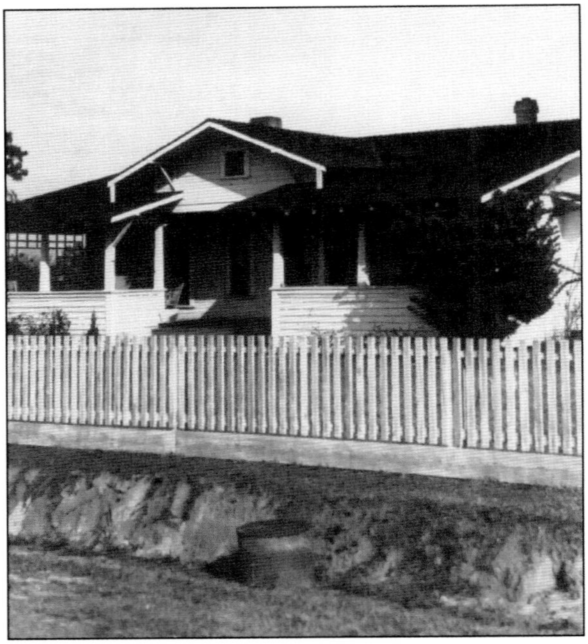

This is the Hunter home. Joe R. Hunter was elected treasurer of the Florida State Beekeepers Association on October 20, 1920, and served as the first county clerk in Gulf County from the early 1920s until the 1940s. His home was located just behind the courthouse in Wewa, and he walked to work each day. He and his wife's family (the Isabells) were some of the early settlers of Wewahitchka. (EMK.)

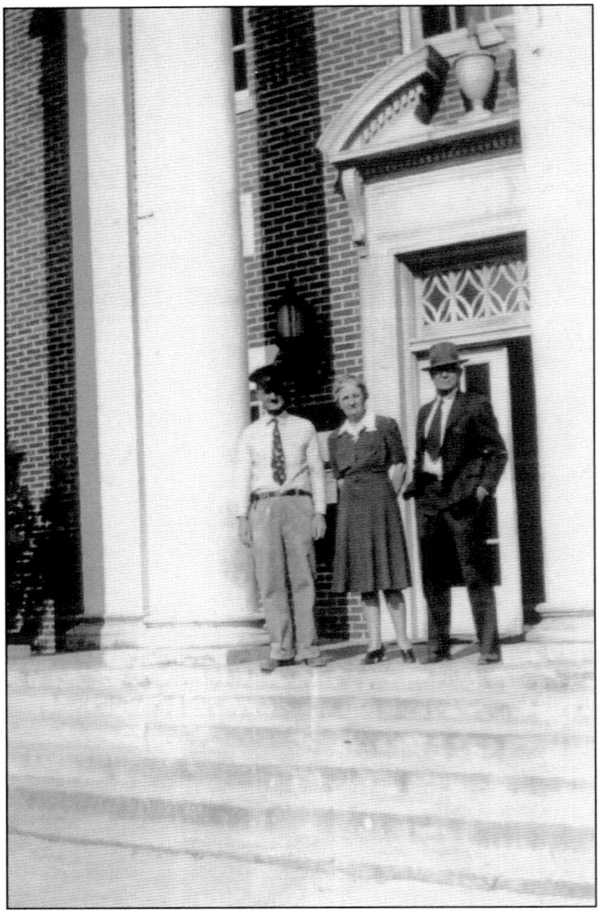

Frank Lanier (left) stands with Lula and Joe Hunter on the steps of the Wewahitchka Courthouse. Frank came to town in 1889. He served overseas in World War I, and for a time he was employed after his return at the air base in Apalachicola as a convict guard. His last employment was with Sherriff Byrd Parker as a deputy jailor for over 15 years. Frank passed away in the Veterans Hospital in Montgomery, Alabama, in 1956. (EMK.)

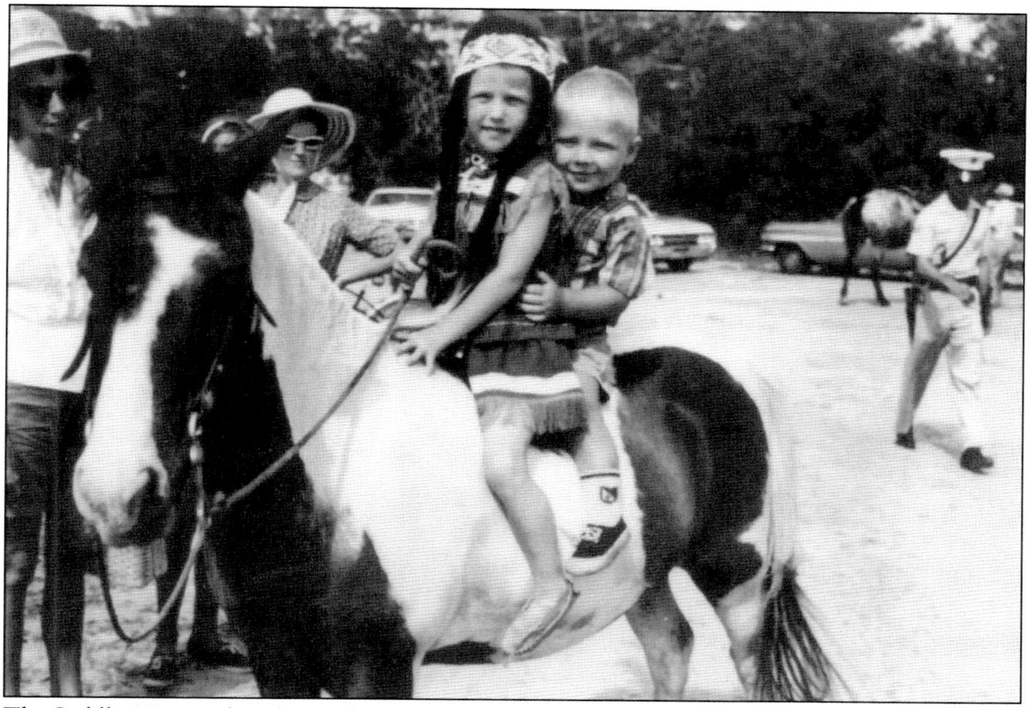

The Saddlin' Seminoles of Wewahitchka, Florida, have taken top honors at horse shows in several Southern states. At the 1966 Peanut Festival in Dothan, Alabama, they won seven blue ribbons out of seventeen offered in competition. The have performed smartly in parades and at state fairs around the South. Pictured here are Ross Stripling's grandchildren Margaret McMillion (in Indian costume) and Stevie Stripling on their pony, joining in the fun. (JJT.)

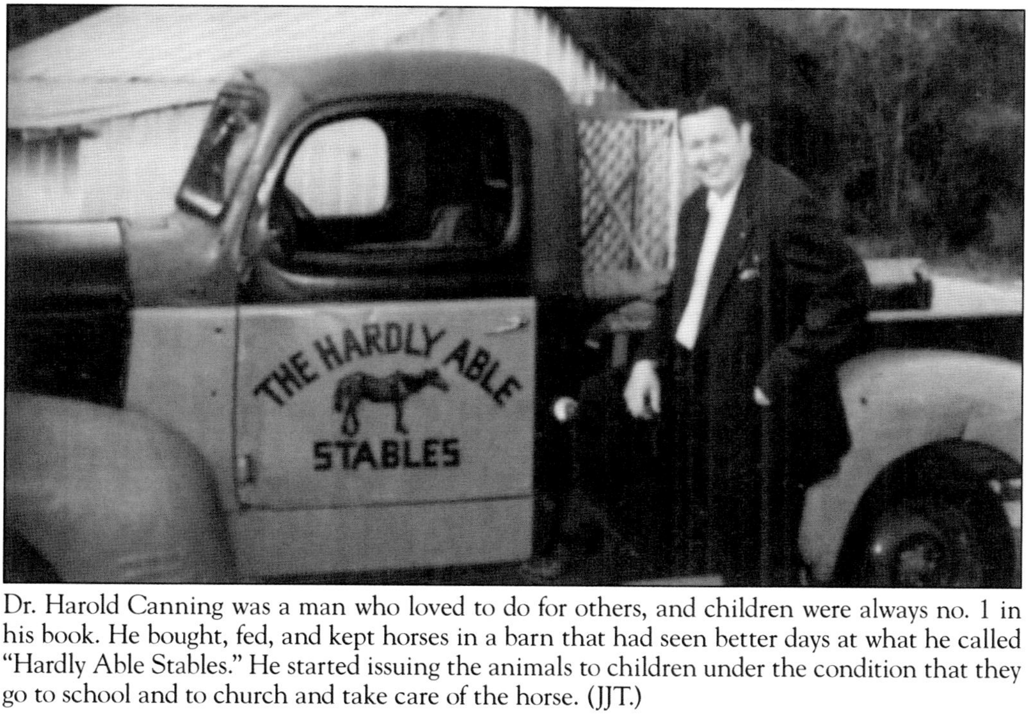

Dr. Harold Canning was a man who loved to do for others, and children were always no. 1 in his book. He bought, fed, and kept horses in a barn that had seen better days at what he called "Hardly Able Stables." He started issuing the animals to children under the condition that they go to school and to church and take care of the horse. (JJT.)

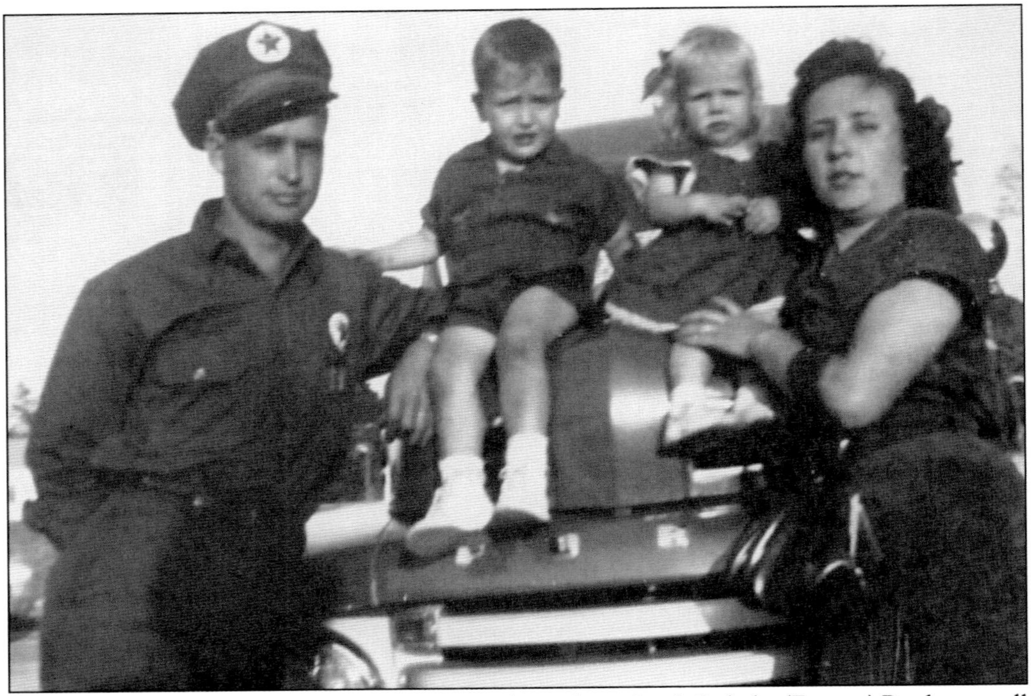

Haywood Borders, his son Charles, daughter Linda Gayle, and wife Ophelia (Fortner) Borders are all pictured with of their family truck in front of their Texaco gas station, which was built in 1950 and was later turned into a Gulf station; it was located on Main Street in Wewahitchka. (LBS.)

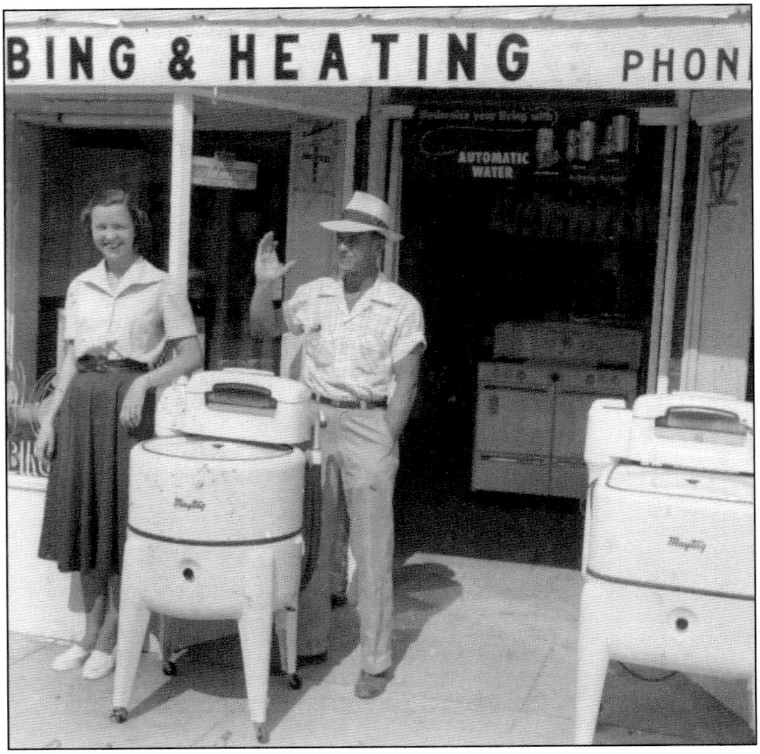

Betty and Bobby Rish stand in front of the Wewahitchka Plumbing & Heating store, located across from the Buy Rite Drug Store in town. The building had been constructed many years before and became Wewahitchka Plumbing & Heating around 1952, maybe a little earlier. Years later, it was changed to West Florida Gas. (DJRW.)

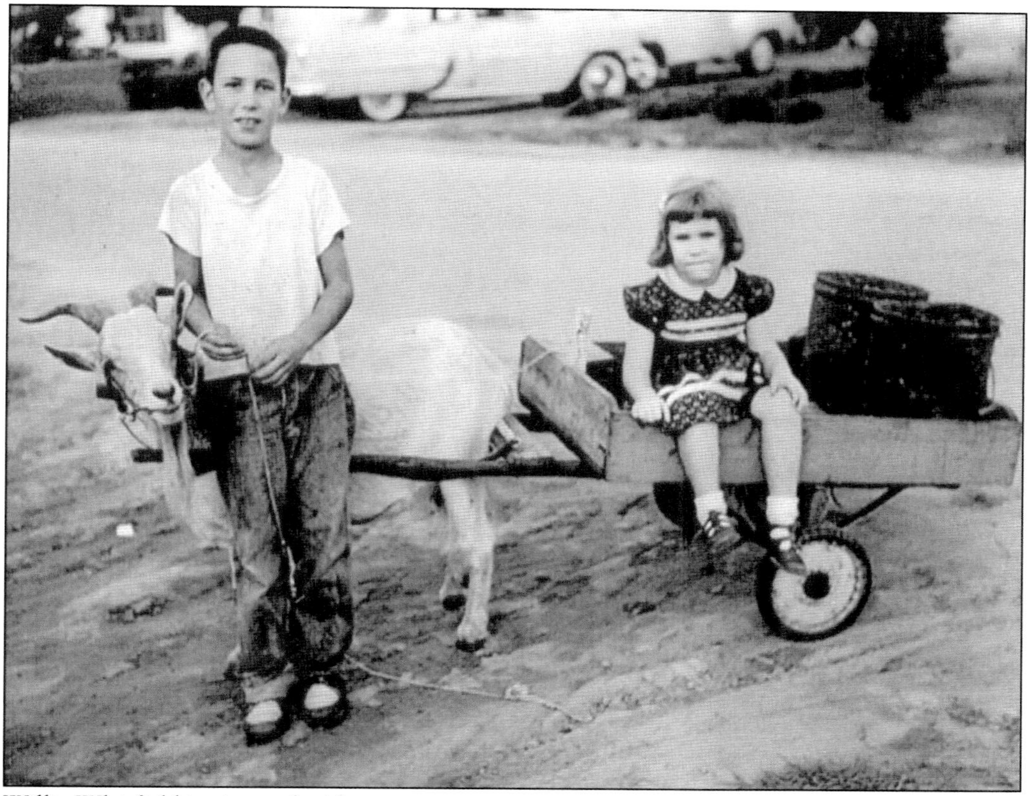

Willie Whitfield is pictured with a goat called Old Nick. Willie used the cart to go around town gathering food for his hogs. When the goat slowed down, he would grab its tail, and it would start trotting. This picture was taken at his cousin Connie Whitfield's fourth birthday party (she is the girl in the cart) in October 1958. Willie gave everyone rides in his cart. (CW.)

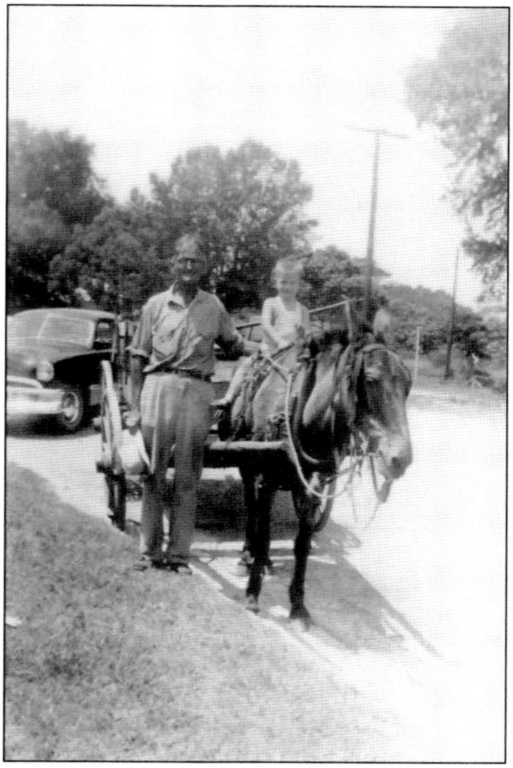

Walter Pitts picked up garbage, and his mule was named Pet. If Walter spent too much time talking to someone, Pet would leave and go home. In this photograph, Walter is giving little Al Millergren a ride. (EMK.)

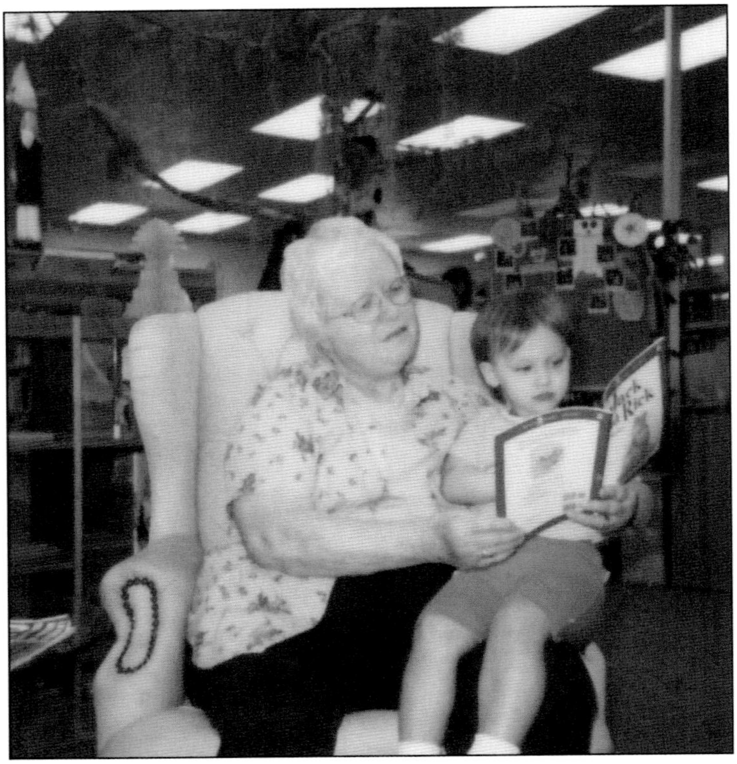

Ann Matlock retired after spending 31 years as a librarian. She began her service when the library was in a small nook in the old courthouse. Here, she is seen in her last years before retiring, reading a book to an unidentified child. (WLIB.)

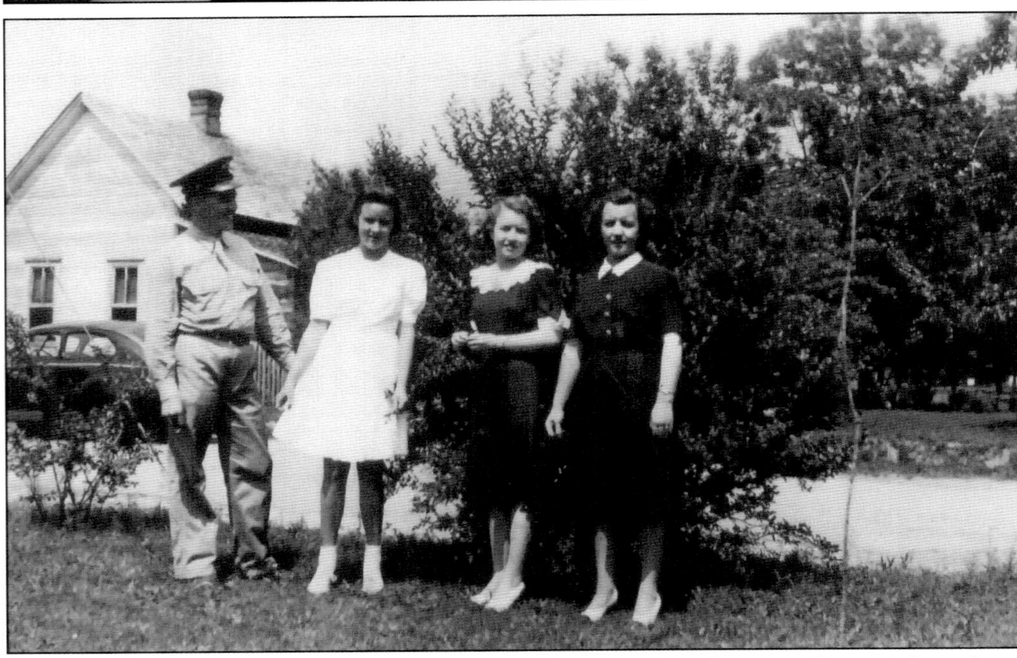

James Franklin Rish Jr. is pictured around 1945 in his Army Air Corps uniform while on leave and visiting his sisters, from left to right. Amy Lou (Musgrove), Marguerite (Brock), and Jeanette "Sister" (Floyd), the eldest. Their parents, James F. Rish Sr. and Fanny Lou (Gibson), married in 1916. James Sr. was a beekeeper, cattleman, and farmer. Fanny Lou was a true homemaker; before her marriage, she had been schoolteacher and taught first grade here for one year. (JER.)

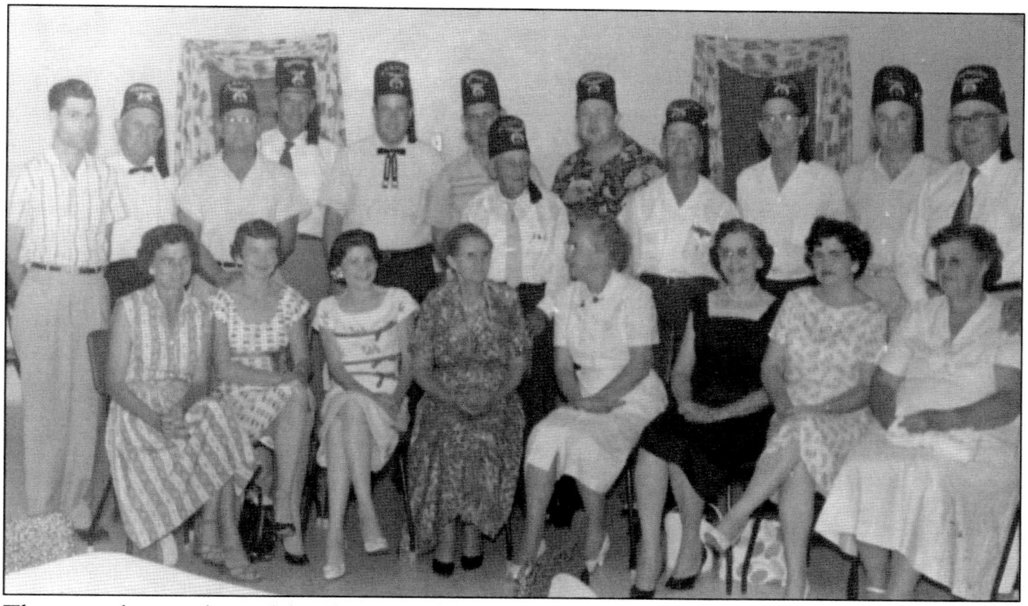

These are the members of the Shriners Club of Wewahitchka and their wives. The men are, from left to right, David C. Gaskin, two unidentified, Thomas McDaniel, Frank Graddy, unidentified, Roy P. Rish, Dr. Harold Canning, unidentified, Dave Gaskin, George Core, and unidentified. The ladies are, from left to right, unidentified, Tweeta Gaskin, Violet "Sis" Graddy, unidentified, Lucy Rish, Annie Gaskin, Cornelia Canning, and unidentified. (BB.)

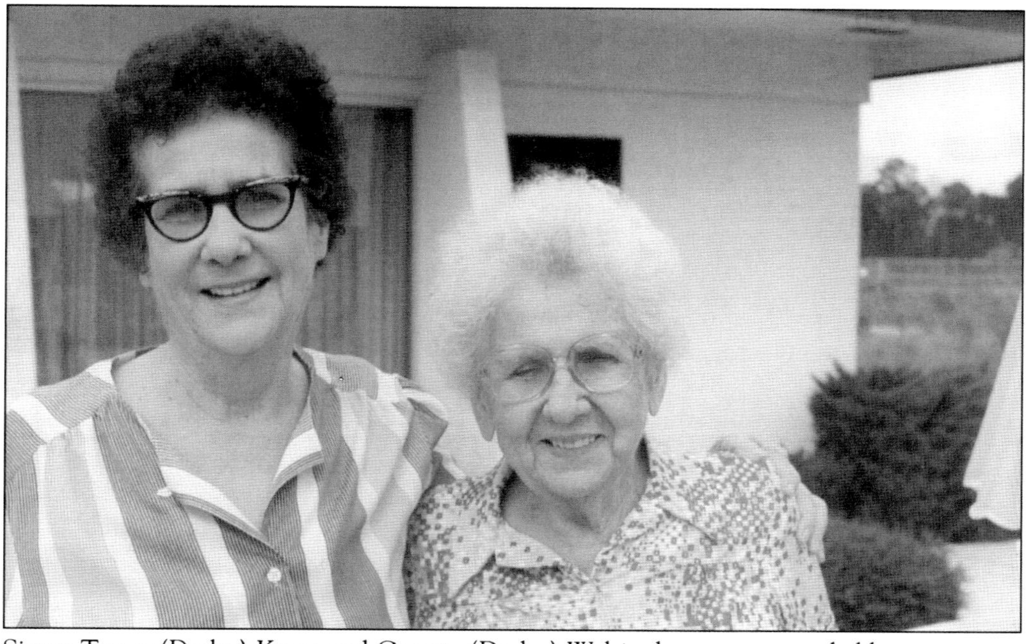

Sisters Treasy (Darley) Kemp and Cosetta (Darley) Walsingham, two remarkable women, are pictured here at a family reunion held in 1984. Extraordinarily strong in their Christian faith, they persevered in the face of adversity in their lives. Treasy was widowed with two teenage children, and Cosetta had problems with severe rheumatoid arthritis; yet they never gave up and were never defeated. They were inspirations to many, especially their children and a niece, Henrietta Darley Branch. (HDB.)

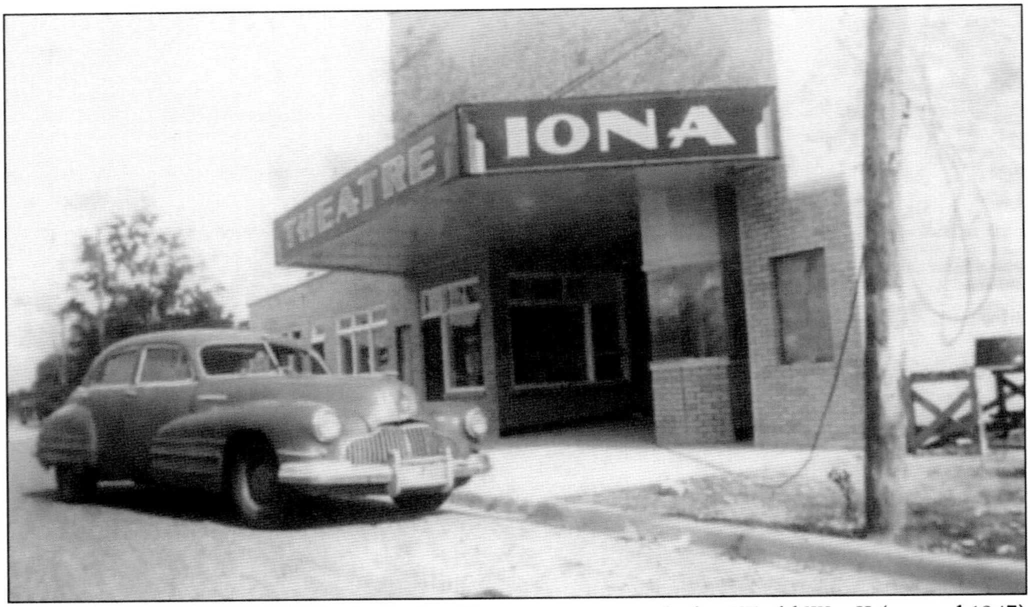

The Iona Theater, owned by Rudy Gaskin Sr., was constructed after World War II (around 1947) and purchased from Mattie and S.E. McDaniel. After Gaskin ran the theater, it was leased to a Mr. Wilson and his wife, Betty. The price of admission when the theater first opened was 11¢ for children and 25¢ for adults. Refreshments were a nickel. In 1960, the theater burned. (SMC.)

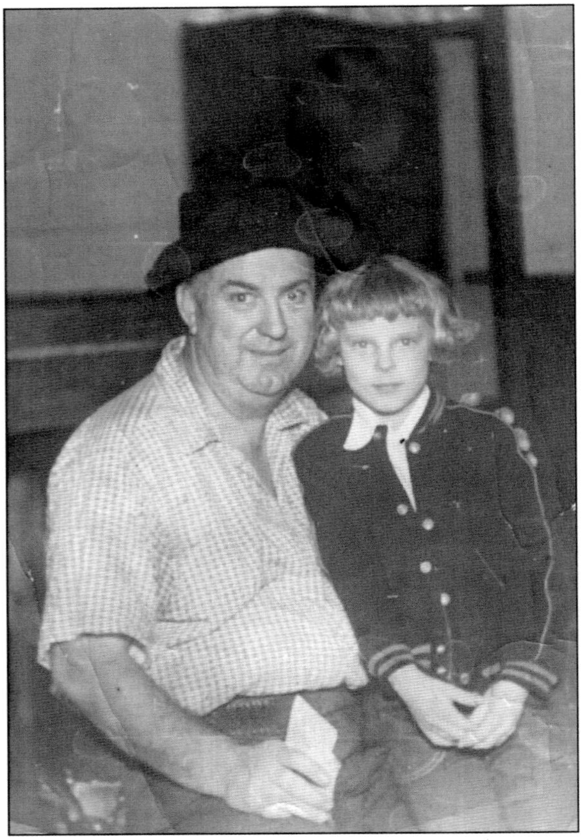

Lester Alvin Burnett, better known as Smiley Burnette, was a well-known country music performer and comedic actor who appears in many Gene Autry westerns. Burnette would show up now and then when Autry's movies were playing, and kids loved getting their photographs taken with him. In this shot, he is sitting with little Carol Ann Longshore, at the Iona Theater in 1954. (CALC.)

"Preacher" is what everyone called him, but his given name was Jonathan Harrell Glass. A lifelong resident of Wewahitchka, Preacher was married to Patricia Teat of Apalachicola for over 25 years, and they had two girls, Darlene and Sherry Glass. He was an employee of Gulf County, serving as chief of police for the city of Wewahitchka for over 19 years. Both he and Patricia passed in 1990. (BGW.)

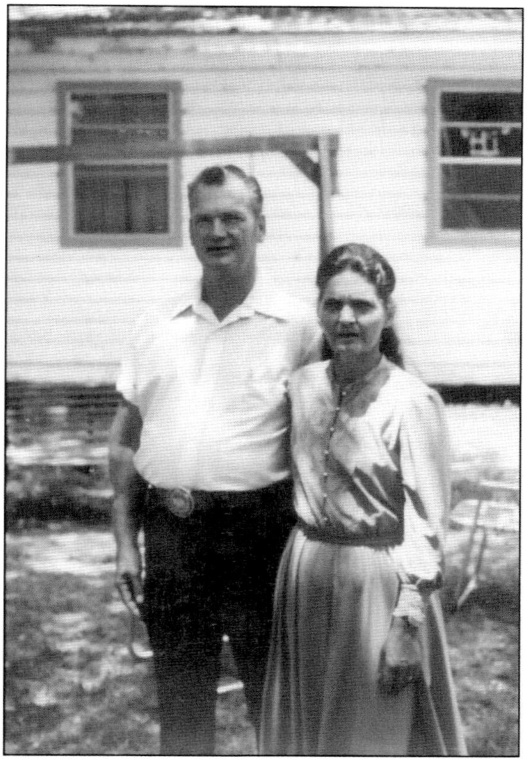

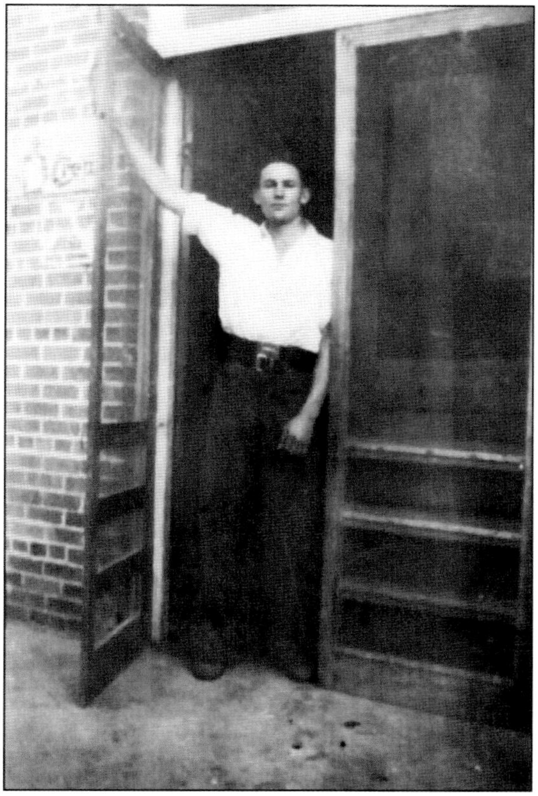

Frank Britt, son of Sam and Irene Britt, stands in the doorway of his mothers' Britt Café back in the late 1930s. (CBW.)

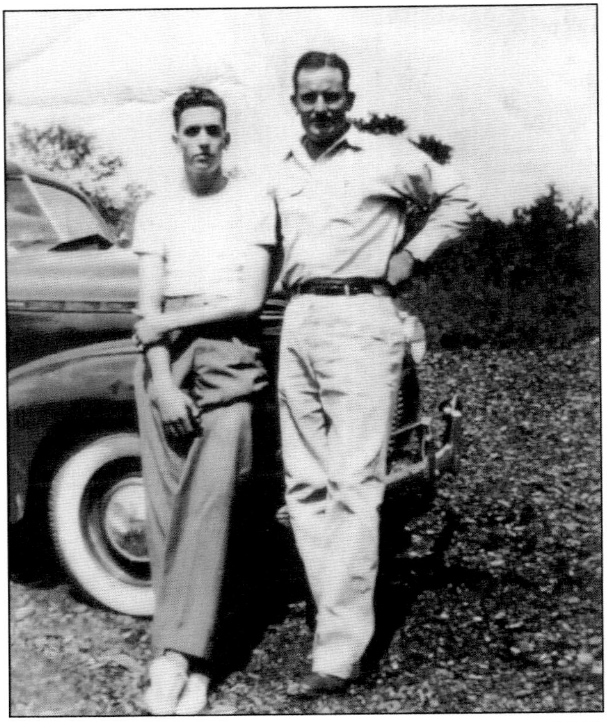

Thomas McDaniel (right) and Frank Britt were not only best friends, they were both members of the Wewahitchka Volunteer Fire Department in 1956. Thomas also was manager of the Wewahitchka baseball team in 1957. William Franklin Britt was the youngest of four sons born to B.F. and Hettie McDaniel Britt. Frank primarily worked for the US Army Corps of Engineers and operated the Standard Oil station in Wewahitchka. (PMM.)

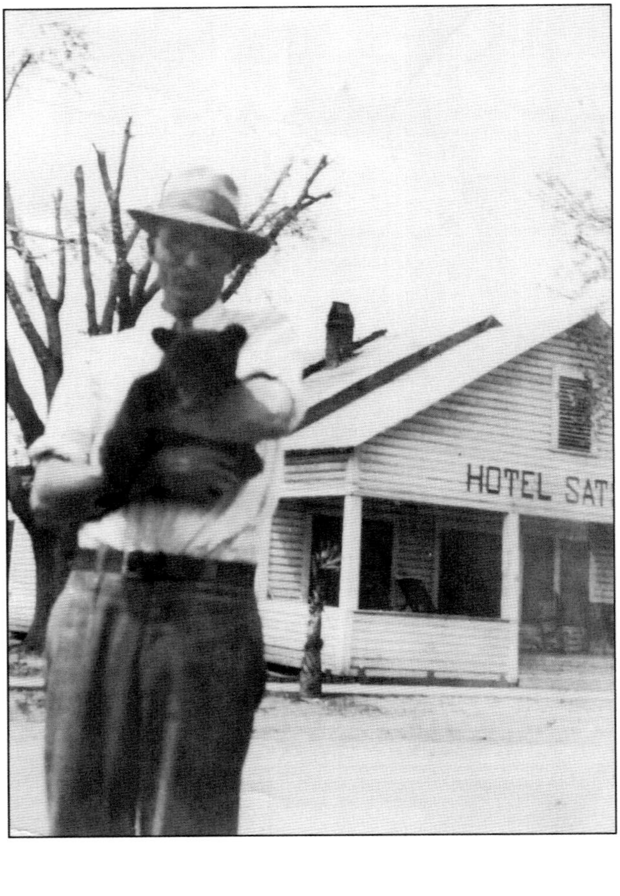

Lorna (McDaniel) Millergren's twin brother, Jim B. McDaniel, is standing in front of the old Hotel Satsuma with his trained bear. They are also remembered for riding around town on a white horse. (EMK.)

Five

Hunting and Fishing Season

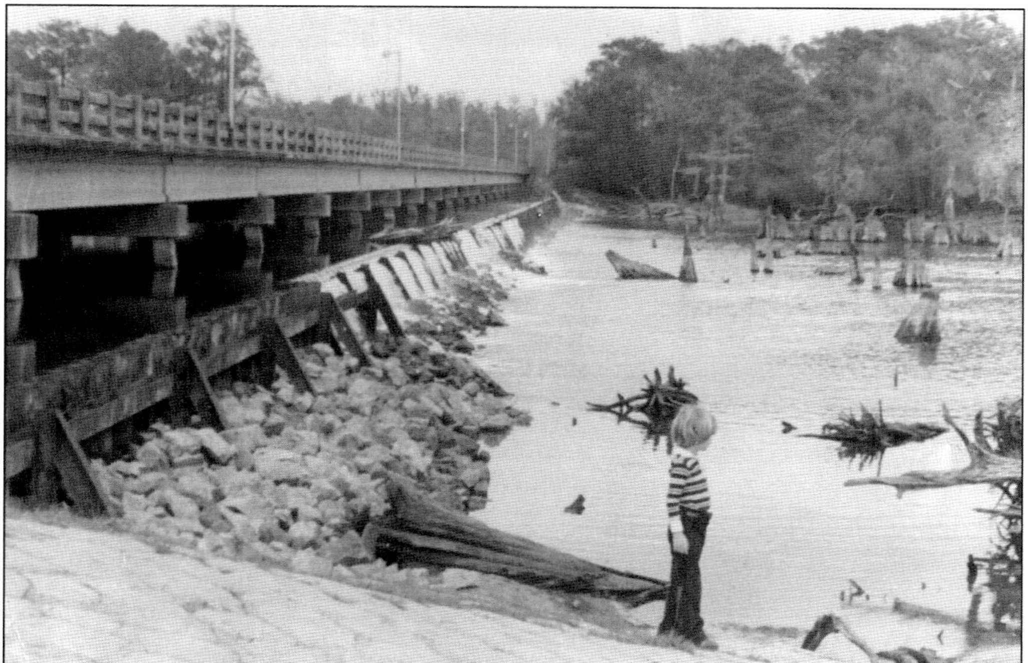

Travis Allen Gillenwater, the son of Bernadette "Bunny" Bandjough-Gillenwater, was six years old in 1978. Here, he is checking out the water at the Dead Lakes Dam when it was still working; water can be seen flowing over the dam and onto the rocks below. (BB.)

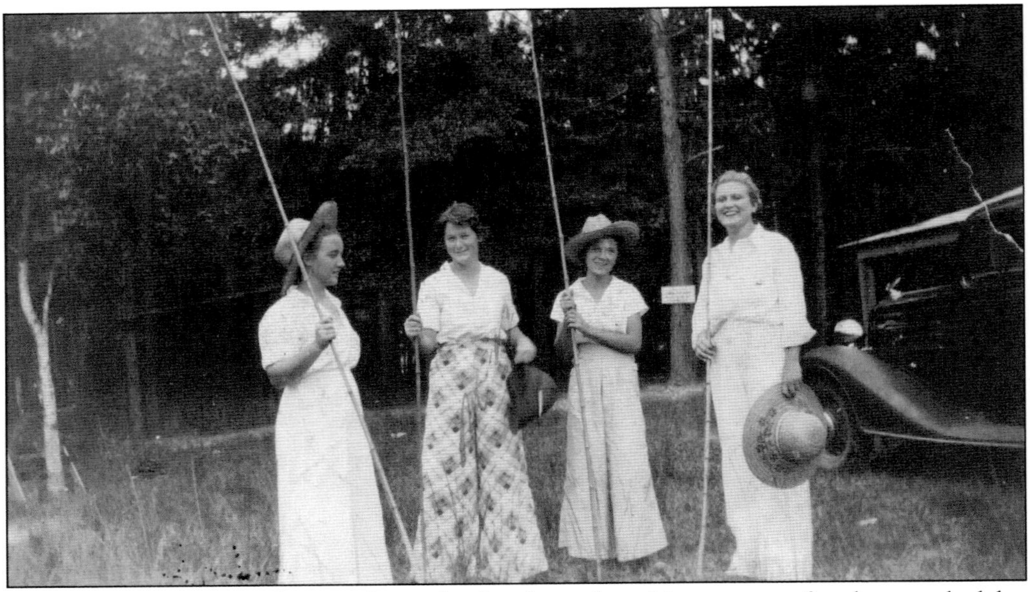

The fish are going to stand a poor chance for their lives when this party gets after them on the lake. Special attention is paid to the comforts and pleasure of ladies and children visiting the lake by the Idlewood Lodge Management. Pictured, from left to right, are Flavelle Campbell, Neil Bandjough, unidentified, and Florabelle Campbell, wife of Dr. Campbell (a dentist in Wewa). (BB.)

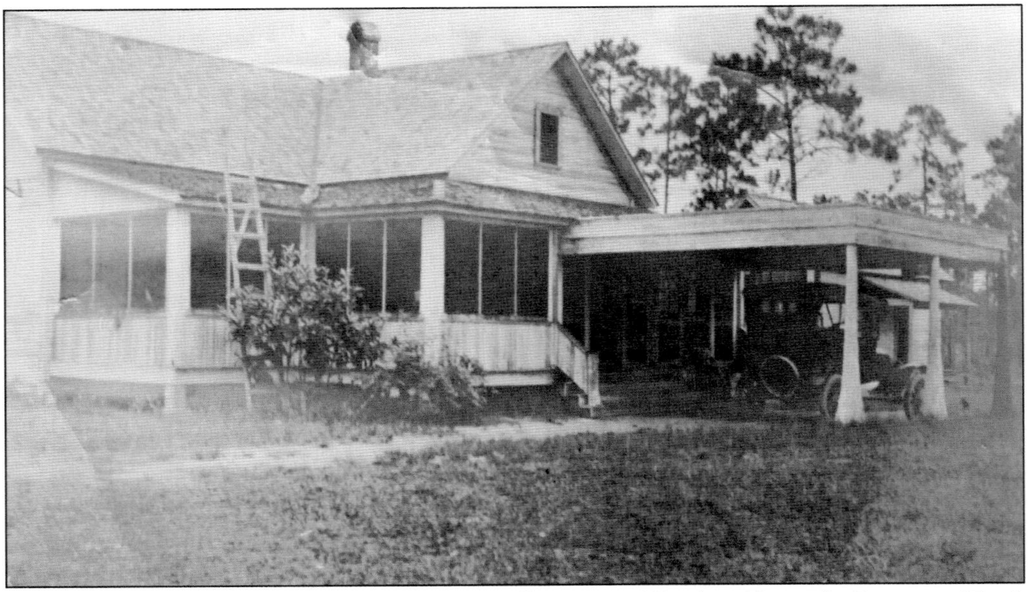

Idlewood Lodge was a fish camp operated by William "Tom" Byrd and his wife, Bramette. Tom's sister Pearl Clark was co-owner and helped in the management. There was a big, central house with a screened porch across the front and a bedroom on each end. Separate guest cottages surrounded the main house and usually held two bedrooms with adjoining baths. (CALC.)

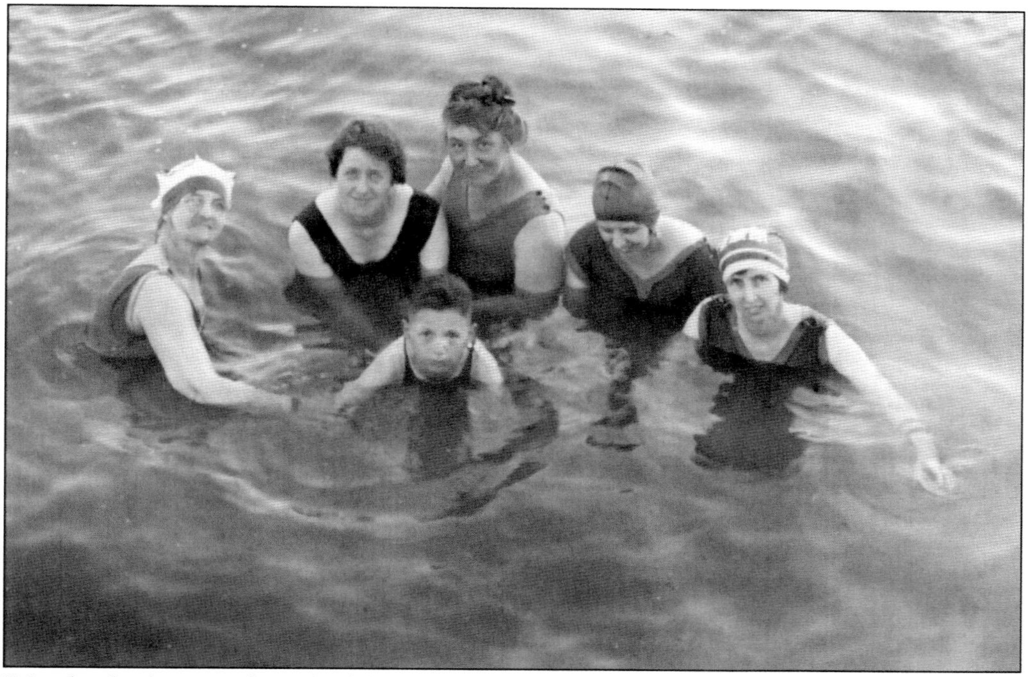

"He who drinks water from this lake will someday return to it," according to an Indian legend. Indians in the area discovered the Chipola River long before Europeans found it. Here, a group of unidentified people enjoys a swim in the river. (BB.)

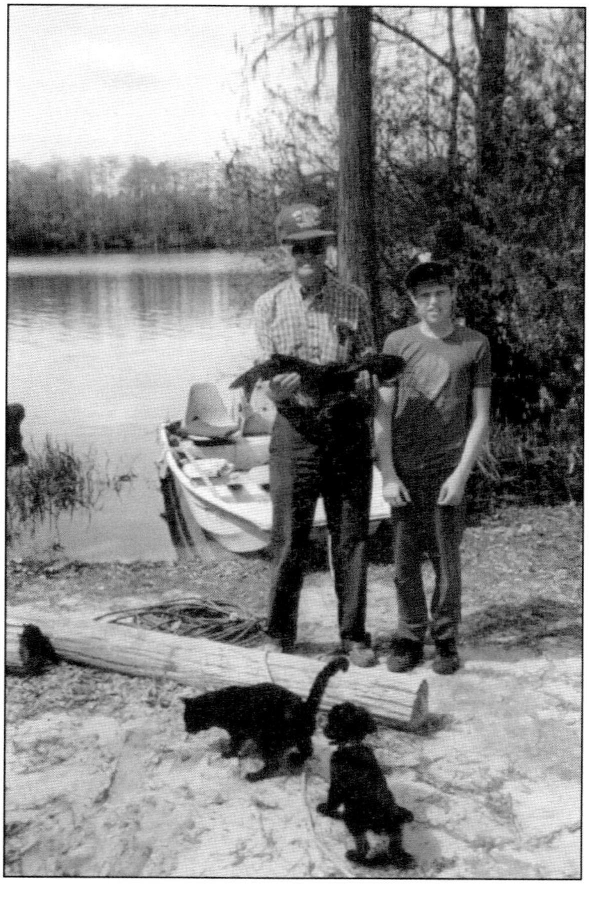

Thomas McDaniel stands here with his grandson Tranum McLemore at Shippey Lake. Young Tranum caught this nicely sized catfish at the age of 13 in May 1990. Grandfather and grandson enjoyed many days together fishing in and around the Dead Lakes areas. (PMM.)

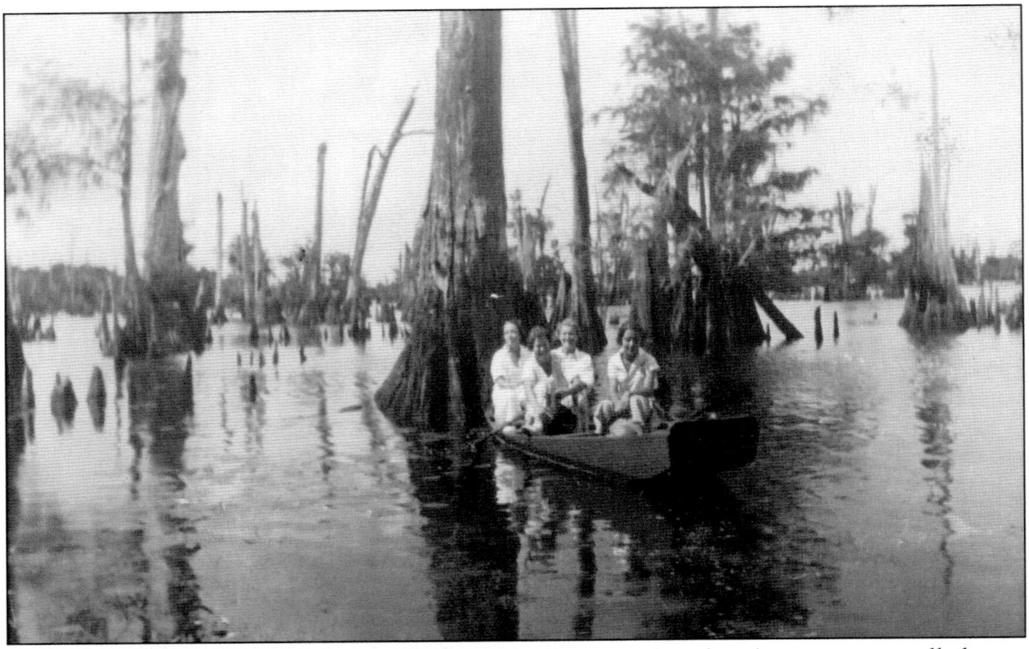

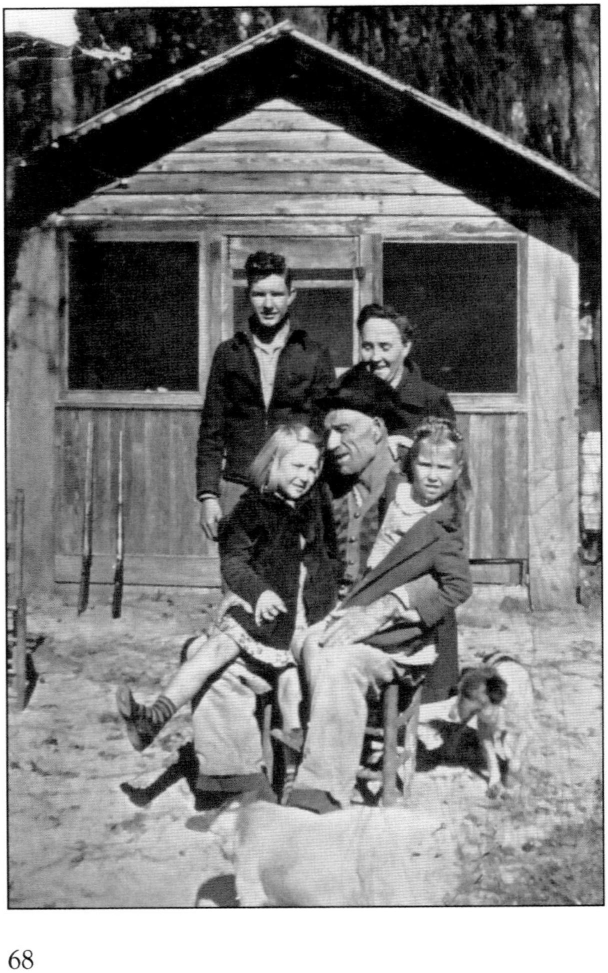

The Chipola, sometimes called Dead Lakes, was used for hunting, fishing, and other recreation. Visitors could always find a boat and bait on hand for fishing. Suffice it to say that there was always all the trout, shellcrackers, and bream that could be wanted. Pictured, from left to right, are Florabelle Campbell, her daughter Flavelle, an unidentified friend, and Nell Connell. (BB.)

This is Fortner's fish camp on the Dead Lakes. In front, John Elton "Elk" Fortner holds his daughters Jean (left) and Edna Pearl Fortner (right). Standing are Herman Fortner and his sister Violet. (LBS.)

Bramette (Farmer) Byrd (left) and her sister-in-law Pearl Clark were co-owners of the Idlewood Lodge. This was a fishing resort, and many fishermen from neighboring states came here to enjoy fishing in Dead Lakes. Gus Russ (right) was not just an employee but also a friend to the Byrd family; he was one of the most reliable and best fishing guides on the river. (CALC.)

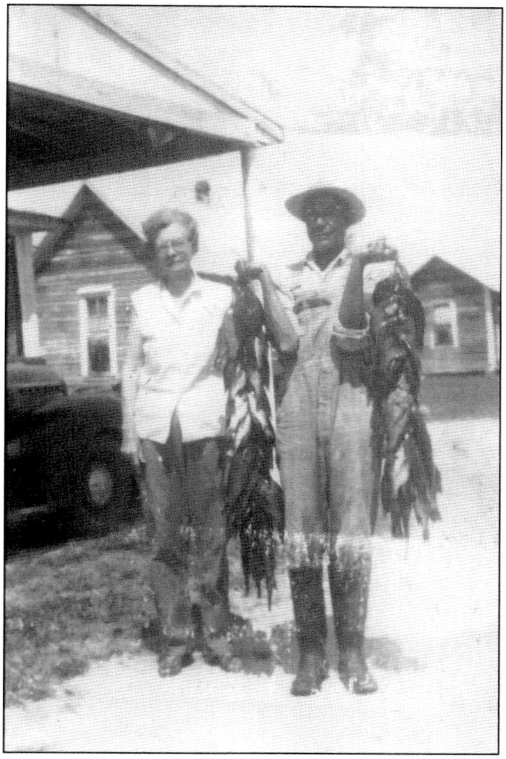

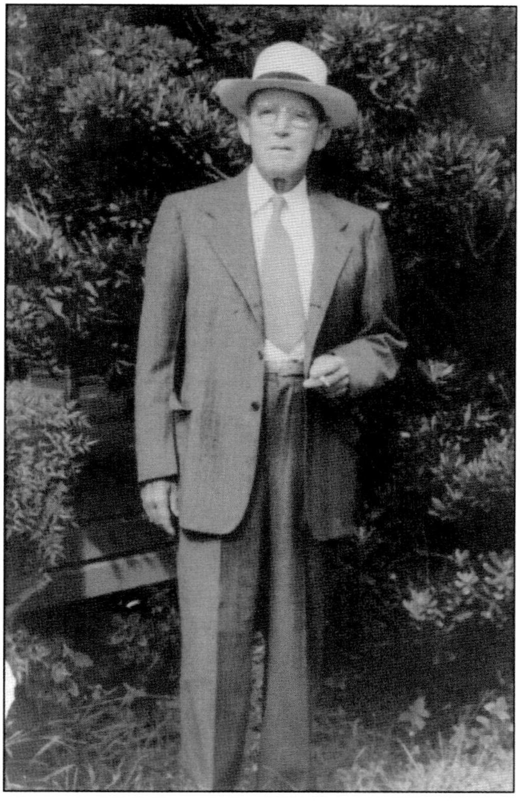

William Thomas Byrd, manager of the Idlewood Lodge and a civil engineer, was the first state surveyor for the state of Florida. He was the best-informed man in North Florida in the land-surveying business. Byrd was born in Virginia, and was an employee of the C&O Railroad in West Virginia before coming to Florida to accept a position on the Internal Improvement Board during the John Martin administration. (CALC.)

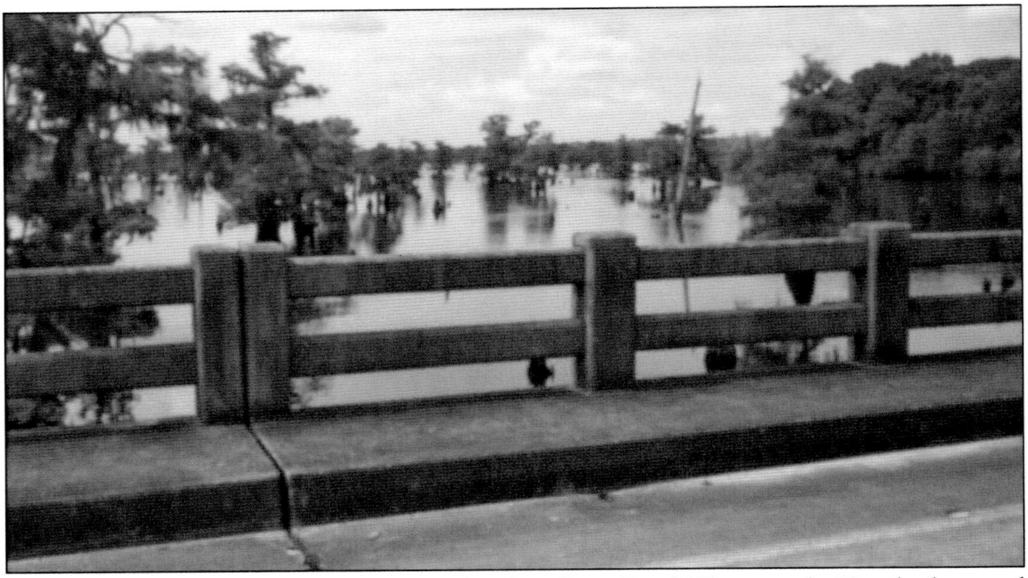

This view is looking north to the Dead Lakes from Dam Road. This stretch, 10 miles long and roughly a mile wide, spreads out into the flatlands at the southern reach of the narrow Chipola River—it straddles the Calhoun County–Gulf County line and is locked at the southern end by a man-made dam, which a few years ago reinforced the natural obstruction that had kept it from merging with the Apalachicola River. (Author.)

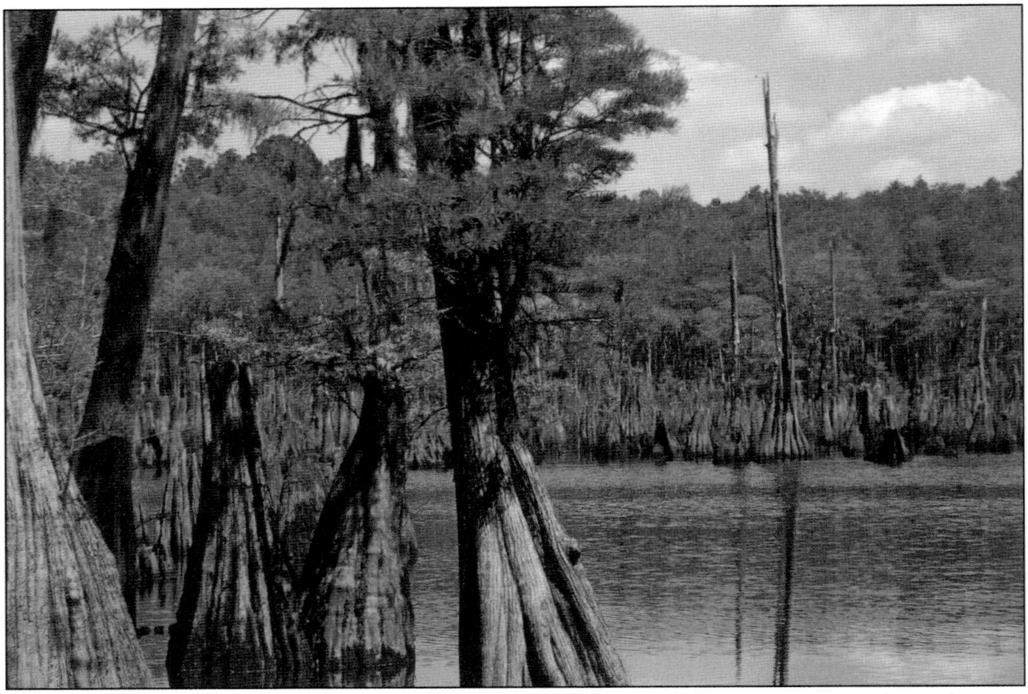

The Dead Lakes is a strangely beautiful, 6,700-acre lake with dark, tannic waters that is located on the Chipola River near the town of Wewahitchka. It is a well-known fact that the lake was once nothing more than a large cypress swamp. The Dead Lakes was formed when the rising level of river bottom forced the river waters outward and into the swamp, flooding it. (Author.)

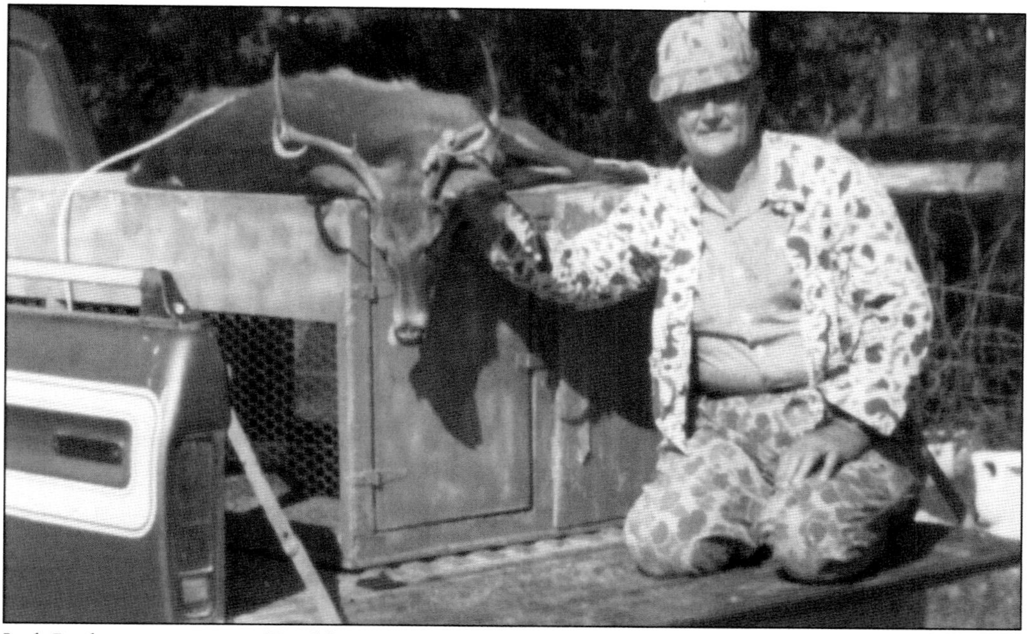

Jack Pridgeon, a native of Buckhorn, was a longtime resident of Wewahitchka. Jack was the owner of several businesses during his lifetime. His love was of hunting and fishing served him right up until he passed away around 1978. In this photograph is the last deer that he killed. (RMP.)

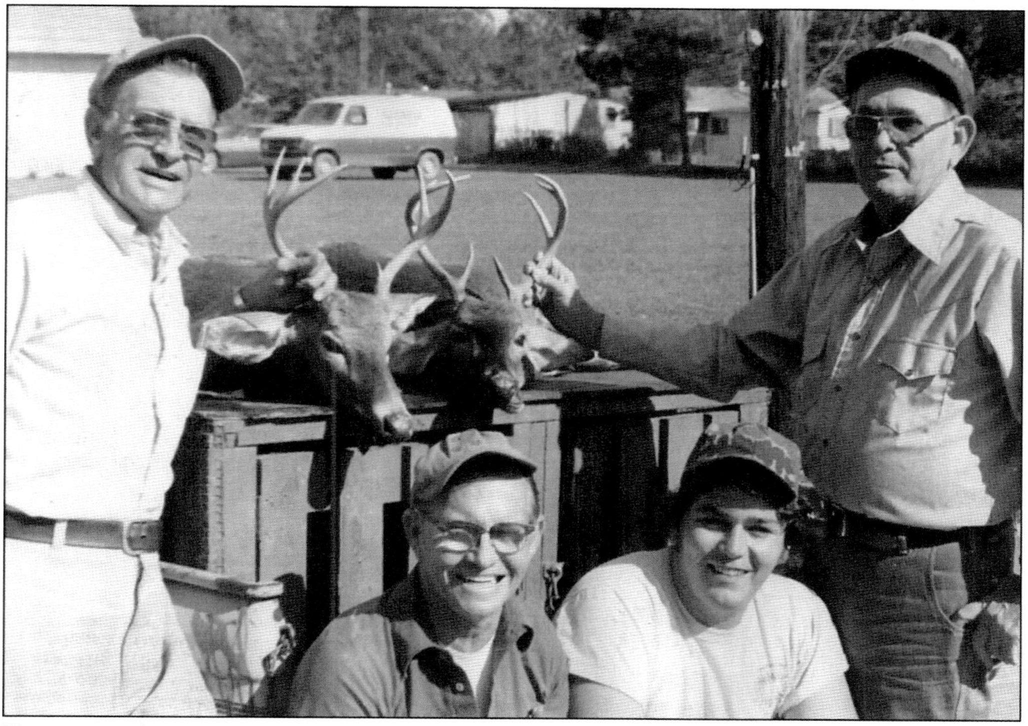

Hunting is a big sport in Gulf County, and every year, the men ride around showing off the deer that they killed on the backs of their trucks. Pictured here around 1973 are some local hunters from the Wewahitchka area; they are, from left to right, Thomas McDaniel, Jess Hand, Chuck Sexton, and Dave Herring. (BH.)

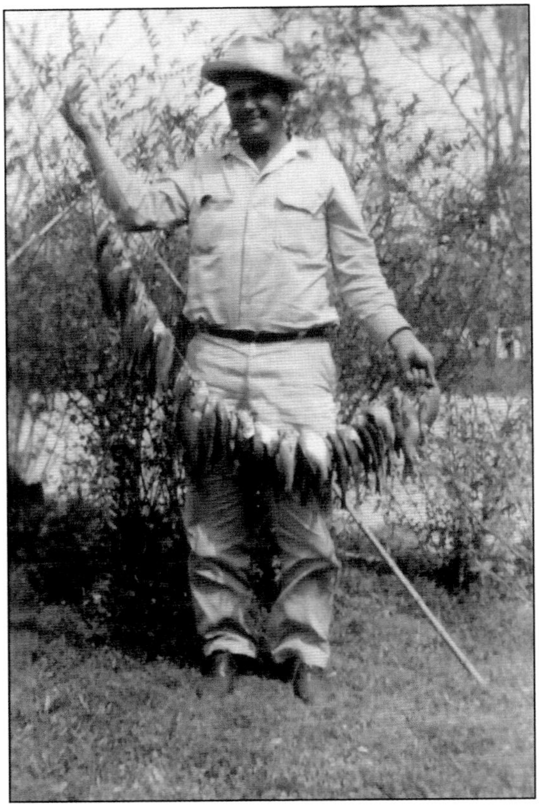

Pictured here in 1950, Native American Joel Edwin Poole, known as "Joe," grew up in Gordon, Alabama. In 1938, he moved to Wewahitchka to begin work at the paper mill in Port St. Joe. He was drafted into the Army but was later injured and discharged. Joe was an avid fisherman. He fished every chance he had, right up until his death in 1991, and taught all his girls how to fish. (JJ.)

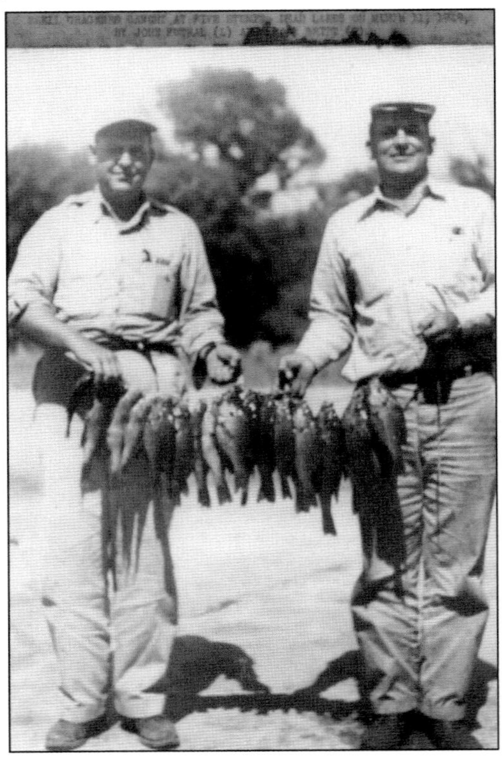

Frank Britt (right) and his fishing buddy John Futral caught this nice string of shellcrackers (freshwater fish) on the Dead Lakes at Five Stumps in March 1949. Wewahitchka resident Britt was the owner/operator of the Standard Oil service station on Main Street at this time. (CBW.)

Boys pose on a bridge with their fish. They are, from left to right, Jerry Roberts (sitting on the bridge rail), Billy Ray Rogers, Craig Bright, and Doug Gray (holding the fish). (BH.)

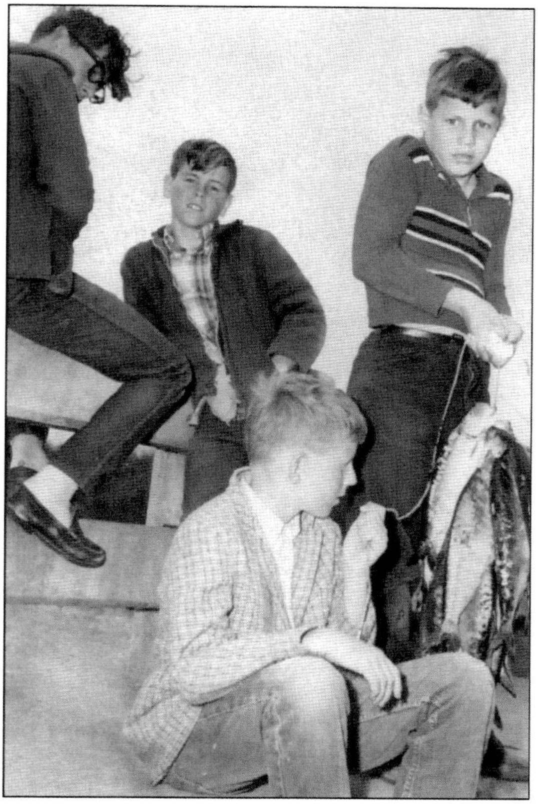

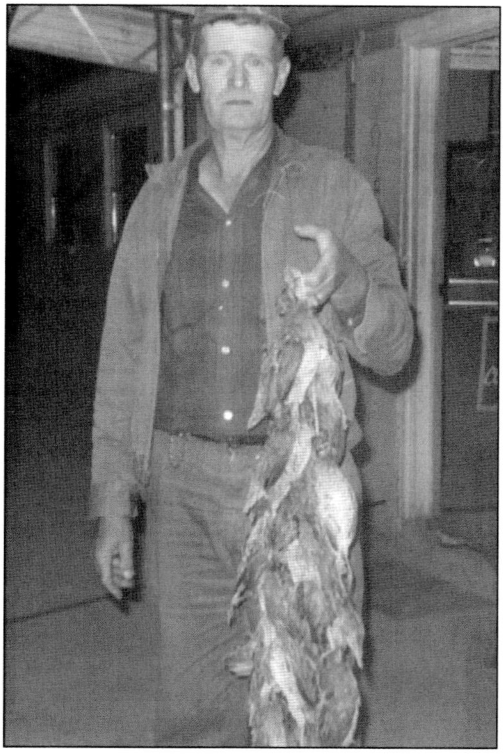

Otis Davis, seen here in about 1956, was owner and operator of the Davis Bait and Tackle shop out on Highway 22. He not only liked selling fish bait but was also a pretty good fisherman. Here, he shows a nice string of freshwater fish from the Wetappo Creek area. (IDC.)

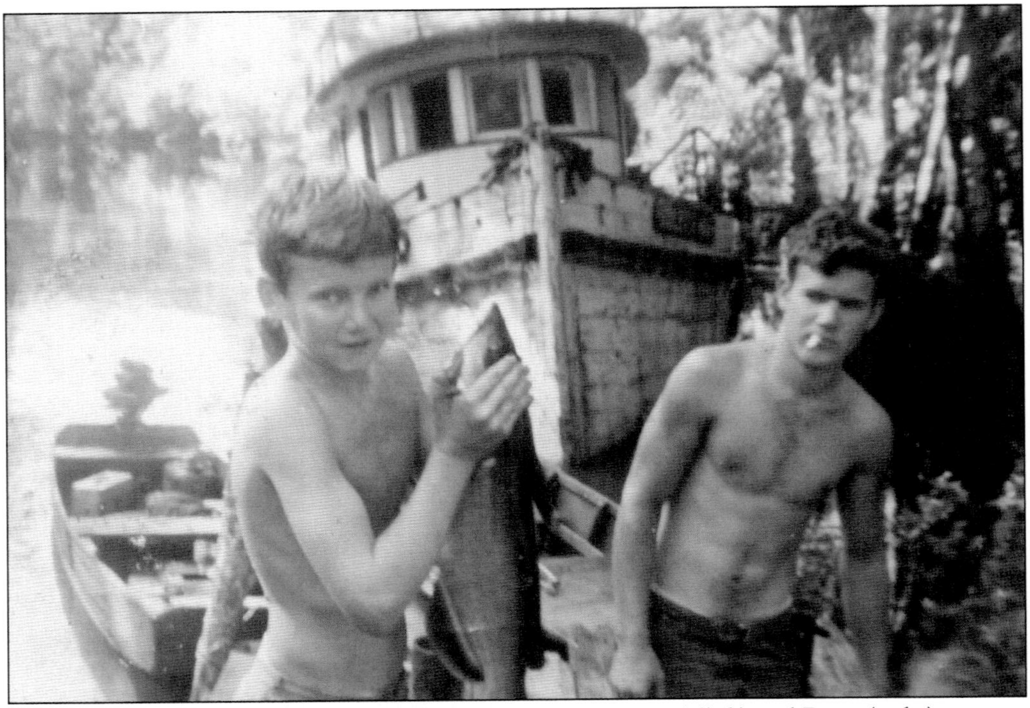

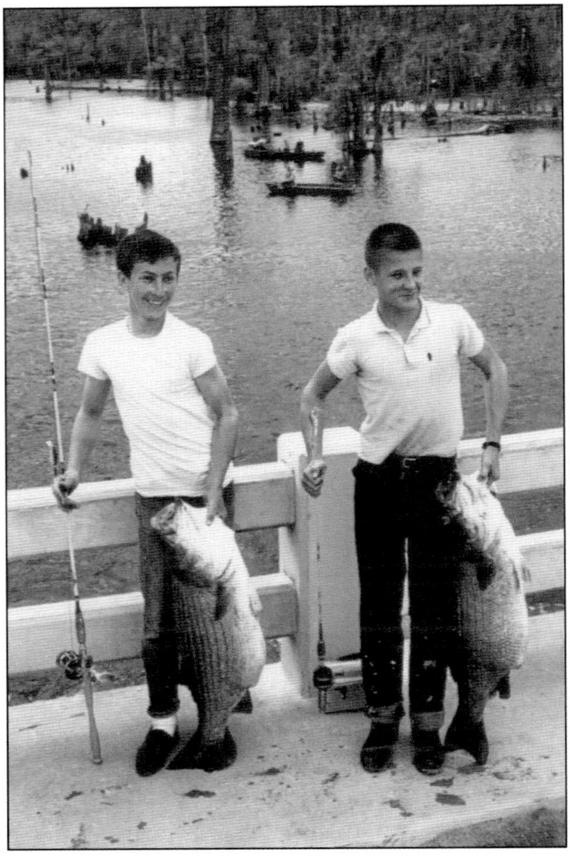

Broward (left) and Doug (right) Nunery, sons of Elmer and Betty Nunery, grew up on the Dead Lakes and enjoyed spending all their free time fishing and hunting in the swamps around Wewahitchka. (JNC.)

As a young lad, Brad Brown (right) caught this 40-pound striped bass, or striper, while his friend Tommy Lane (left) caught one that weighted in at 35 pounds off the Dead Lakes Dam, on the very same day in 1963. Brown's father was so proud of the photograph that he had it sitting on a shelf in his shoe shop in town for many years. (PMM.)

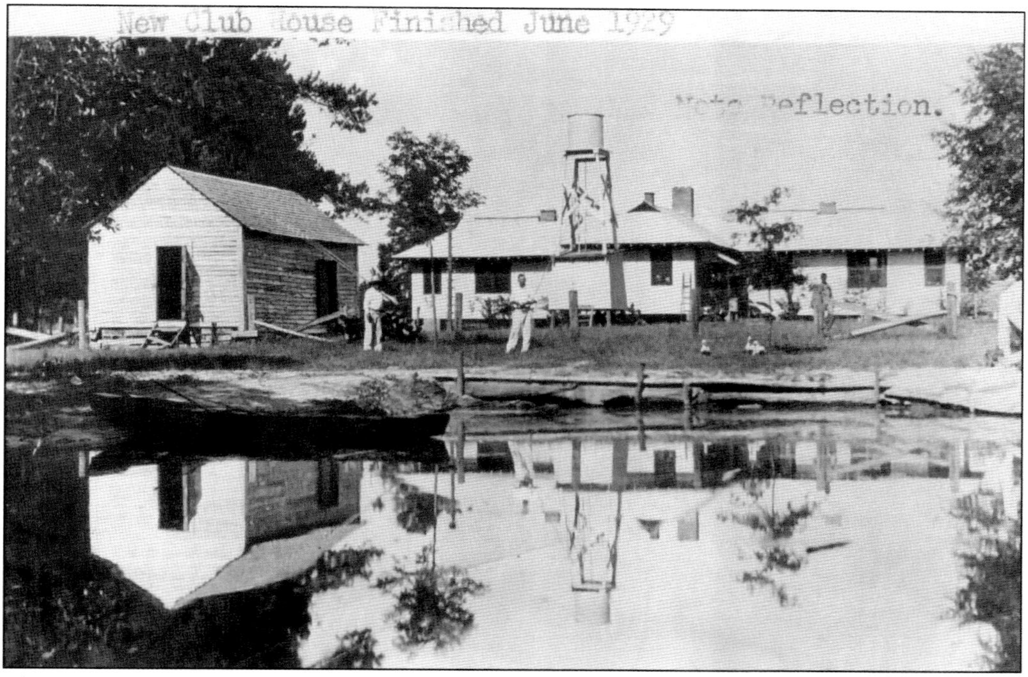

There were many fishing lodges and camps in and around the Dead Lakes area; in this photograph is one that was completed in June 1929. It is not identified by name, but George Core labeled the photograph "New Club House." He also made note of the reflection seen in the water. (GC.)

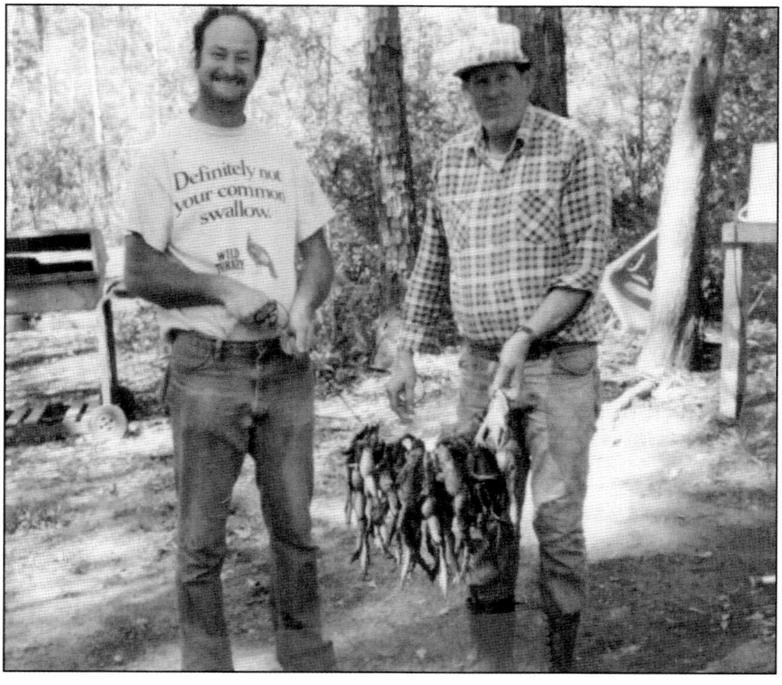

Enjoying a weekend at Brake fish camp, near Sauls Creek, Ronnie Brake (right) and good friend Joe Paul Wages hold up a nice string of frogs. Joe was born in Wewahitchka almost 40 years ago. His parents, Leroy and Betty Wages, were actually in the Sauls Creek area during hunting season when Betty when into labor, and the clinic in Wewahitchka was where Joe was born. (Author.)

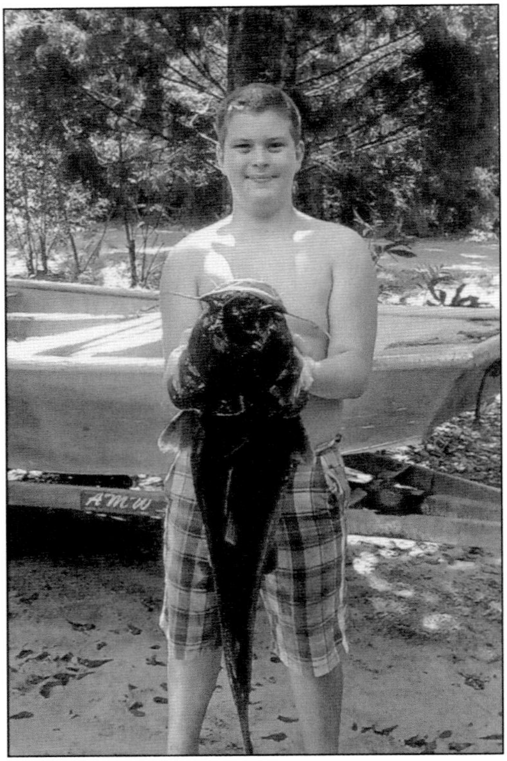

At the age of 12, River Rollins, son of Bo and Kandi (Ward) Rollins, caught this 26-pound flathead catfish near Bryant's Landing in Dalkeith during the summer of 2014. Rollins is the grandson of Melvin and Wanda Ward of Howard Creek. (KWR.)

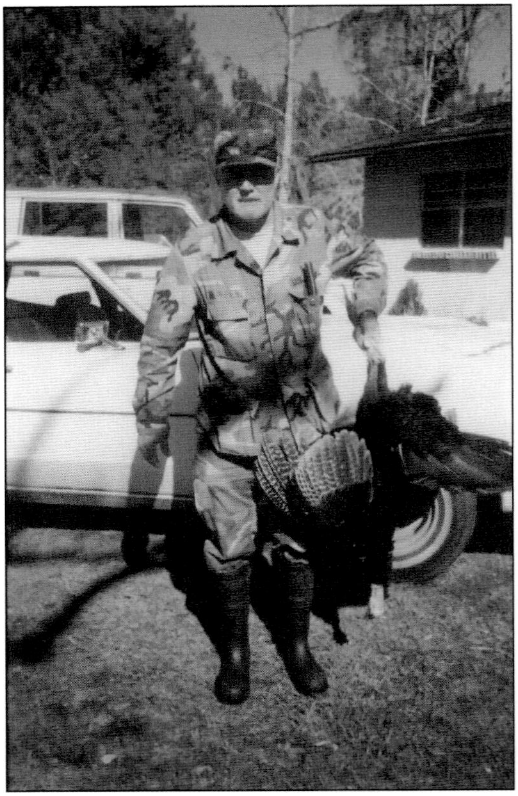

Jenning Davis Jr. is pictured with his big kill of the day. This turkey will look great in the middle of the Davis family's Thanksgiving dinner table. Jenning was born and raised in Gulf County; he worked at the paper mill for over 30 years in Port St. Joe until it closed and was employed at the Gulf County Prison for another eight years. He is now retired and spends his time with family or out hunting. (WD.)

Six

Unsung Heroes

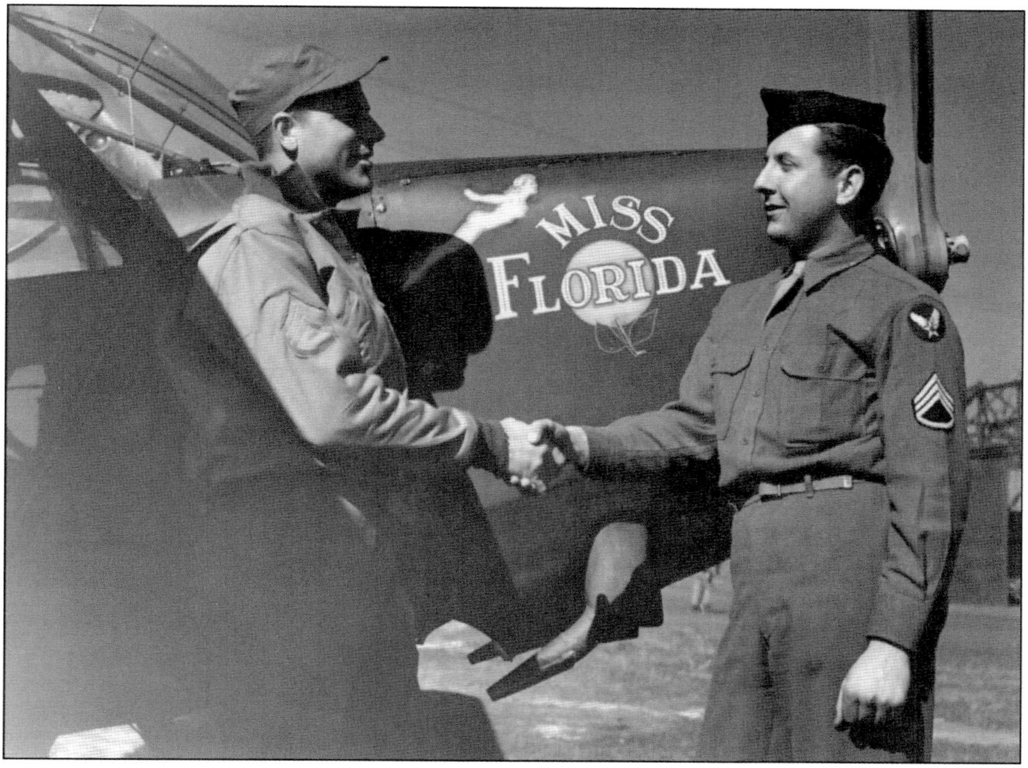

An unidentified solider (left) and Riley McDaniel stand in front of the airplane *Miss Florida*. This picture was in a box of photographs McDaniel had when he married just after the war. The man on the left may be Alton Ward. The photograph was taken during World War II while Riley was still in the Army Air Corps. (SMC.)

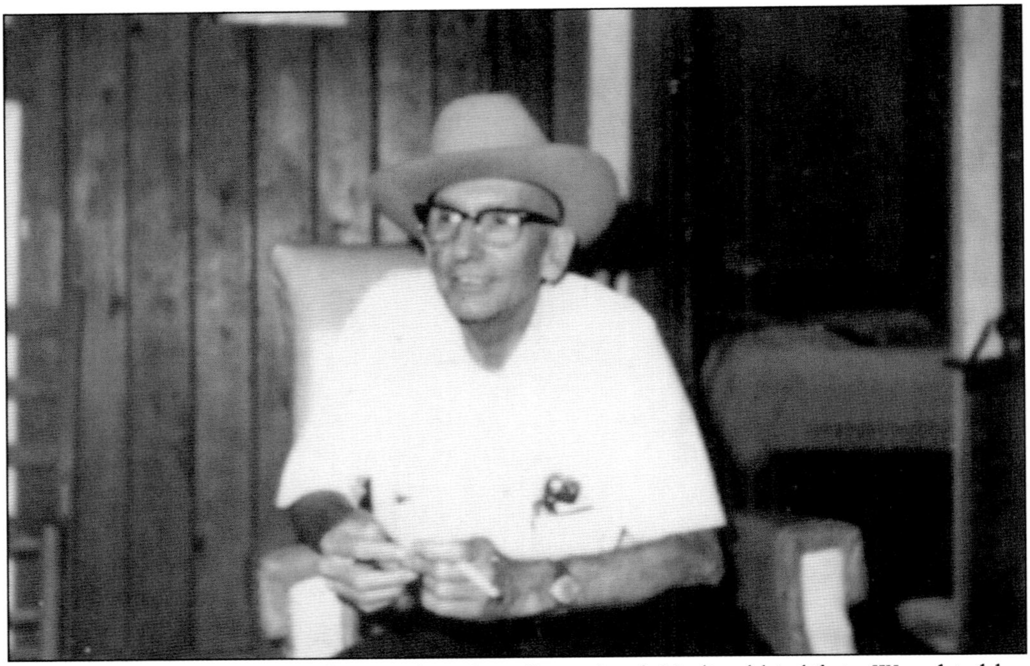

Alfred Jackson "Jack" Connell was a friend to all mankind. He lived his life in Wewahitchka. After completing school, he worked for the St. Joe Paper Company as a machinist and for the State Road Department before becoming a lawman, a career that lasted over 18 years. He served as Wewahitchka's police chief and was deputy sheriff for Gulf County sheriff Byrd Parker. Jack was loved by all. (BB.)

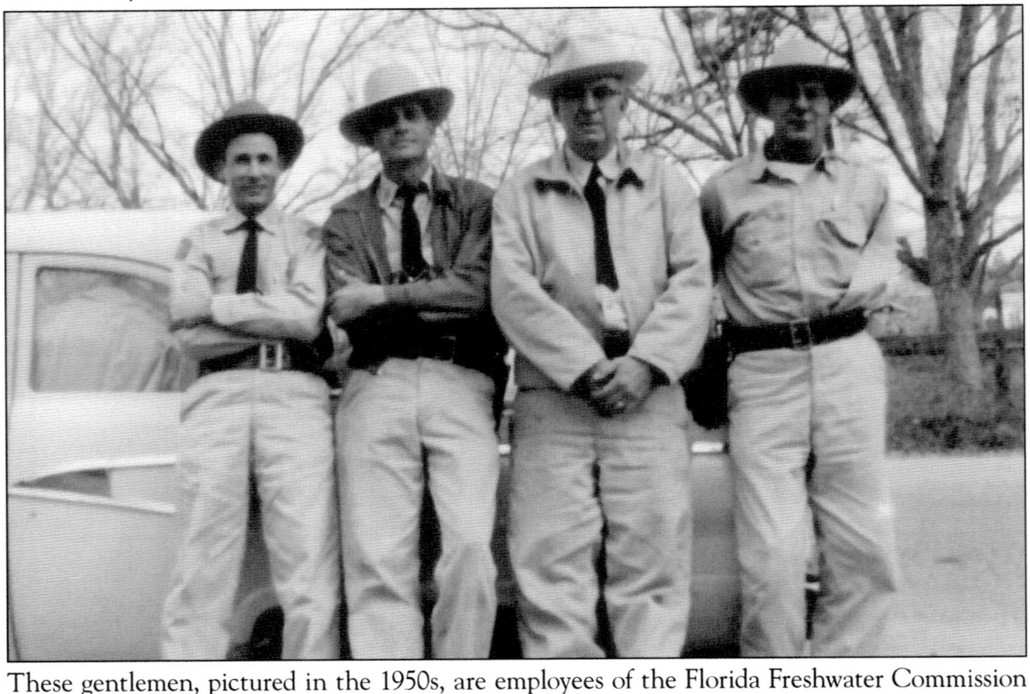

These gentlemen, pictured in the 1950s, are employees of the Florida Freshwater Commission and were known as local game wardens. They are, from left to right, Carl Culbreth, Thomas McDaniel, Sam Husband, and Pete LeGrone. (PMM.)

Carl Daniel Dean was the son of Daniel Webster and Eula F. (Ramsey) Dean of Wewahitchka, Florida. This photograph was taken during his service on February 6, 1947. Carl entered the Army in November 1946 and served in the occupation of Japan until November 1949. He and his wife, Mytrice (Alford), have three children—Phillip Thomas (married Laura Guilford), Sharon Diane (now Clark), and Sandra Jean Dean (now Flowers). (MAD.)

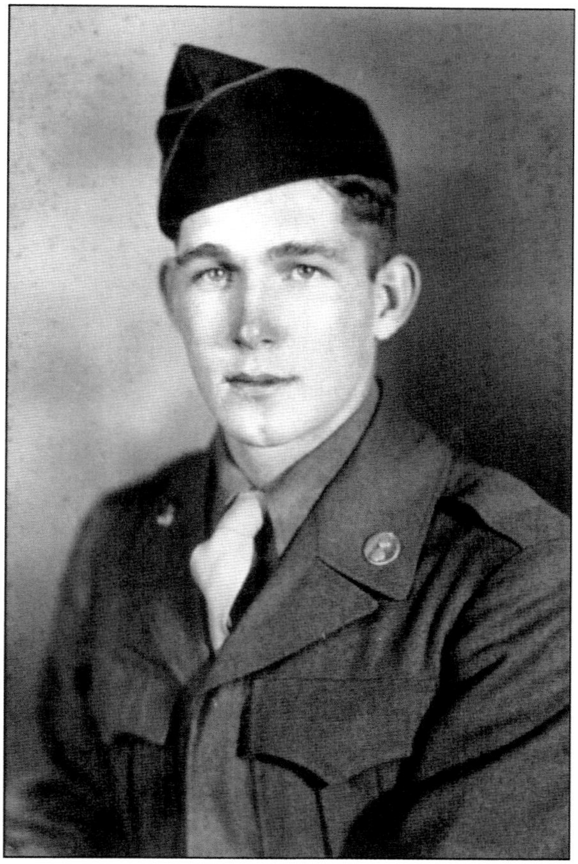

Mytrice Dean worked with the Gulf County Health Department for more than 30 years. She is married to Carl Daniel Dean of Wewahitchka, Florida, and they have three children. They both are now retired and enjoying their time spent with family. (MAD and BB.)

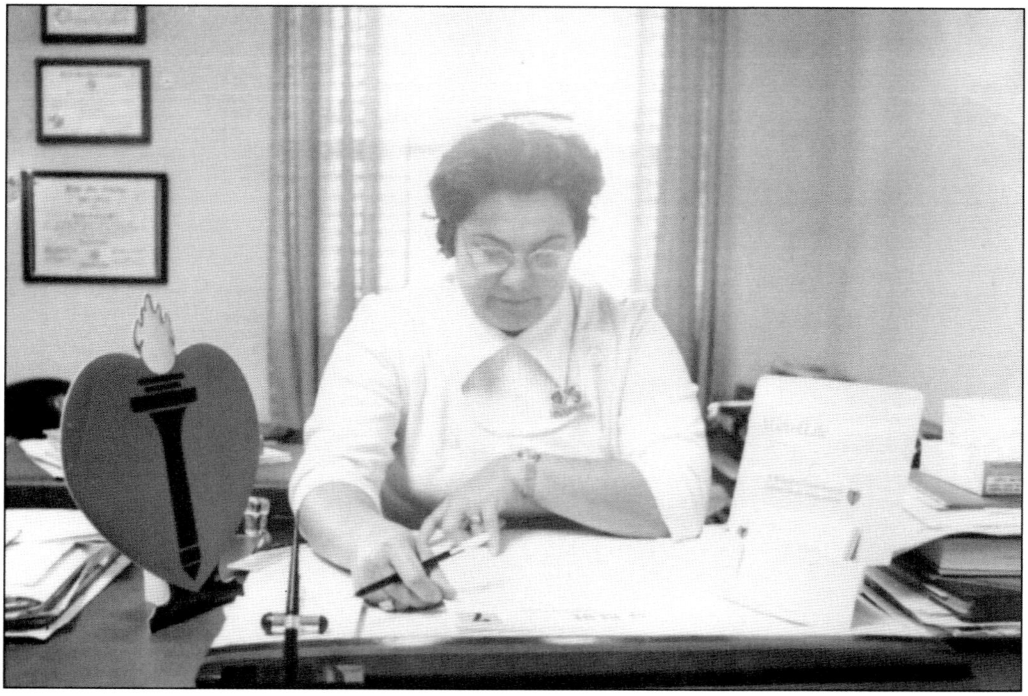

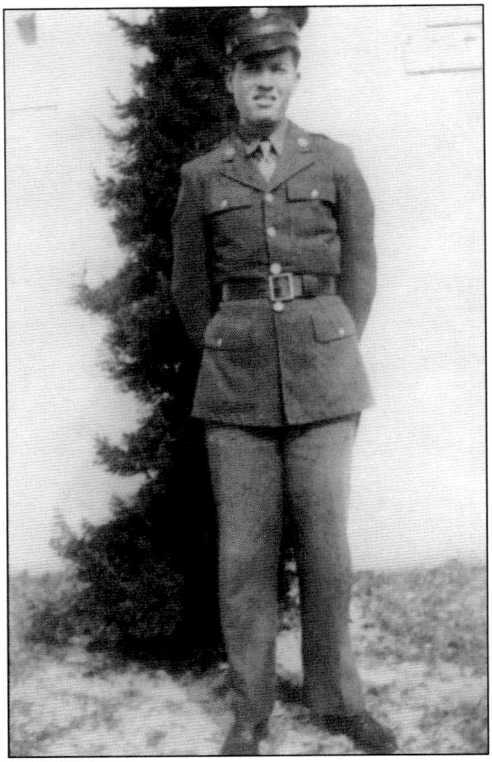

J. Foyal Pitts was the son of George W. and Marium L. (Richards) Pitts. He was born in 1920 and died in 1988. J. Foyal served in the 78th Armored Field Artillery Battalion and was discharged in 1946. He was a technician fourth grade, Medical Detachment, and he serve some time at Normandy and was always spoken well of. He was married to Mary Lee Davis, and they had two girls, Mary Ann and Brenda. (MPF.)

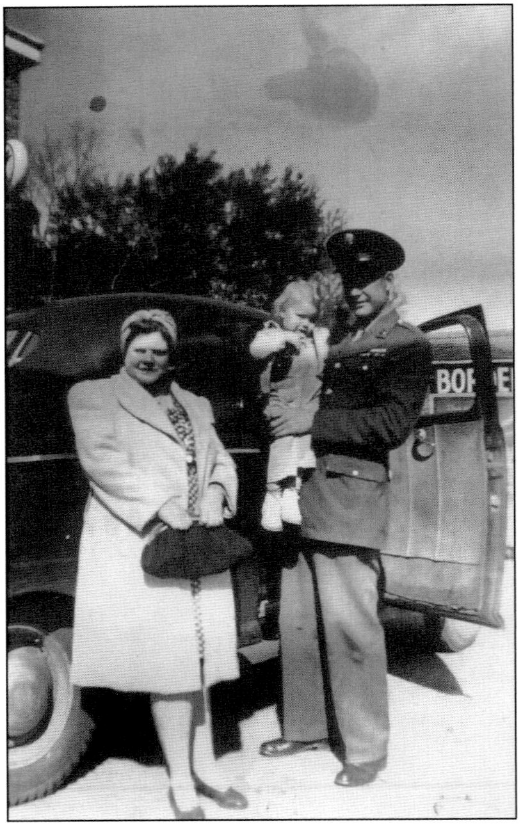

Joe Poole is pictured with family member Fredna Price-Siebe and his daughter Gayle. While living in Wewahitchka in about 1940, Joe met and married Jewel Hughes, was drafted into the Army, and was stationed in France. He was severely injured and pronounced dead twice. After many surgeries, he received a medical discharge and returned home to his family in Wewahitchka. Joe and Jewel had two more daughters, Darlene and Sharon Poole. Joe passed away in January 1991. (JJ.)

Riley Gaskin McDaniel grew up in Wewahitchka and met his wife, Mary Frances Rogers, while she was working in Dr. Redfern's drugstore. They married in 1946. Riley decided to rejoin the Air Force, and served for 20 years until his retirement. As he advanced in rank, he became a first sergeant. The McDaniels moved back to town in 1963, and they later relocated to Georgia. (SMC.)

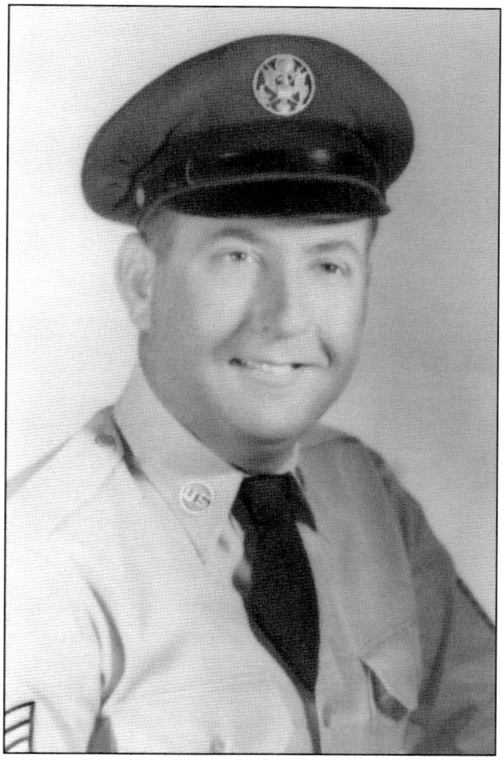

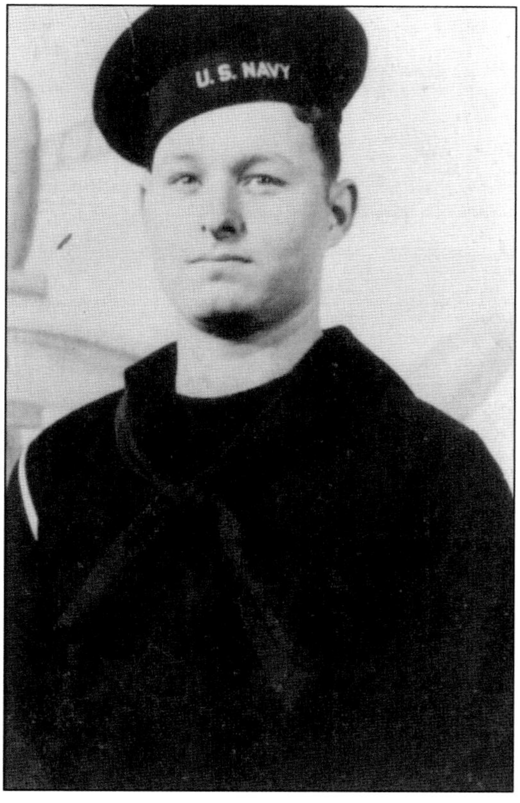

Farmer Forehand, who served in the US Navy during World War II, was born in 1925 and died in November 2000. He worked as a boilermaker (retiring in 1987) and also enjoyed working with his bees that made wonderful tupelo honey. He and wife Onita (Price) Forehand had three children—Earl, Evelyn, and Debbie. (FFW.)

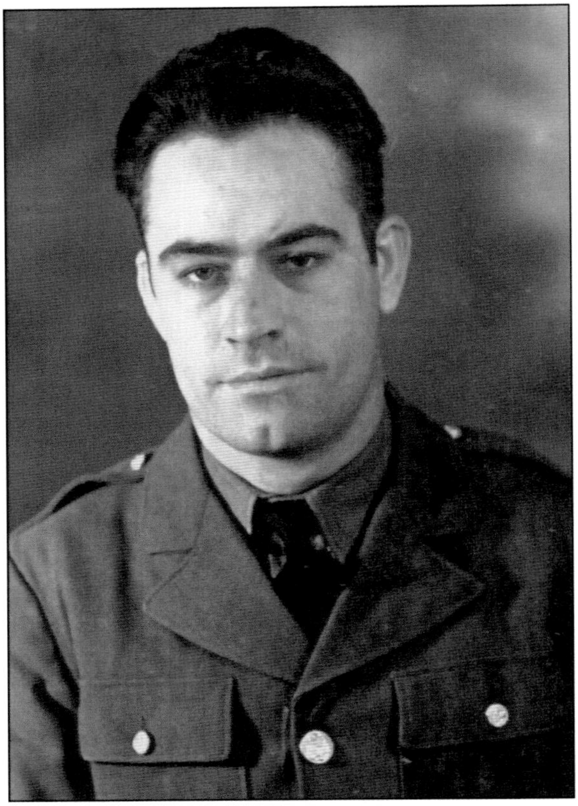

Leroy Fortner was the son of Stephen M. and Belle (Gaskin) Fortner. He married Bernice Kemp and was father to Charles "Scootsie," Sue, Willie Joe "Dude," and Faye Fortner. He is pictured here when he served in the Army during World War II. (FFW.)

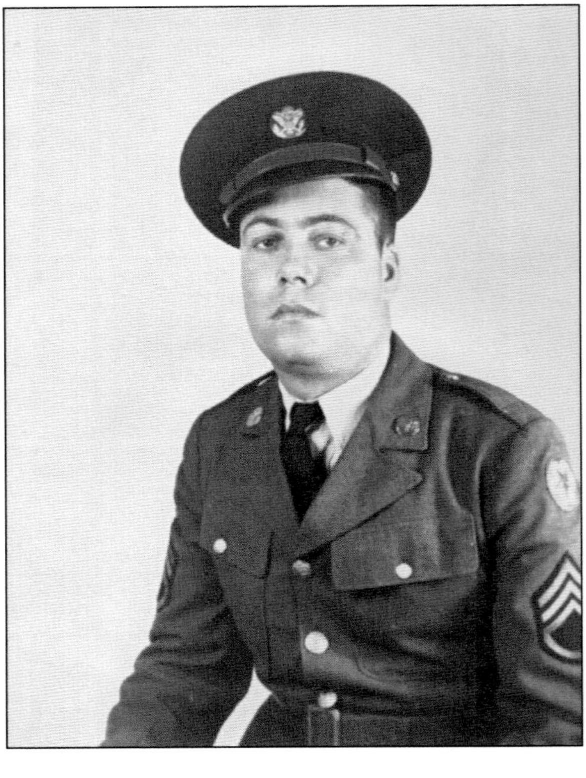

Sam M. Fortner (November 30, 1918–February 4, 1966) served in the Army as a private during World War II and was the son of Stephen M. and Belle (Gaskin) Fortner. Commonly called "S.M.," he was husband to Pauline (Cotton) Bailey Fortner. He is buried in Pine Memorial Cemetery in Calhoun County, Florida. (FFW.)

Susan Diane Carter (now Maurice) graduated from Wewahitchka High School in 1974; she enlisted in the Air Force and served for over six years (1978–1984). Maurice is retired now and enjoying time with her husband and children in Texas. (SMC.)

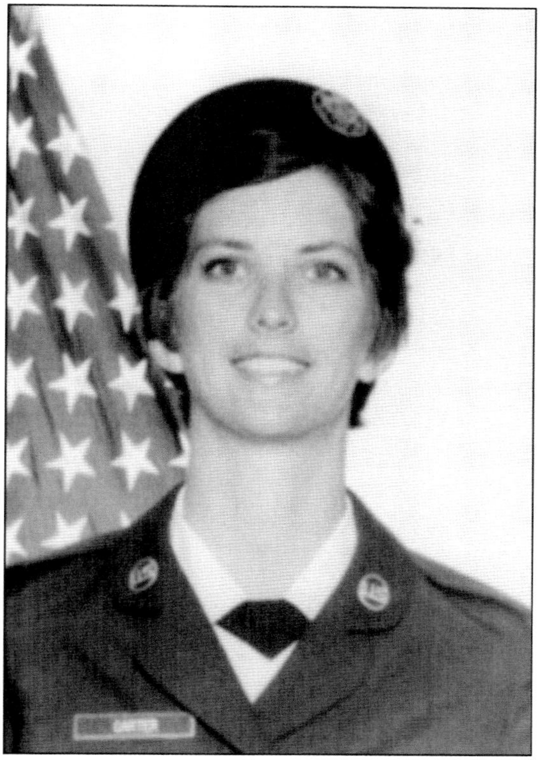

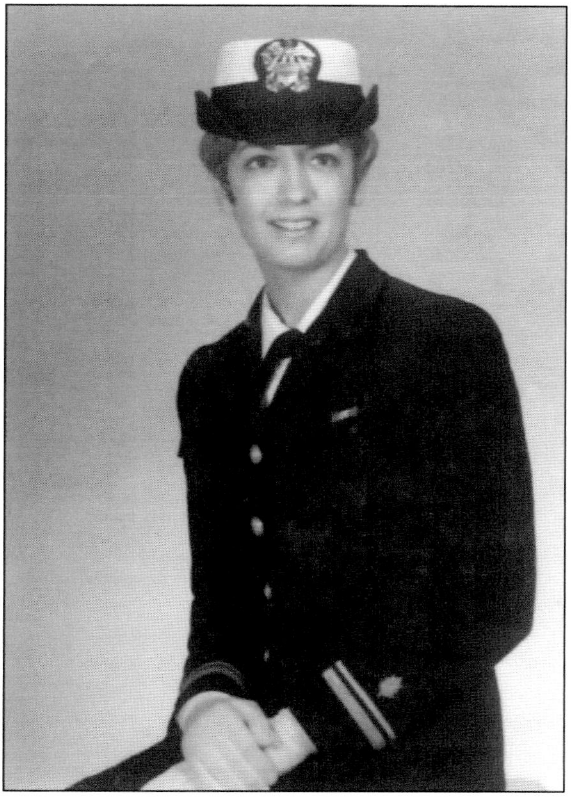

Sandra F. (McDaniel) Causby is the daughter of the late Riley Gaskin McDaniel and Mary Frances Rogers McDaniel. She served as a Navy nurse from 1968 and as an Air Force nurse from 1971 to 1990, and she retired in January 1990 as a lieutenant colonel. She and her husband now live in northwest Florida. (SMC.)

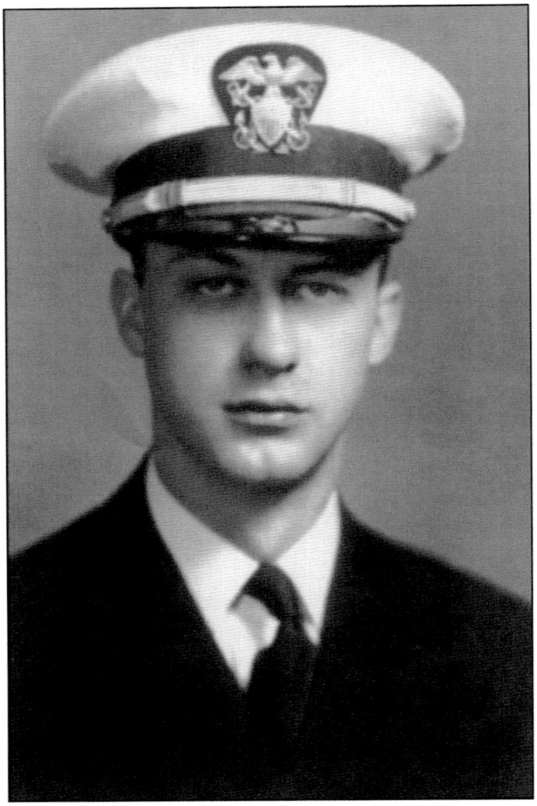

After college, Edward Anthony "Ed" Bandjough joined the Navy. While stationed at the Navy base in Panama City, he met and married Nell Connell. He served in Saipan during World War II, and in about 1943 was stationed at Adak, Alaska. His wife and daughter were allowed to join him there in the 1950s. Bandjough reached the rank of lieutenant. Upon returning to the Lower 48, the family came back to Wewahitchka and settled there. (BB.)

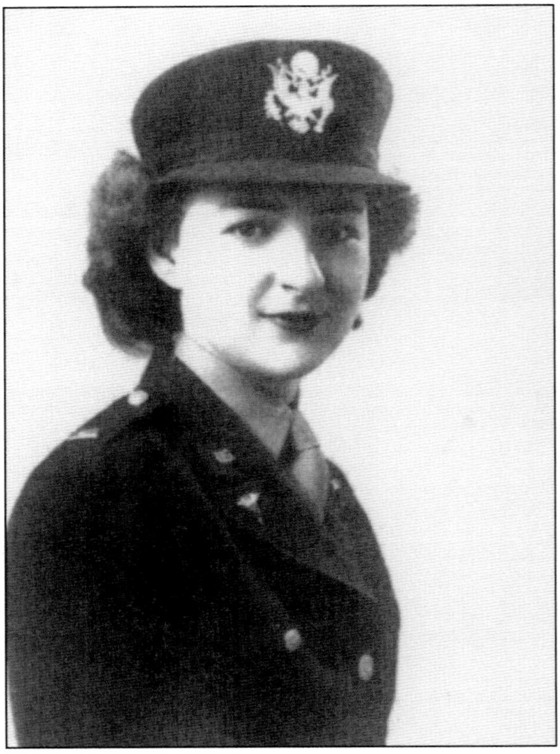

Nellie Wade was born in Pennsylvania. After competing nursing school, she joined the Army and was sent to Kyoto, Japan, from 1945 to 1947. Nellie is proud to be a World War II combat veteran. She is a mother, a grandmother, and a great-grandmother, and she still is a nurse at the age of 90 for Dr. Michael Barnes. Nellie is an inspiration to all who know her. (TWM.)

Sandra Abreu Batson joined the Women's Army Corps in the mid-1960s. The corps was disbanded in 1978. (SAB.)

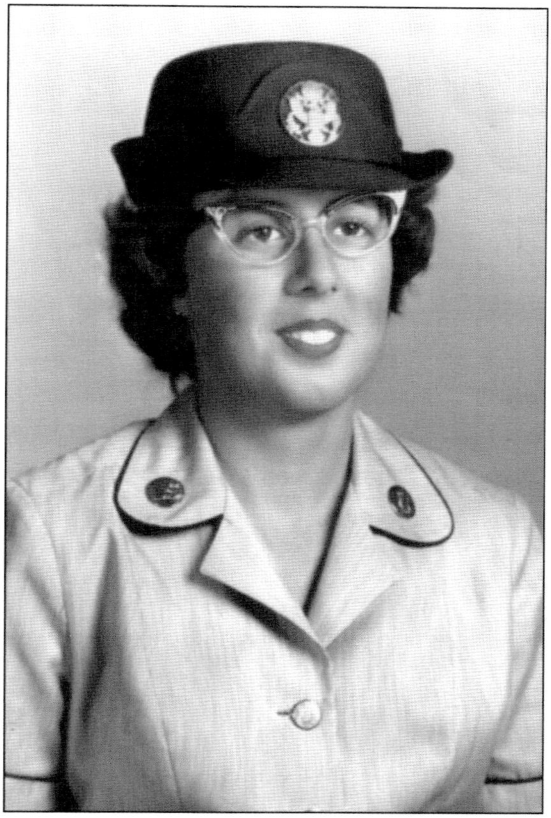

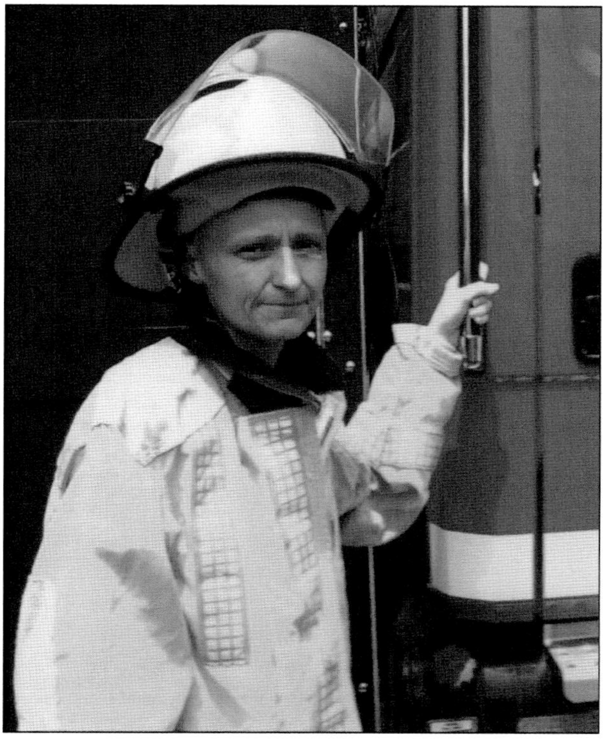

The Gulf County Board of County Commissioners recognized Lisa (Davis) Blankinchip as chief of the Dalkeith Volunteer Fire Department and the first female chief of Gulf County, Florida. Her outstanding service to her community and dedication to the fire department earned her the respect of all her fellow firefighters. Lisa passed away at home on November 7, 2007. (WD.)

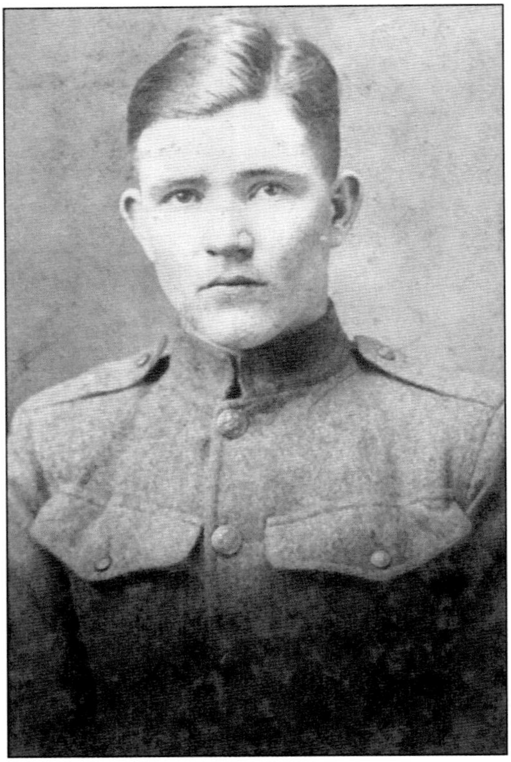

William Elias Branch Jr. was born in 1898 in Calhoun County, Florida. He was a private first class in the US Army from May 1917 to December 1918, and he served during World War I in France. He lived in Abe Springs and the Marysville Communities in Calhoun County before moving to Gulf County and Wewahitchka after the deaths of seven family members, including his wife and child, during a flu epidemic. (HDB.)

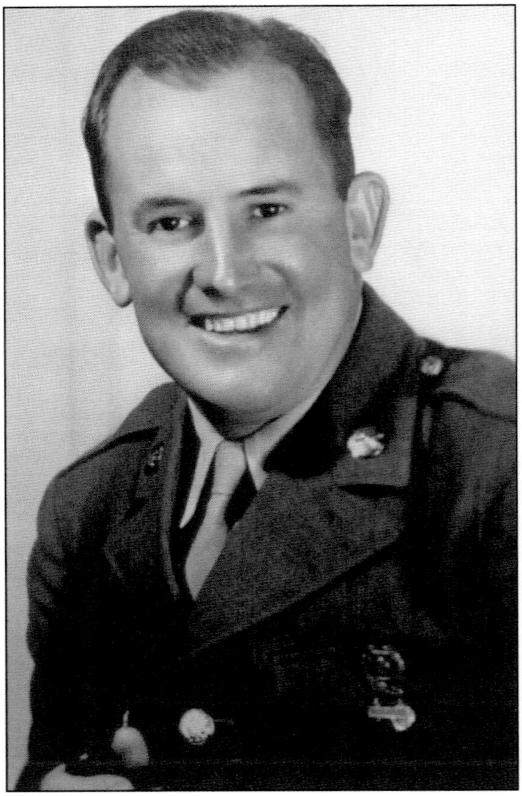

William Franklin Britt was the youngest of four sons born to B.F. and Hettie McDaniel Britt. He fought in the Battle of the Bulge, with the 97th Infantry Division of Patton's Third Army, and then did six months of occupation duty in Japan following the end of the war. Frank primarily worked for the US Army Corps of Engineers, although he operated the Standard Oil station in Wewahitchka for 10 years. (CBW.)

David Carl Gaskin was the son of Dave and Annie Gaskin. He served in the Air Force and was a tail gunner during World War II. At one time, he served under James Stewart, the famous actor. Later, Gaskin went to the University of Florida. He was an attorney, and he married Tweeta Byrd. They have three children—Jerry, Pam Gaskin Sumner, and Jan Gaskin Traylor. (SMC.)

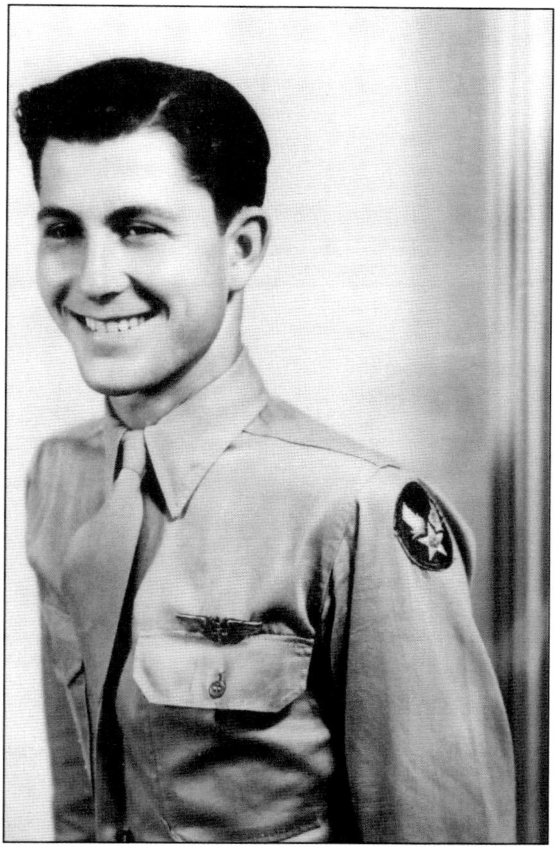

Preacher Glass was a lifelong resident of Wewahitchka. He was a fine law officer, though he was not a highly educated person. He had worked as an employee of Gulf County, even driving an ambulance, before serving as chief of police for the city of Wewahitchka for over 19 years. Glass likely will be remembered as a man who made his mark in Gulf County when life was less complicated but more dangerous. (BGW.)

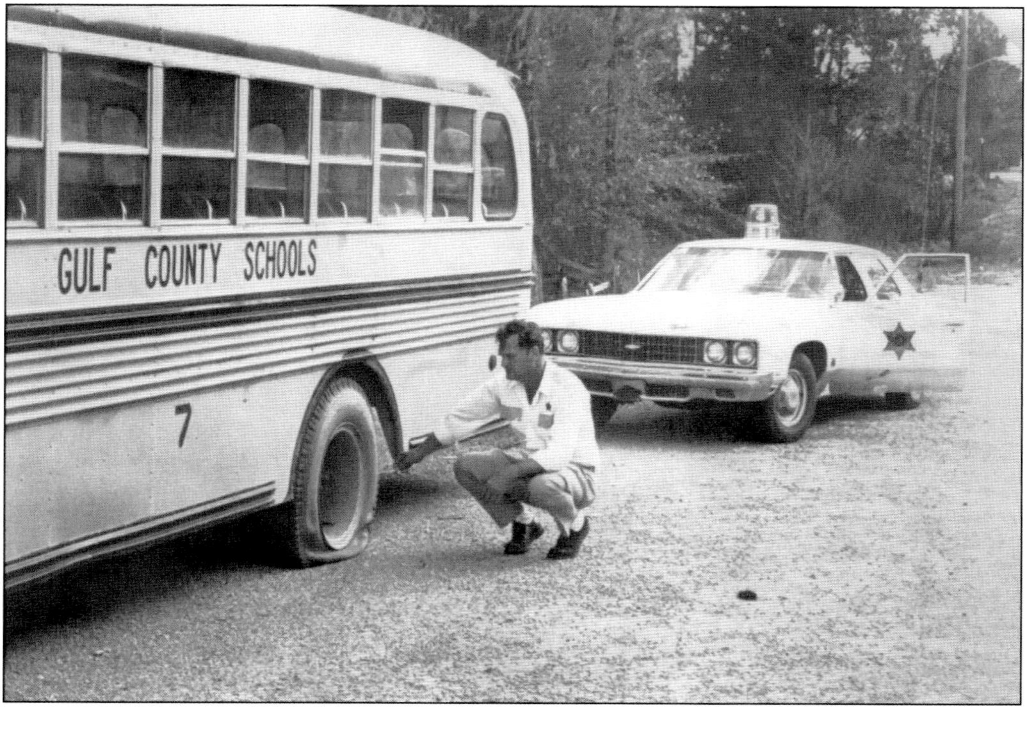

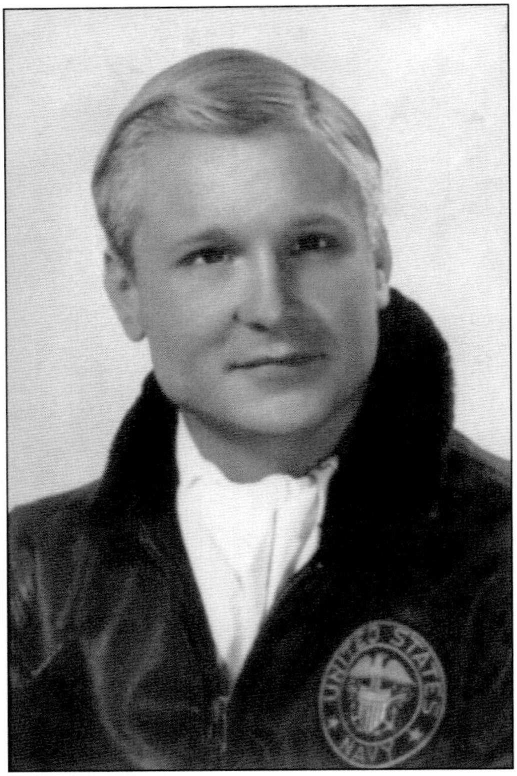

Robert Glenn Brown, born in Hazlehurst, Mississippi, moved to Wewahitchka in the 1940s. Brown was a civil servant at Tyndall Air Force Base and a veteran of World War I, serving in the US Army Corps. He operated a shoe shop for many years and enjoyed fishing. Brown passed away in May 1996. (SB.)

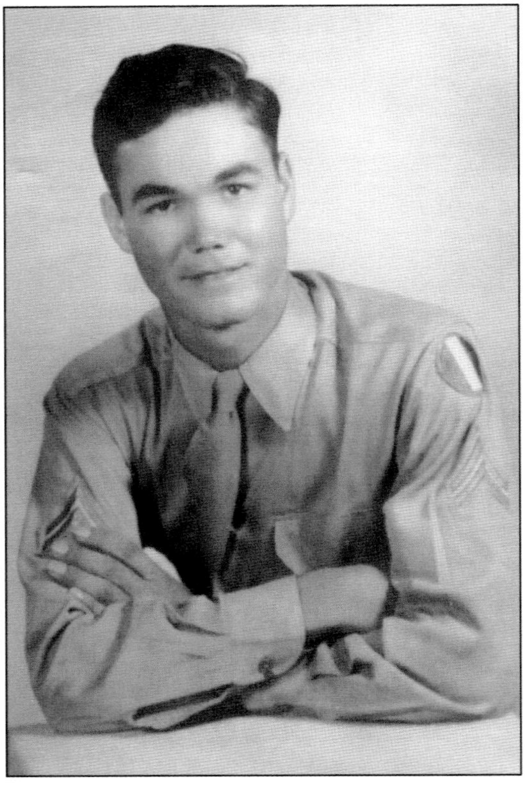

Upon graduating from Georgia Military College in Milledgeville, Alfred Layfett Whitfield joined the Army and was stationed in Germany during World War II. After two years in the Army, he attended Auburn University and graduated with a bachelor of science degree in agricultural engineering. For many years, Whitfield worked in beekeeping, farming tupelo honey. He later served as director of member services at the Gulf Coast Electric Cooperative. (CW.)

Jerry Turner served in the US Army. He did his basic training in 1965 at Fort Jackson, South Carolina, and later went to Vietnam from 1966 to 1967. He is married to Dr. Canning's daughter Joey and is living in Wewahitchka. (JJT.)

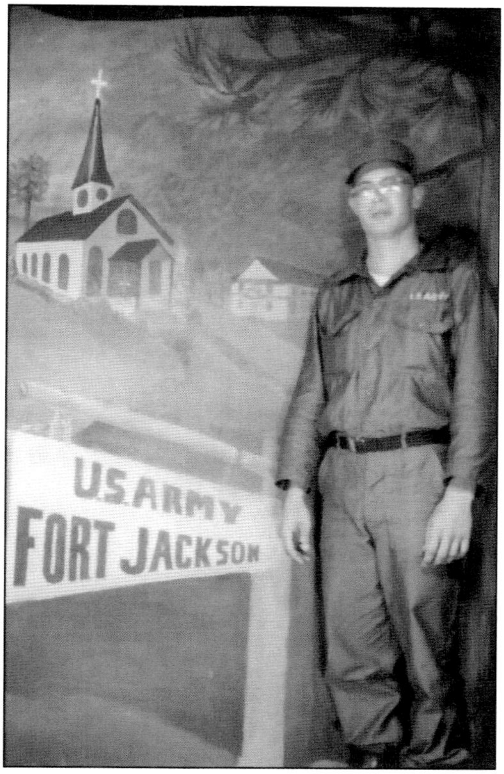

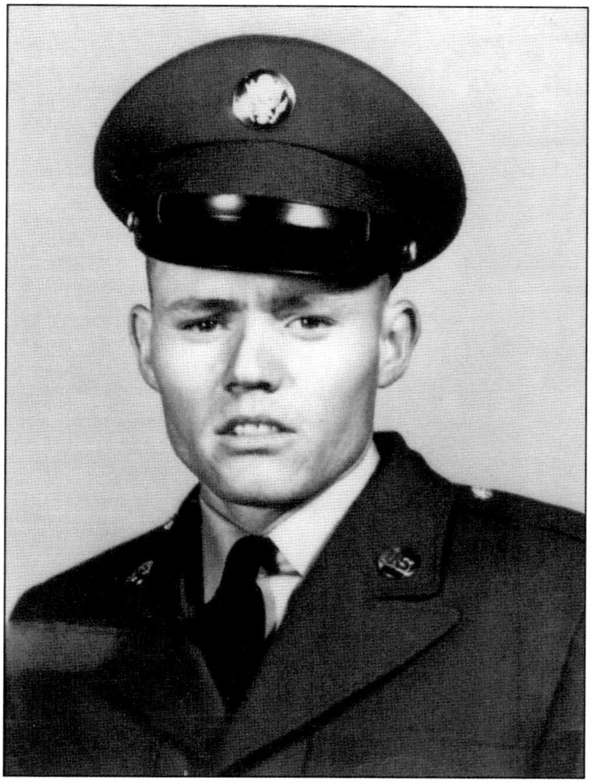

William Jennings Davis Jr. was born in 1944 in Gulf County and joined the Army in 1965. He went to Fort Jackson, South Carolina, served three and a half years, then joined the Army Reserve. He came back and worked for over 30 years at the paper mill in Port St. Joe. He spent another eight years working at the local prison, and today he is retired and enjoying being with family and going hunting. (WD.)

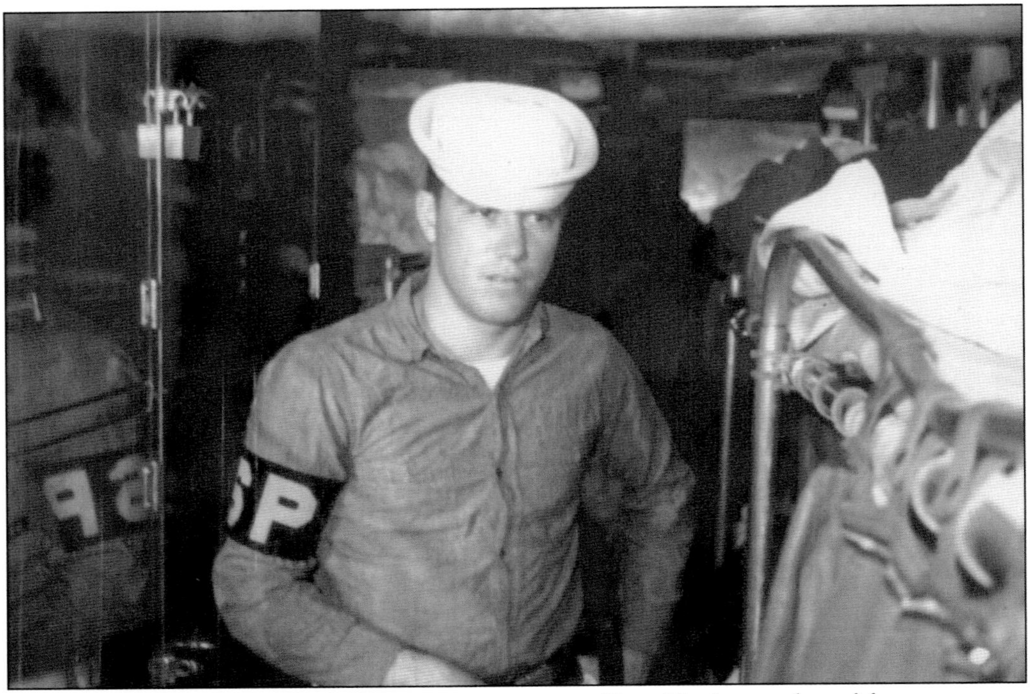

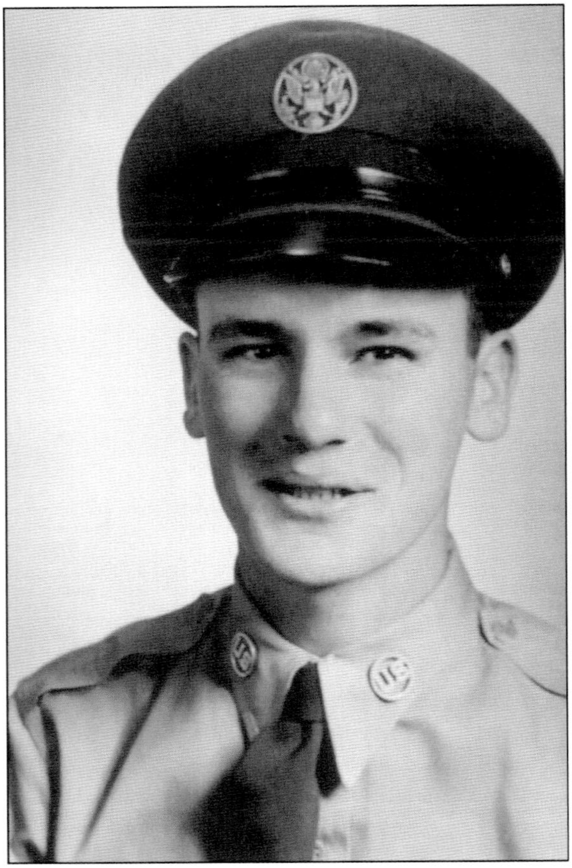

Gene Hanlon graduated from Wewahitchka High School and entered the Navy. He served honorably in Vietnam and received a Meritorious Unit Citation, a Vietnam service medal; two campaign medals with two stars for combat action; and one Top Gun Award. Gene retired after over 20 years with the US Postal Service and is proud of his heritage and his hometown of Wewahitchka. (GH.)

Fred Greer, husband of Feraldine Hall, came to Wewahitchka in 1955. He served in the Air Force during the Korean War from 1950 to 1954. He worked for the St. Joe Paper Company and spent all his free time fishing and hunting. (FHG.)

William H. Linton served in the Navy during World War II and lived in Gulf County since 1937. A graduate of Florida Southern College, he earned his master's degree in education from Florida State University. He worked for the Gulf County School System for 35 years as teacher, coach, and administrator, retiring in 1977. William passed away on October 28, 1991. (THL.)

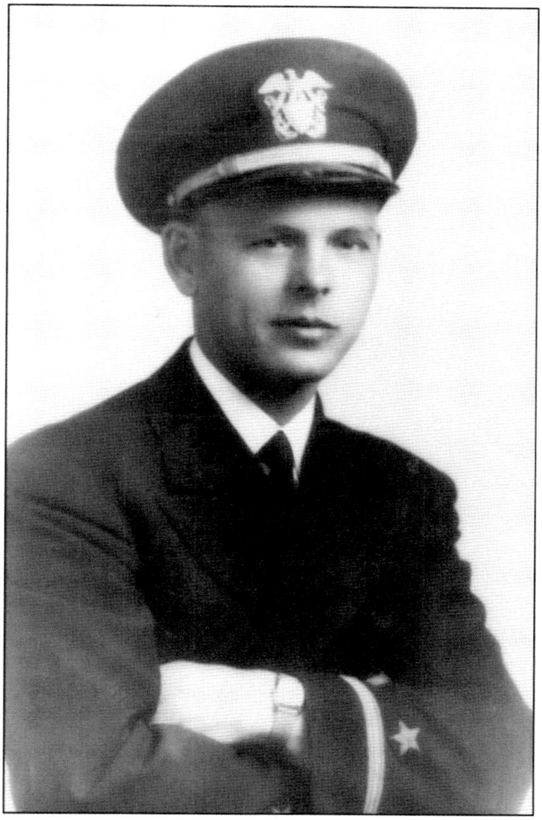

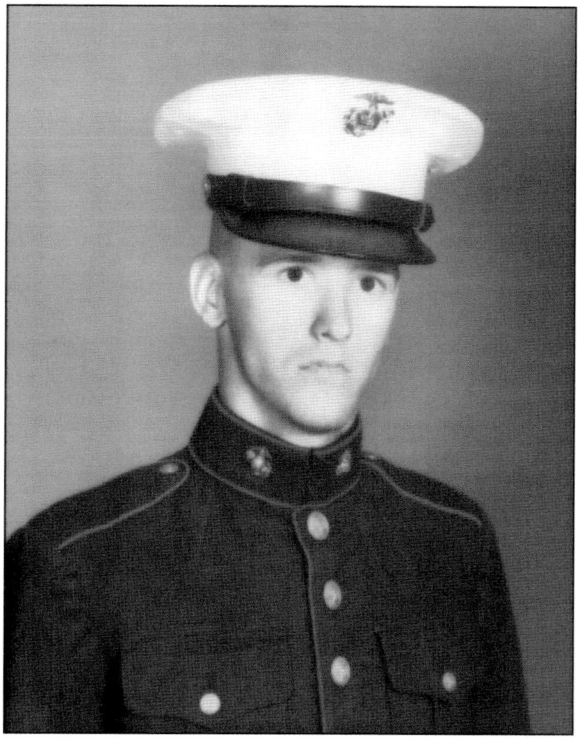

John Strength, lance corporal, served in the 4th Motor Transportation, 4th Marine Division, from May 1965 to May 1971. (SSW.)

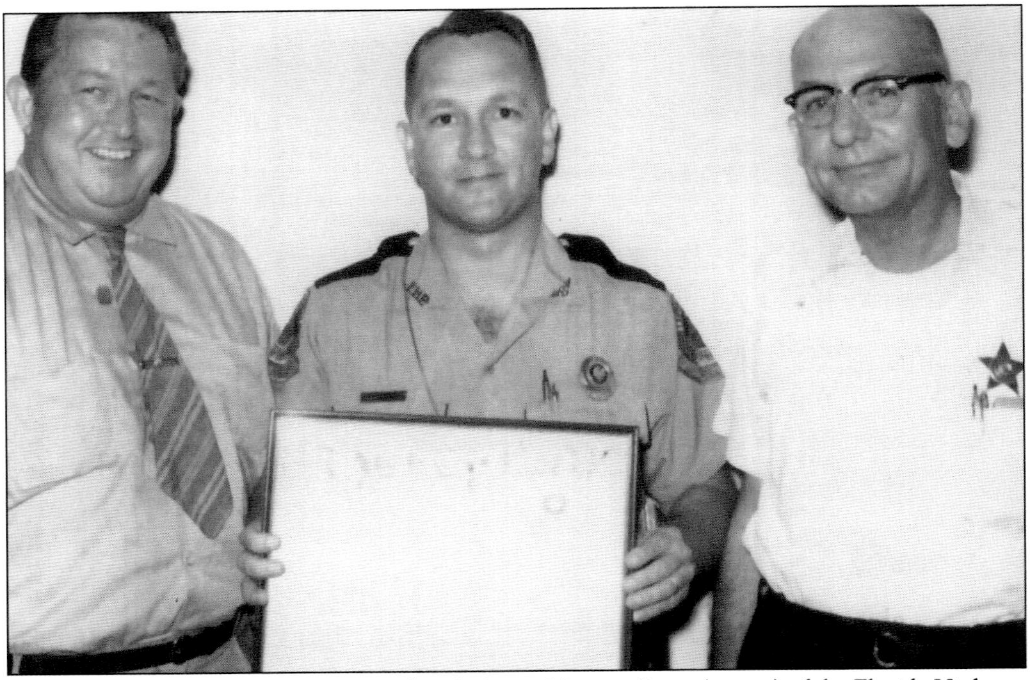

Dr. Harold Canning, mayor, is pictured with Angus Newton Petty (center) of the Florida Highway Patrol and Jack Connell (right), Wewahitchka's police chief, in the 1950s. (BB.)

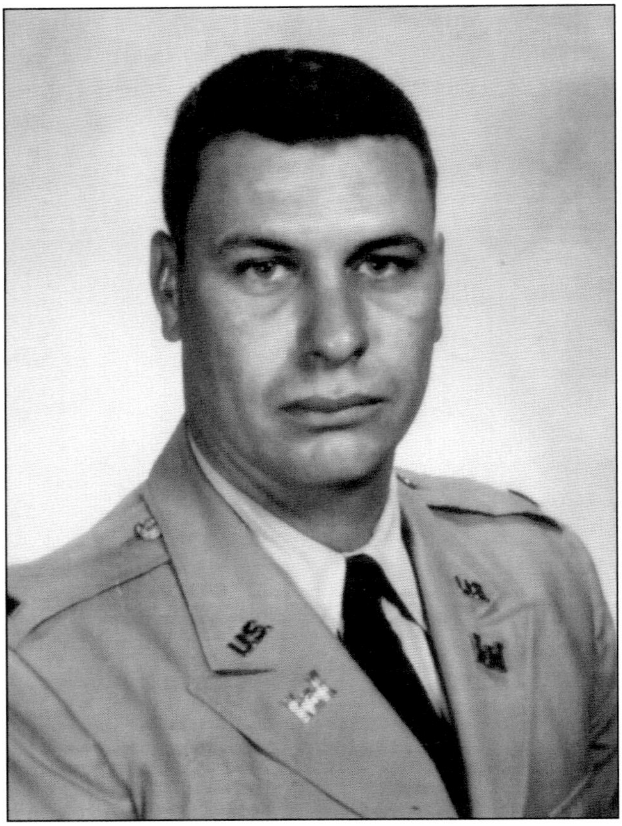

William L. "Bill" Tillman joined the Army National Guard in September 1954 at the Fort Coombs Armory in Apalachicola. He served 16 years there, obtaining a commissioned officer rank of first lieutenant. Later, as a captain, he was transferred to Head Quarters Company and served on battalion staff in Panama City. Captain Tillman faithfully served the US Army and the state of Florida for over 32 years before retiring honorably. (KGT.)

Seven

Olden Days

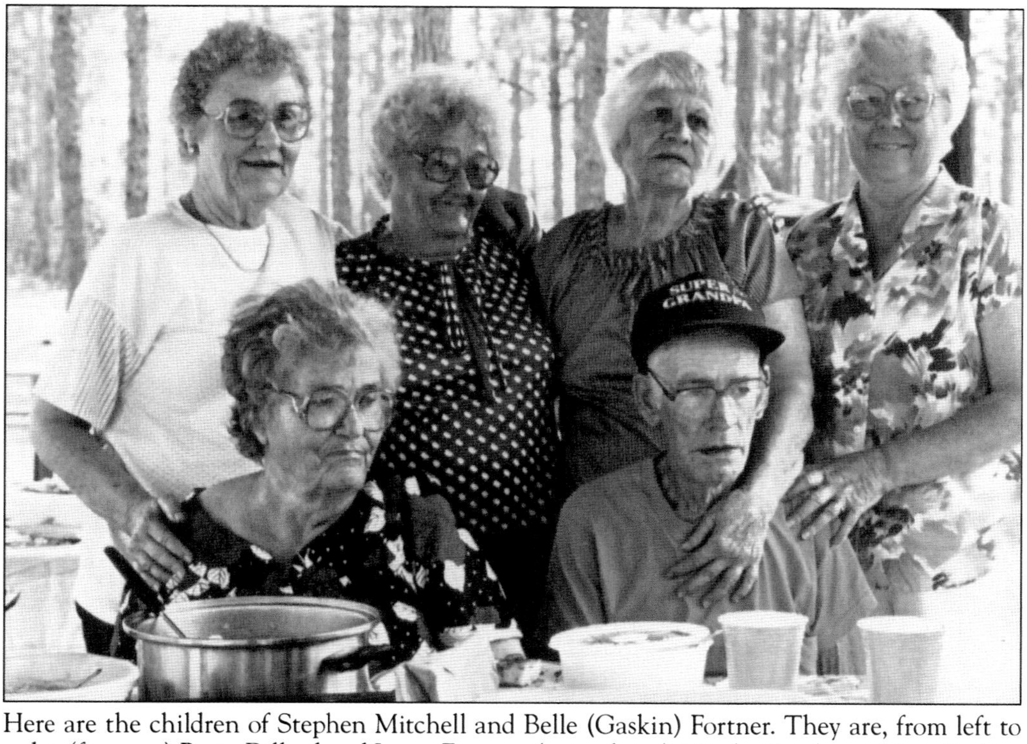

Here are the children of Stephen Mitchell and Belle (Gaskin) Fortner. They are, from left to right, (first row) Betty Dillard and Leroy Fortner; (second row) Martha Stephens, Mary Barlow, Estella Chason, and Hazel Forehand. Little did they know that this would be their last reunion: the following year (1989), their brother Leroy died. (FFW.)

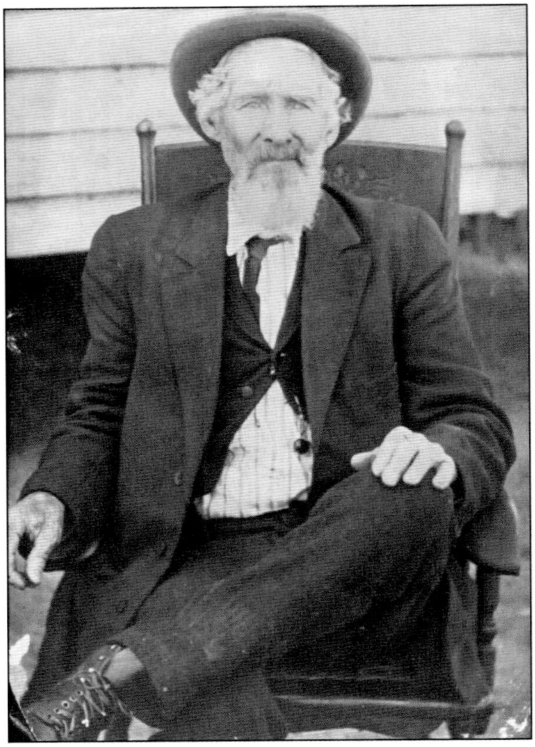

William "Bill" Strange, born in 1838 in Dooly County, Georgia, died in 1929, in Wewahitchka, Florida, and is buried in the Roberts Cemetery. Bill and his wife, Eliza, lived at Juniper Creek, near Frink, from 1861 until 1882. They moved to Wetappo Creek, near Early, Florida, and stayed there until approximately 1899. They then moved to Farmdale, Florida. William moved back to Wewahitchka after Eliza's death in 1914. (LBS.)

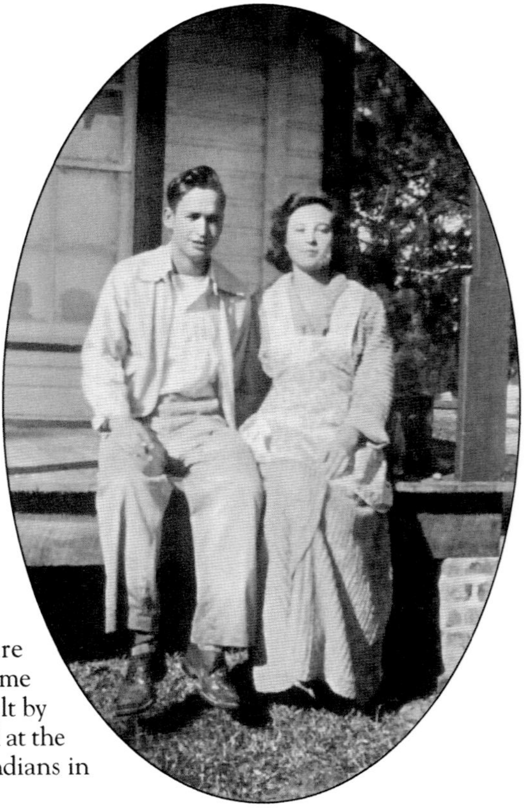

Haywood and Ophelia (Fortner) Borders are pictured sitting on the front porch of their home the day after their wedding. The house was built by Haywood's father, Cordie Borders, and is located at the site where the Richards family was killed by Indians in the early 1830s. (LBS.)

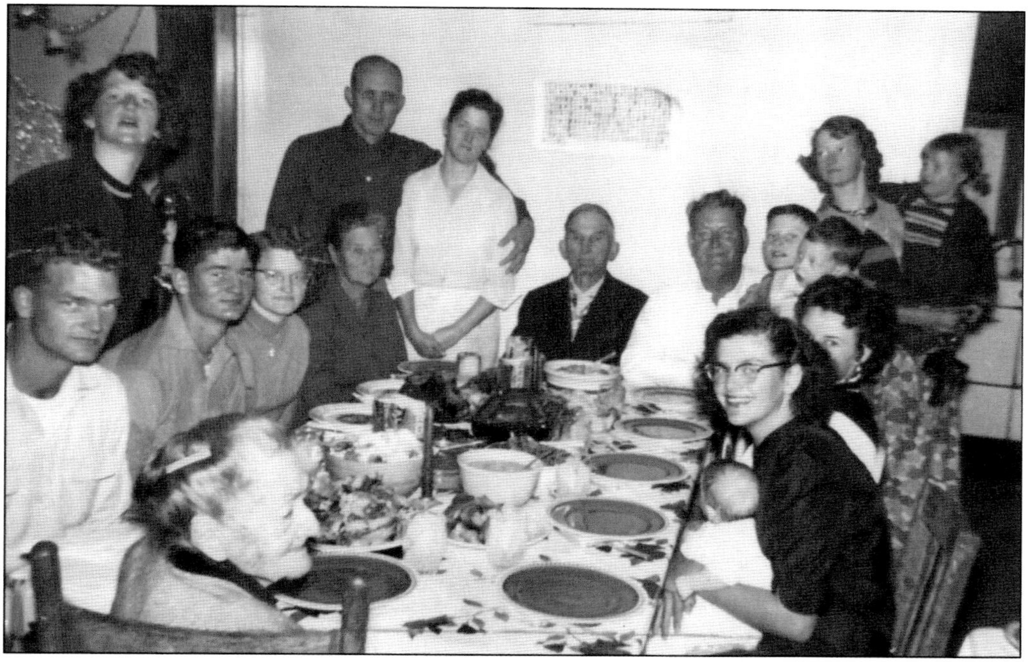

The families of Cecil Glass and Walter Pitts are pictured here in the late 1950s. Clockwise around the table, from bottom left, are Preacher, Joe, Sallie (standing behind Joe), Pearl Glass, Granny Hooker, Rev. Charles and Louise Keith (standing at the far end), Walter Pitts (seated at the head of the table), Cecil, Cecil's daughter Betty Glass (standing and holding Iris Oliver), Johnny Glass (holding Charles Oliver), Doris Glass, Doris's sister Kathryn, and Doris Oliver. (BGW.)

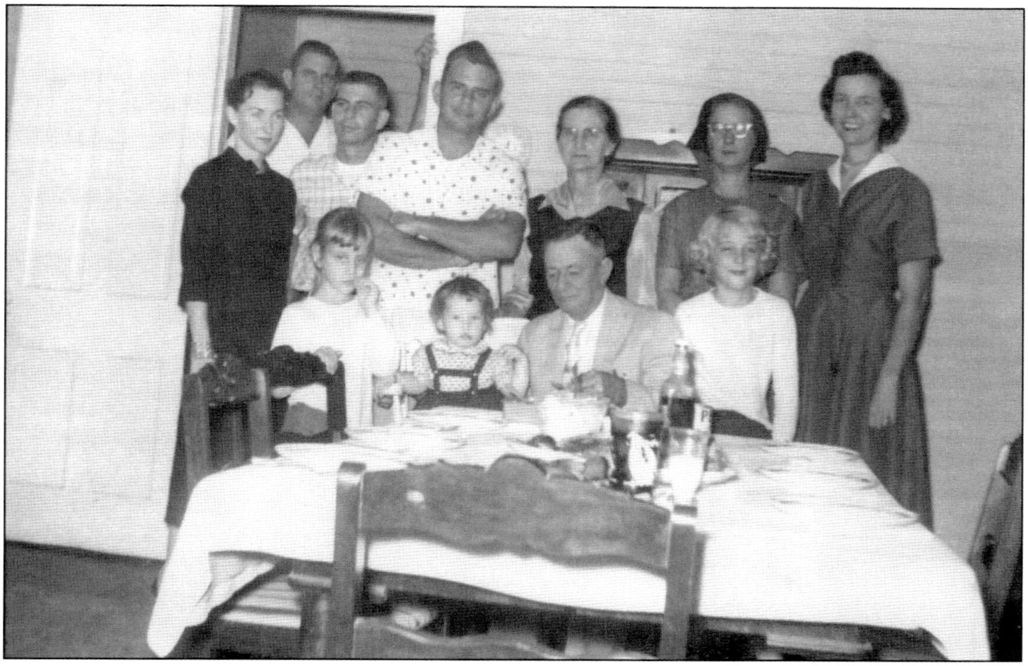

In this photograph of a Rish family dinner from about 1958–1959 are, from left to right, (first row) Erin, Ann, Roy Sr., and Donna; (second row) Carol, Roy Jr., Billy Joe, Henry, Lucy, Doris and Betty. (DJRW.)

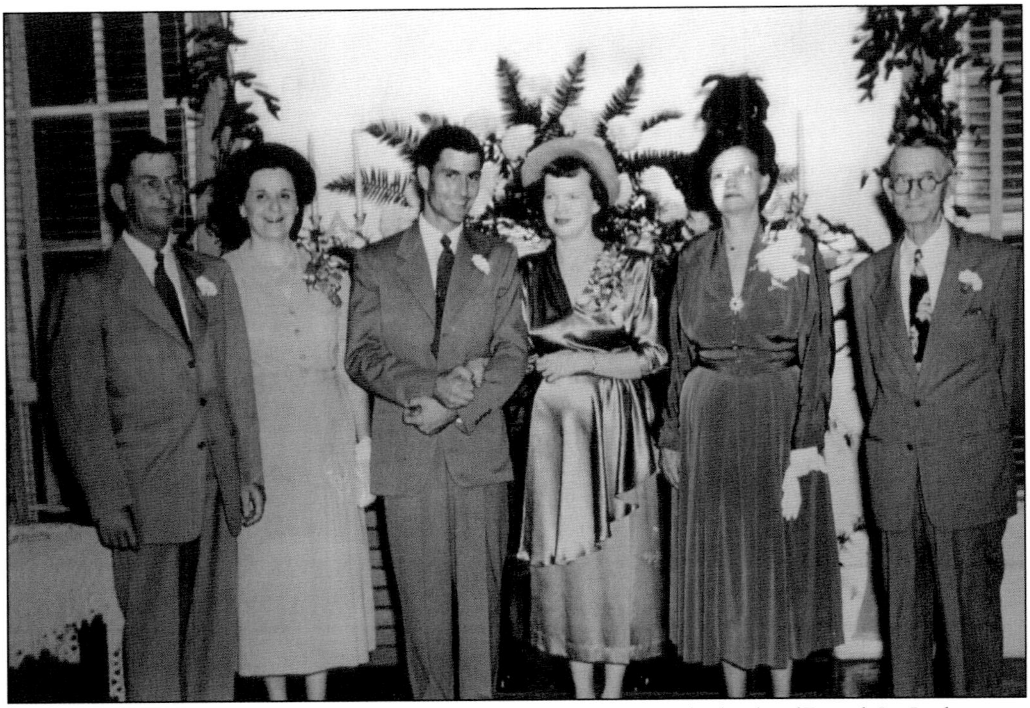

Verre Byrd, daughter of Bramette Byrd of Wewahitchka, became the bride of David C. Gaskin, son of Mr. and Mrs. Dave Gaskin, in the Methodist church on Sunday, September 4, 1949. Pictured here are, from left to right, Dave Gaskin, Annie Traylor Gaskin, groom David Carl Gaskin, bride Verre "Tweeta" Byrd Gaskin, mother of the bride Bramette Byrd, and Rev. W.A. "Billy" Daniels, minister of the Presbyterian church, who officiated at the double-ring ceremony. (PGS.)

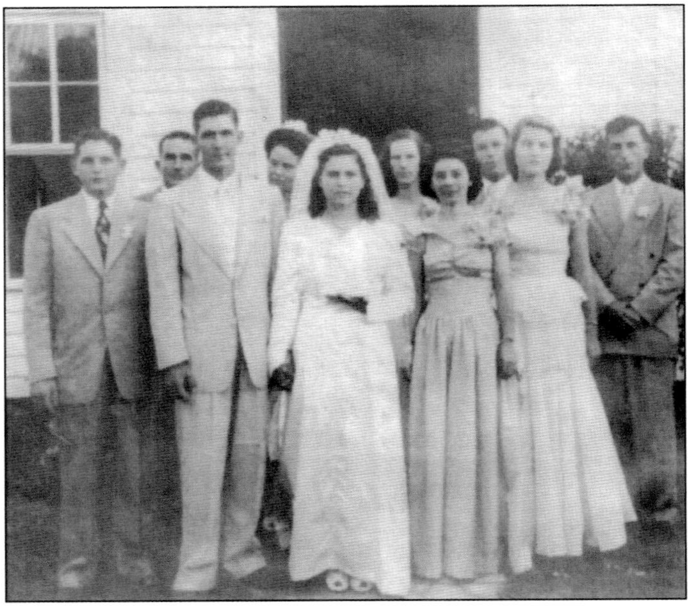

The wedding of Carl Dean and Mytrice Alford was held on July 16, 1950, at the Glad Tidings Assembly of God Church in Wewahitchka. This church was a wooden building located where the Sunday school rooms are today. The happy couple has been married for more than 50 years now. Pictured, from left to right, are Thomas Williams, William Dean, Carl Dean, Eva Williams, Mytrice (Alford) Dean, Joyce ?, Jesse Corbin, Ted Brown, Daisy (Boyette) Fortner, and Ned Brown. (MAD.)

Joseph A. Whitfield (center) was born in Allenton. In 1913, he came to Dalkeith to serve as postmaster, while his father ran a general store. He and his wife, Mae Brown (left), moved to Wewahitchka in 1925. There, he opened the Pride Mercantile Company, but he later sold it to become a beekeeper. Whitfield Apiaries produced tupelo honey for many years. Joseph and Mae had four children, Ernest, Kenneth, Alfred, and Shirley. Also in the photograph is son Ernest Whitfield. (CW.)

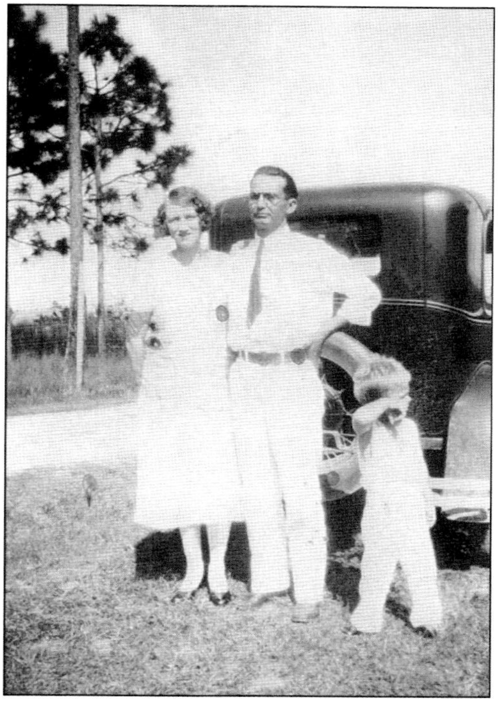

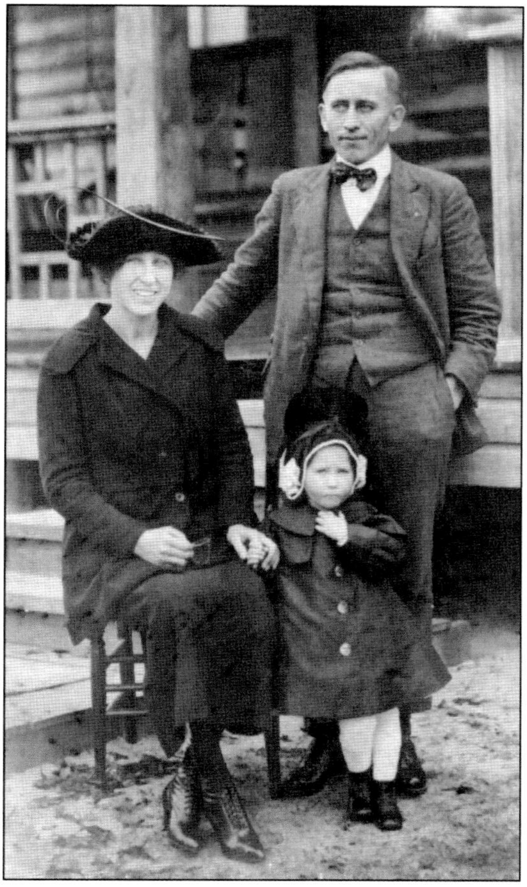

Alf and Lorna Millergren are pictured with their daughter Emmie in about 1920–1921. Later, they had two more children, sons Chap and Nils. Alf was the local postmaster, and Lorna worked in the post office as well. Emmie grew up working alongside her parents as a clerk. Son Nils later became the postmaster, followed by his wife, Hazel (Lamb) Millergren, who became postmistress. Alf was responsible for getting the first doctor for Wewahitchka. (EMK.)

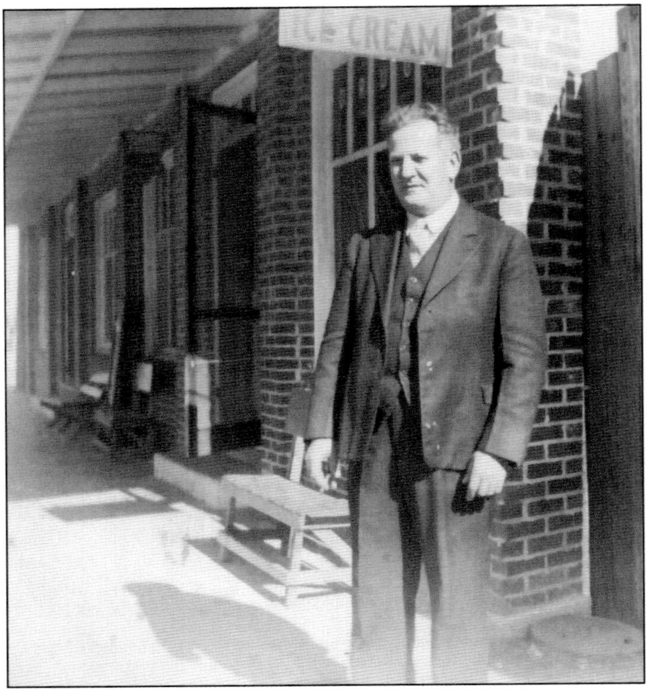

Dr. George Redfern came to Wewahitchka in 1939 with his wife, Florence, three children, and his widowed mother-in-law, Katie Butler. He opened up a drugstore and served as the local dentist and pharmacist in 1940. (PMM.)

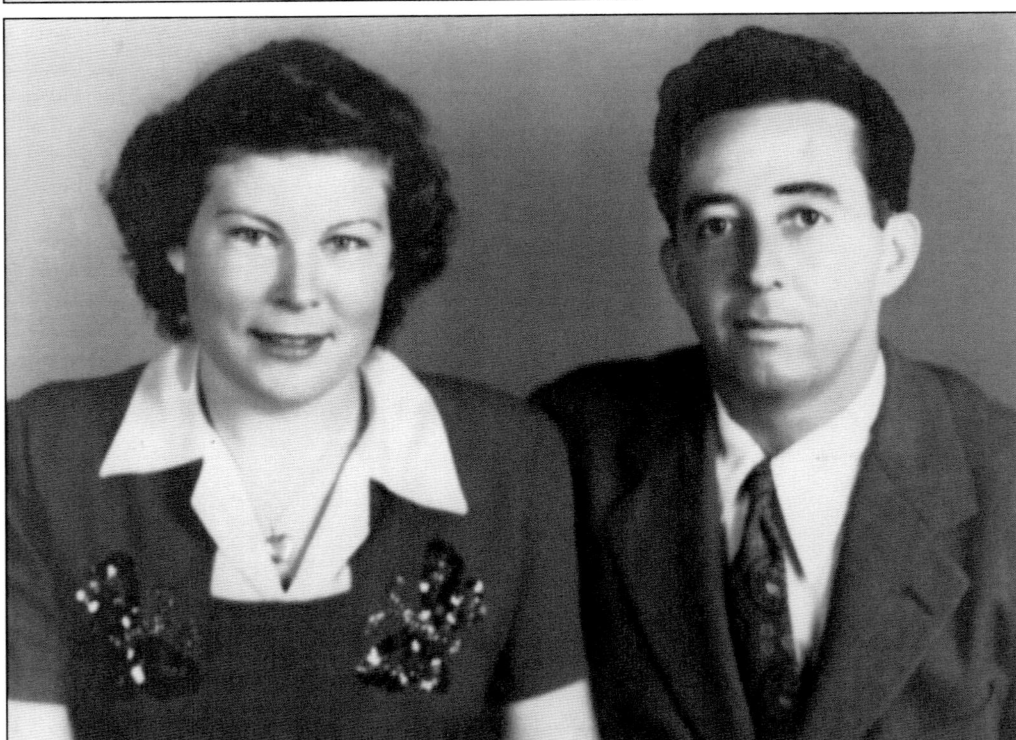

This photograph was taken at the wedding party for Mary Juanita Jones and her new husband, Lawrence Abreu, who were married in Hawaii in 1945 while she was stationed as a Civilian Public Service worker. The couple moved back to the area after the war and Lawrence pastored at the Methodist church in Honeyville, just south of Wewahitchka. (SAB.)

Scottie (Witherspoon) Connell (1868–1948) married William Roy Connell in 1910 on the steamboat *John W. Callahan*. They had nine children, four of them after Scottie went blind. Scottie's blindness was due to life on the river with a common water pump and towels. She got German measles in her eyes from the germs on a towel she used to dry her face. She was pregnant at the time. (BB.)

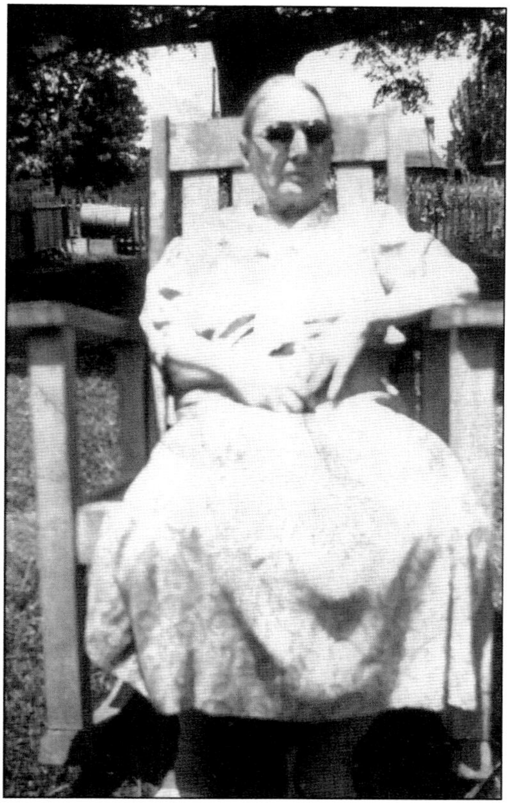

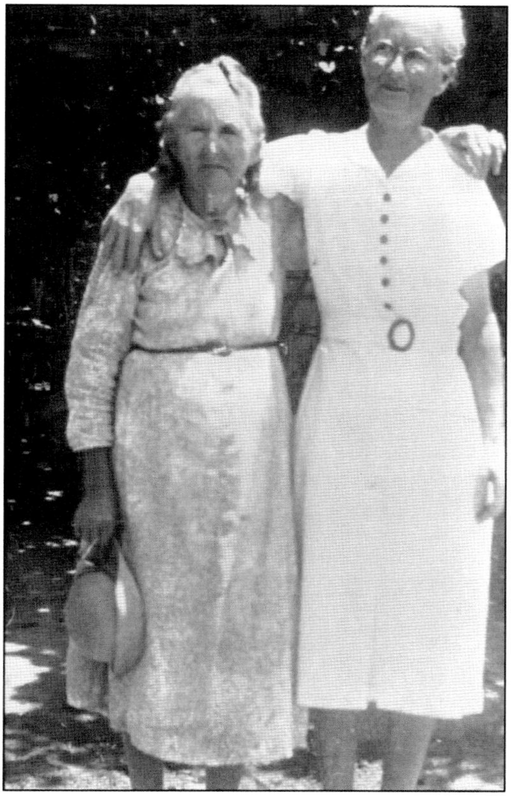

Here are Alice Lee (Daniels) and her mother, Lovie (Strange) Daniels, both of Kinard. Lovie was once the mail carrier there, and she rode on a horse and buggy from Dyer Point to Early, Florida, in around 1907–1909. Alice married John J. Husband, but he died in 1930. She then married Rev. Rufus J. Pitts. He passed away in 1954, and she in 1955. Both women lived in Wewahitchka in their later years. (LBS.)

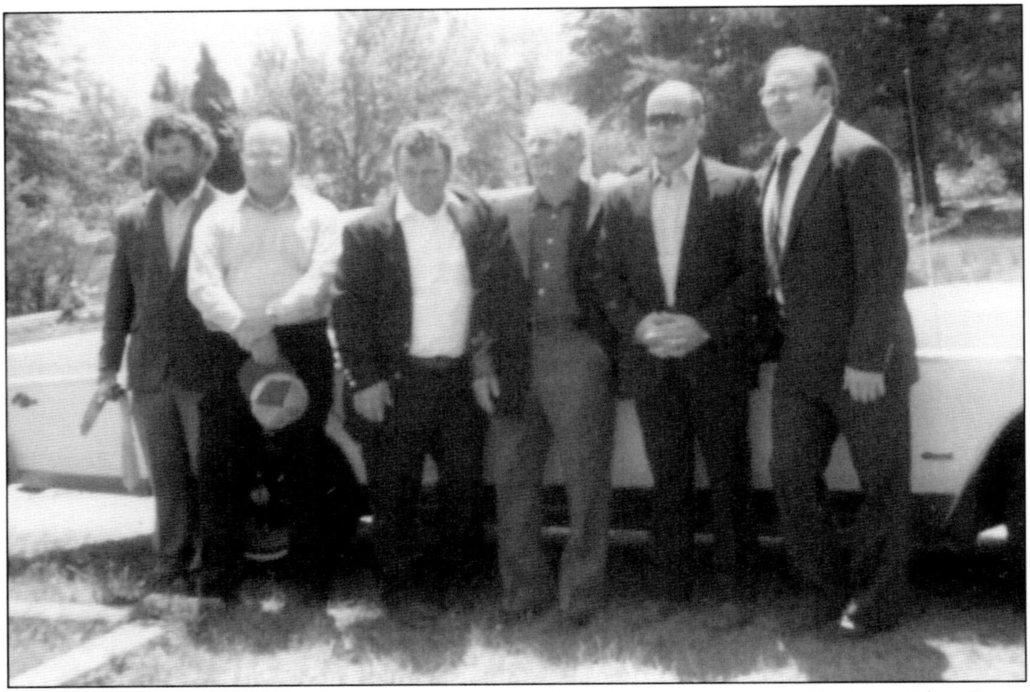

The sons of Ruel Ervin and Dorothy (Redd) Forehand are, from left to right, Alford, Ira, Glen, Ervin Jr., Steve, and Wayne Forehand. This family grew up in Gulf County, and most of them stayed in this area. Ervin and Dorothy are both buried in the Roberts Cemetery in Honeyville. (FFW.)

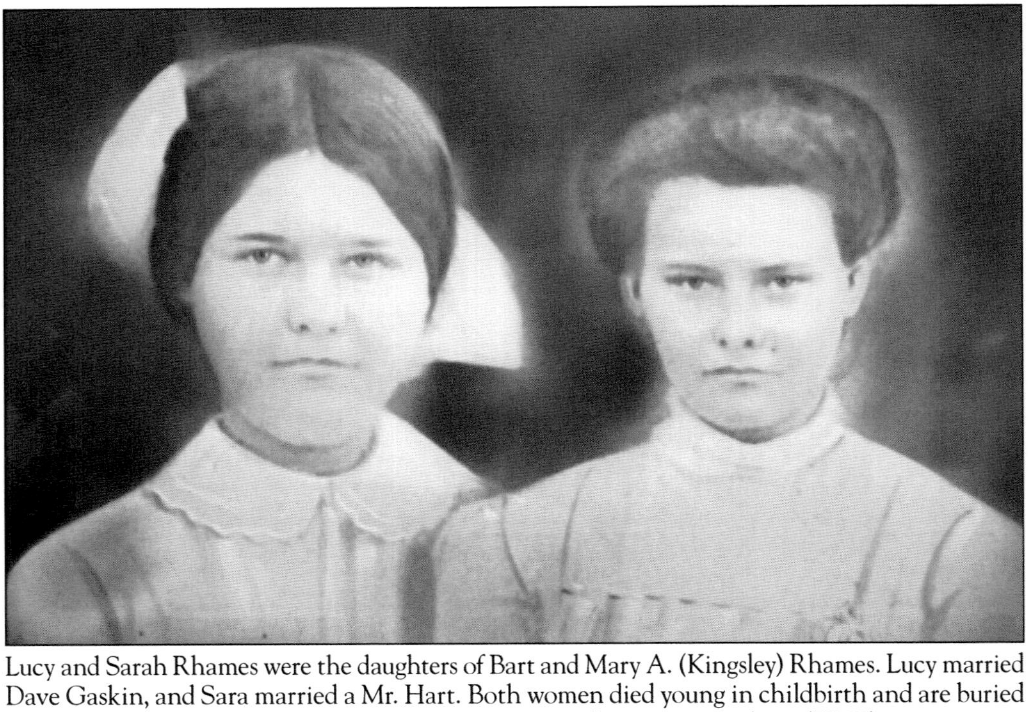

Lucy and Sarah Rhames were the daughters of Bart and Mary A. (Kingsley) Rhames. Lucy married Dave Gaskin, and Sara married a Mr. Hart. Both women died young in childbirth and are buried in the Old Rhames Cemetery on the Gulf County–Calhoun County line. (FFW.)

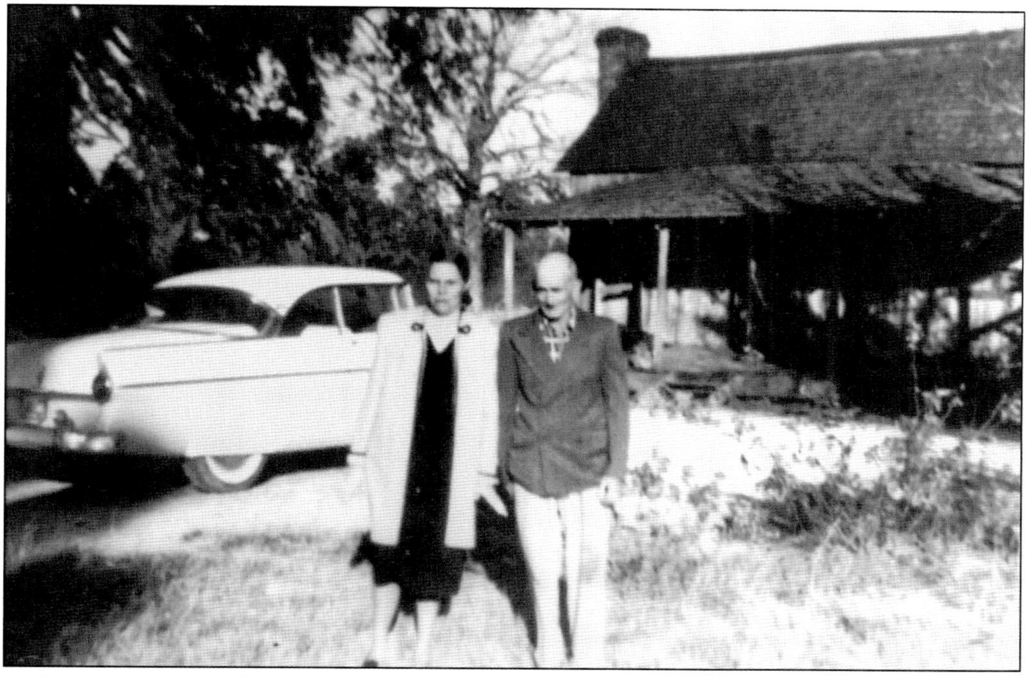

W. Jenning Davis Sr., born in 1908 in Homer, Georgia, came to Florida and met and married Edna E. Whitfield in 1939. He worked in logging, at the paper mill, and in the fishing business. In this photograph, he and Edna are standing in front of the old Joseph Weldon Whitfield homestead. Edna, being the youngest of the Whitfield children, inherited the home and lived there with her family. (WD.)

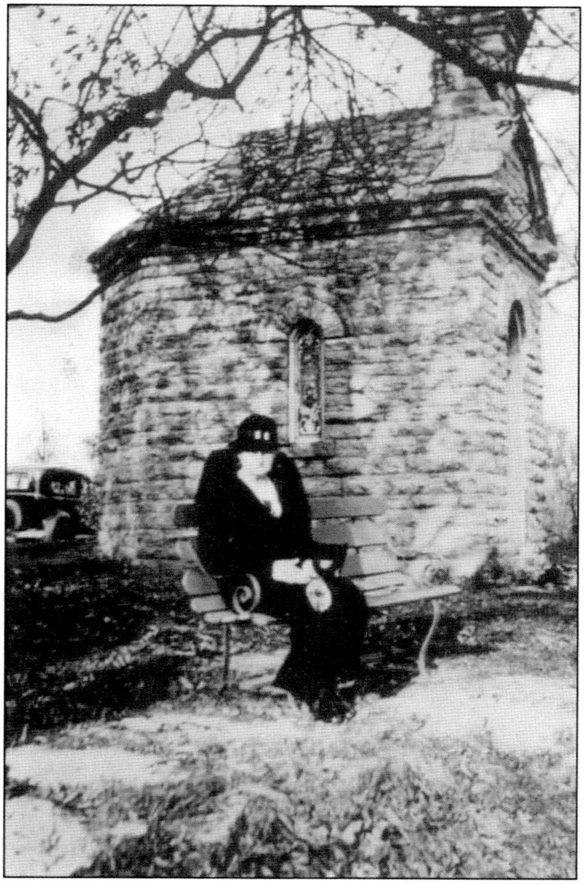

Cornelia Ann (Patterson) Byrd (1861–1927) was a Florida pioneer; she was left a widow with several small children in the early years of young womanhood. She bought 120 acres on the Dead Lakes in 1919 and founded the Idlewood Hotel and Hunting Lodge. Cornelia also ran a boardinghouse in Blountstown and helped many poor young people, including Fuller Warren. (CALC.)

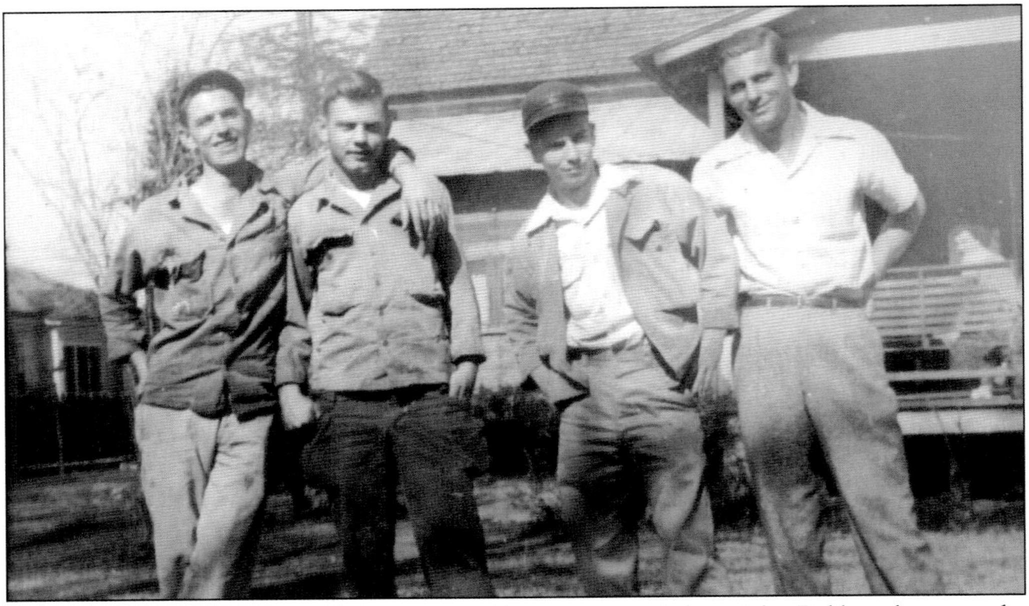

The sons of Roy Sr. and Lucy P. Rish pictured here are, from left to right, Bobby, who opened a heating and plumbing business that later became the West Florida Gas Company; Henry, who worked at the chemical company in Port St. Joe and was killed on the job in 1962; Billy Joe, who opened a law office in Port St. Joe and was elected to the Florida House of Representatives; and Roy Jr., who was a pilot instructor with a government contractor. (DJRW.)

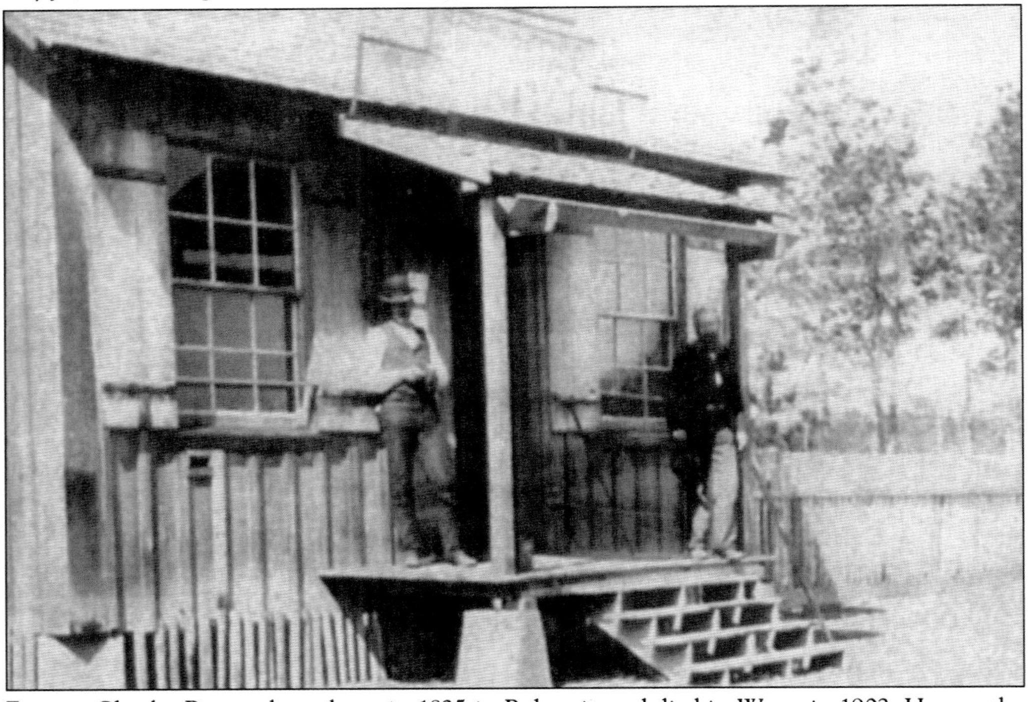

Frances Charles Rummel was born in 1825 in Bohemia and died in Wewa in 1902. He was the postmaster in Wewahitchka after he served in the Civil War. In this photograph provided by Pam Rummel, he is seen on the porch of the Wewahitchka Post Office. It was Dr. John Washington Keyes who hired Rummel to construct the St. John's Church building. (PR.)

Dave E. "Coon" Gaskin was born in 1875 in Georgia and married Lucy Rhames in December 1907 in Blountstown. Lucy died during childbirth in 1922, leaving Dave in Kinard with a house full of children to raise all alone. (FFW.)

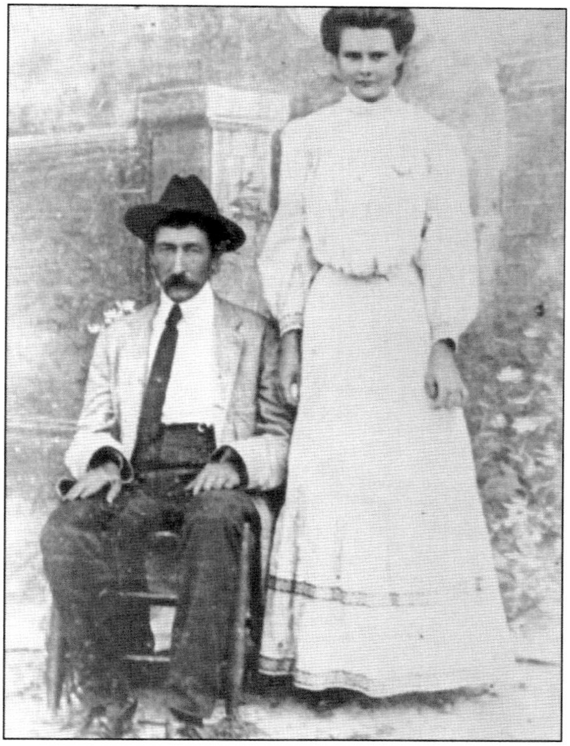

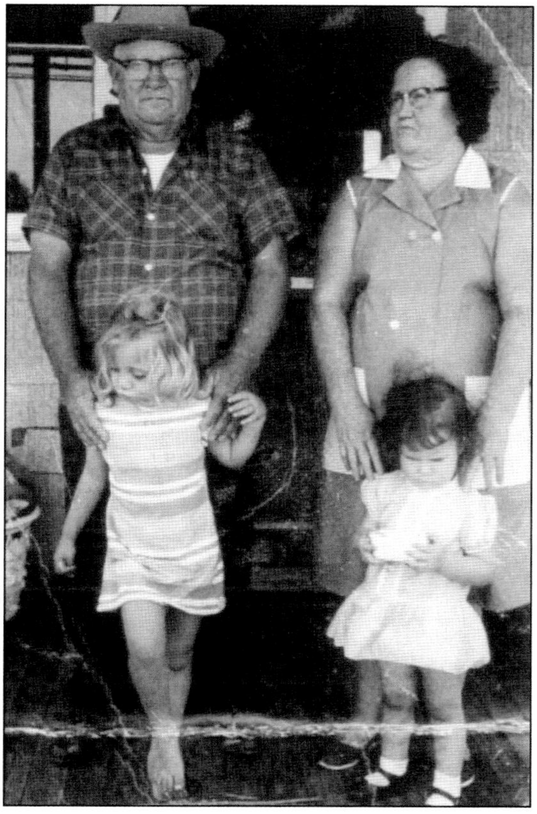

Elmer Gary Nunery married Elizabeth "Betty" Ophelia (Baston), daughter of Tom and Ada Baston of Iola, Florida. Elmer worked for Sheriff Byrd Parker for 25 years as jailor and dispatcher in Gulf County. He and Betty had 12 children—6 boys and 6 girls. In the photograph are granddaughters Susie (left) and Helen (right). (JNC.)

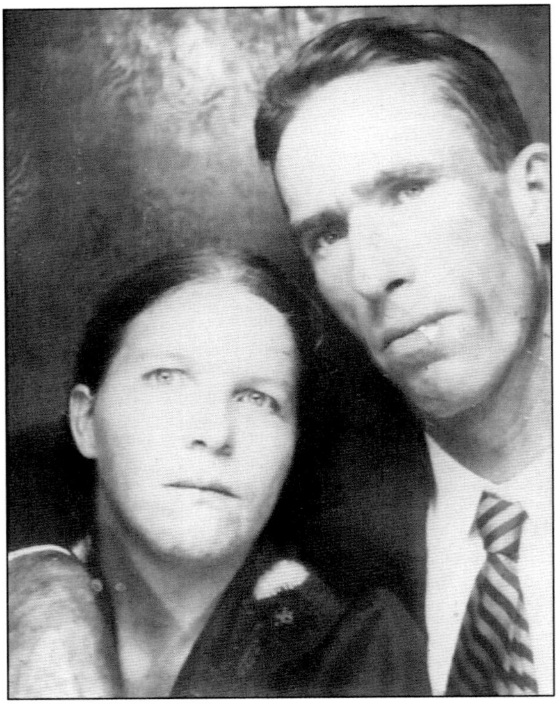

Irvin and Emma (Bryant) Darley were married in 1938 in Wewahitchka. Irvin worked in the shipyard during World War II and later bought his first grocery store on Highway 22. This store was sold, and another was built on West River Road. Irvin was a successful merchant and businessman for many years and was known to be generous to those in need. (HDB.)

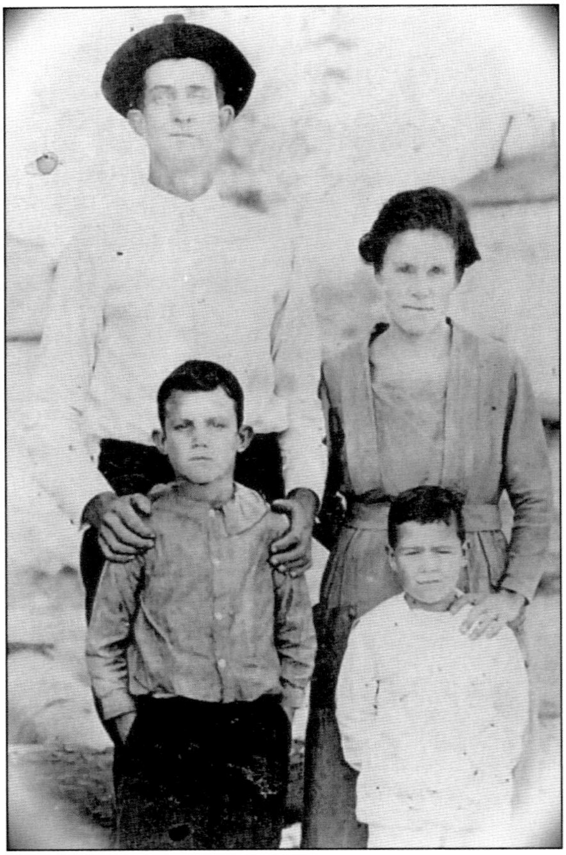

Francis and Lillie Bass moved to Wewahitchka around 1922. Pictured with them are two of their four children, Cage (left) and Paul. Ethel (Whitfield) and Ruth (Linton) were their daughters. Francis worked as a brickmason. When Paul was just a small boy, he worked as a fishing tour guide at his brother-in-law's fish camp on the Dead Lakes. (SBJ.)

Eight

OUT OF TOWN

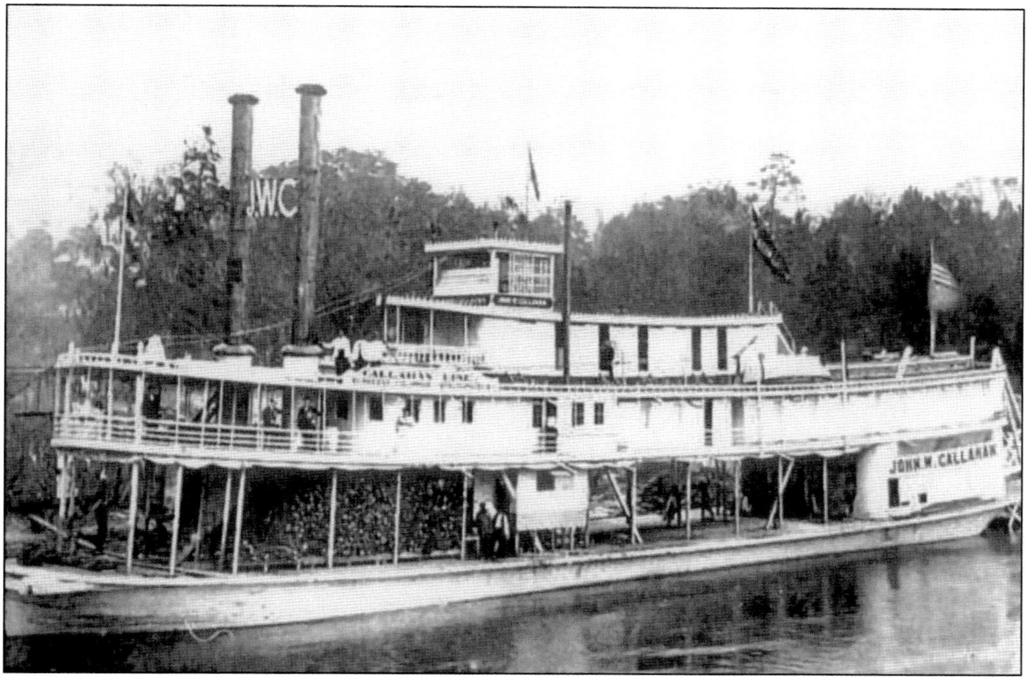

The riverboat *John W. Callahan* was built in 1907 at Apalachicola, which was its home port. It was owned by J.W. Callahan and sold to Tri-State Navigation. Roy Connell was captain of the riverboat, whose normal route was from Bainbridge, Georgia, to Apalachicola. After the *Callahan* sank when it hit a snag in the Chipola River, the company offered Connell another steamboat, the *Albany*. The company changed the vessel's name to the *J.W. Callahan Jr.* (BB.)

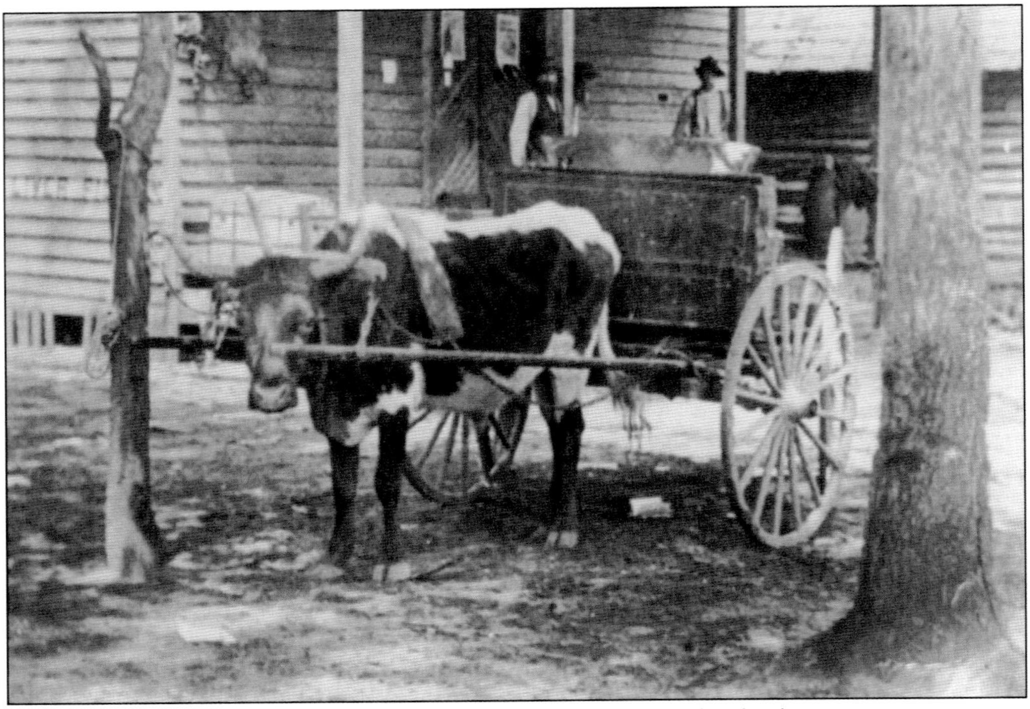

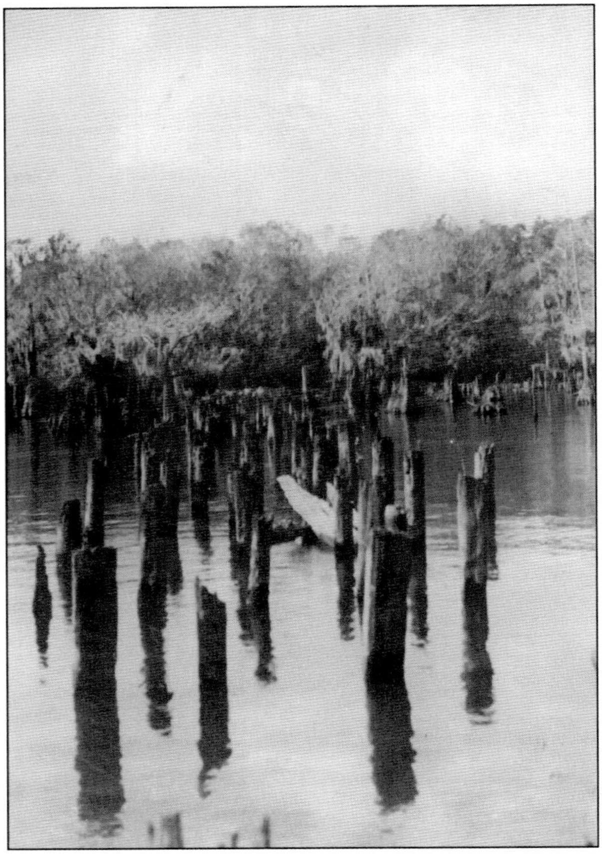

Iola, Florida, does not appear on the 1835 map by David H. Burr showing Florida's towns. The post office was established in 1838, with James Hudson as postmaster. In the early 1900s, there were a number of hotels springing up in Iola; one was the Hotel Iola, which Henry A. Rish operated (in addition to his being the local mail carrier, as shown in this photograph). This hotel later burned in 1925. (Author.)

This view of the old pilings of the Iola & St. Joseph Railroad across the Dead Lakes between Wewahitchka and Iola looks west toward the mainland. The Kodak photograph was taken by Joe R. Hunter on December 3, 1938. (Author.)

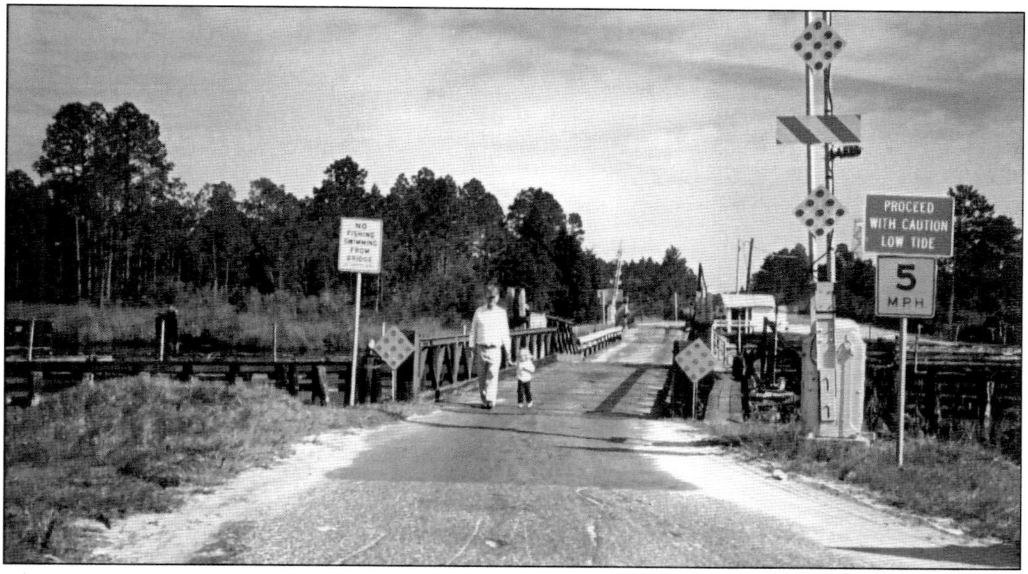

The Overstreet floating bridge was installed in 1932 and operated until about 1988. This was a route that was used for folks from the north to get the beaches in the south of the county. Also, it was used to get across the Intracoastal Waterway. Preston Gibbs is walking his granddaughter Savannah Gibbs across the bridge in this image. Today, a very high concrete bridge is located here. (NRG.)

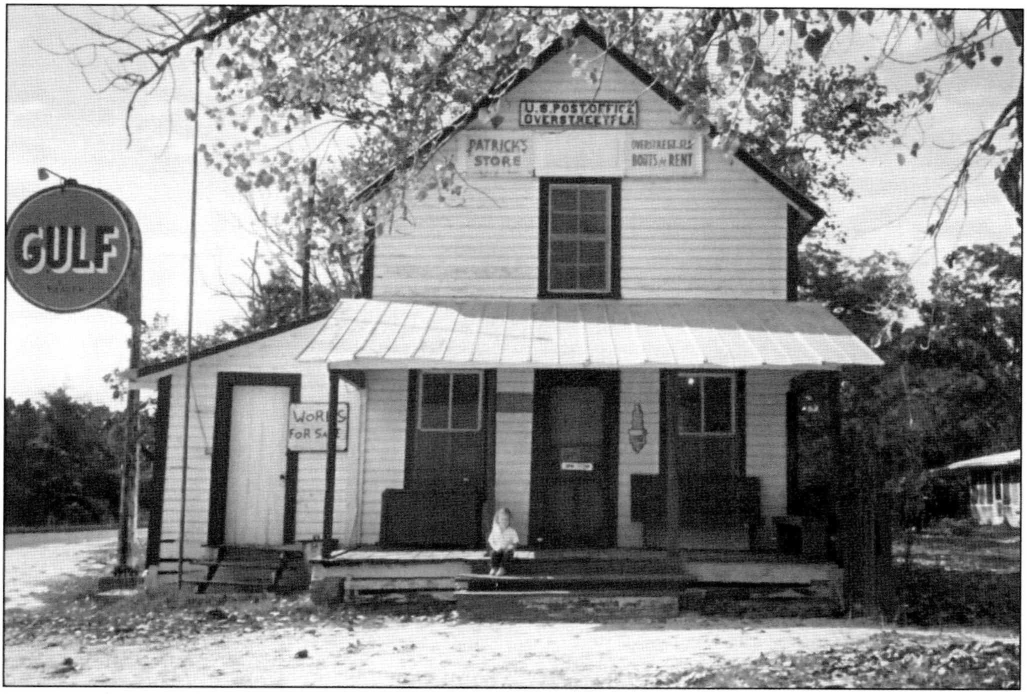

In 1916, the postal inspector, summoned by George Overstreet two years earlier, arrived at this small settlement. The inspector established a post office in "Miss Lillie Scott's corncrib," and the community was officially named. A few months later, the post office was moved across the canal to Thomas Patrick's store, and "Mr. Tom" became the postmaster. Here, Savannah Gibbs sits on the steps of the store. (NRG.)

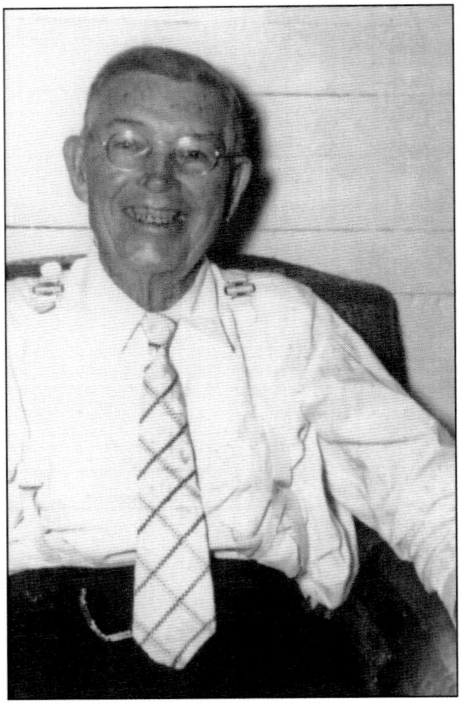

Rufus Jefferson Pitts (1870–1954), a religious man who loved God, had a wonderful sense of humor, playing tricks on just about anybody. During his lifetime, he was a farmer, postmaster, mail carrier, toll collector on the canal, and always a minister. Pitts built a house in Wewahitchka and married Alice Husband. He is pictured here around the 1950s. (Granny Rollins family.)

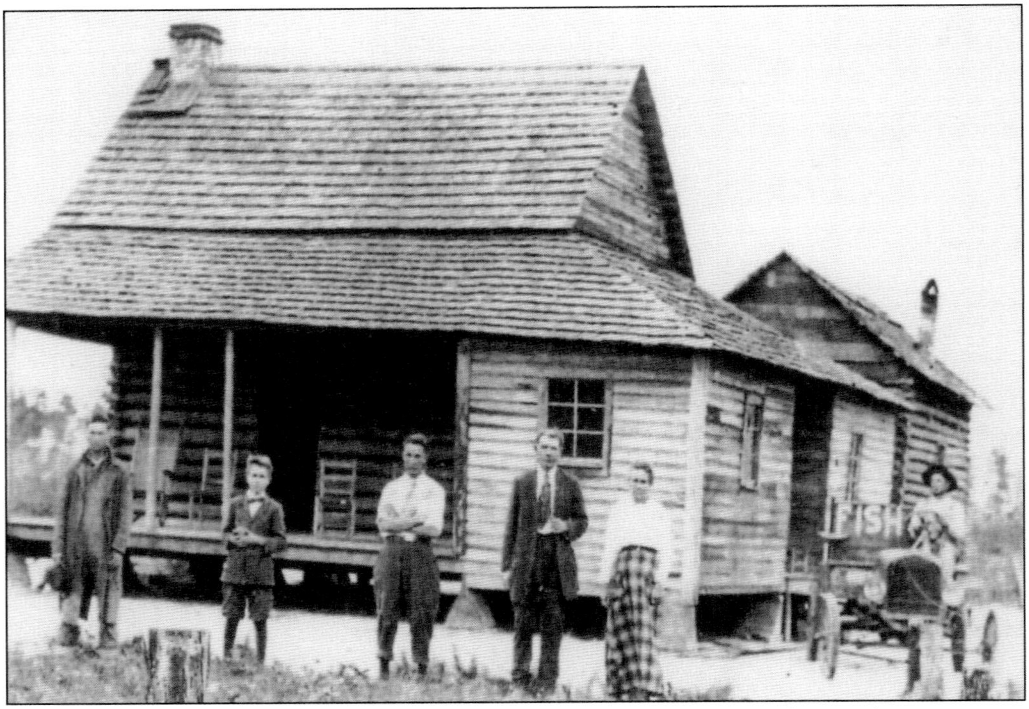

This is the log home of Rufus and Roxie (Bailey) Pitts at Boardbranch. Rufus was the postmaster, and the room built on the right front is the post office. At this time, Walter (Rufus's brother) had the mail route from Boardbranch to Frink. Pictured, from left to right, are unidentified, Joseph Allen Pitts, Charlie Monroe "Jake" Pitts, Rufus Jefferson Pitts, Roxie Delany (Bailey) Pitts, and an unidentified man in the car selling fish. (Granny Rollins family.)

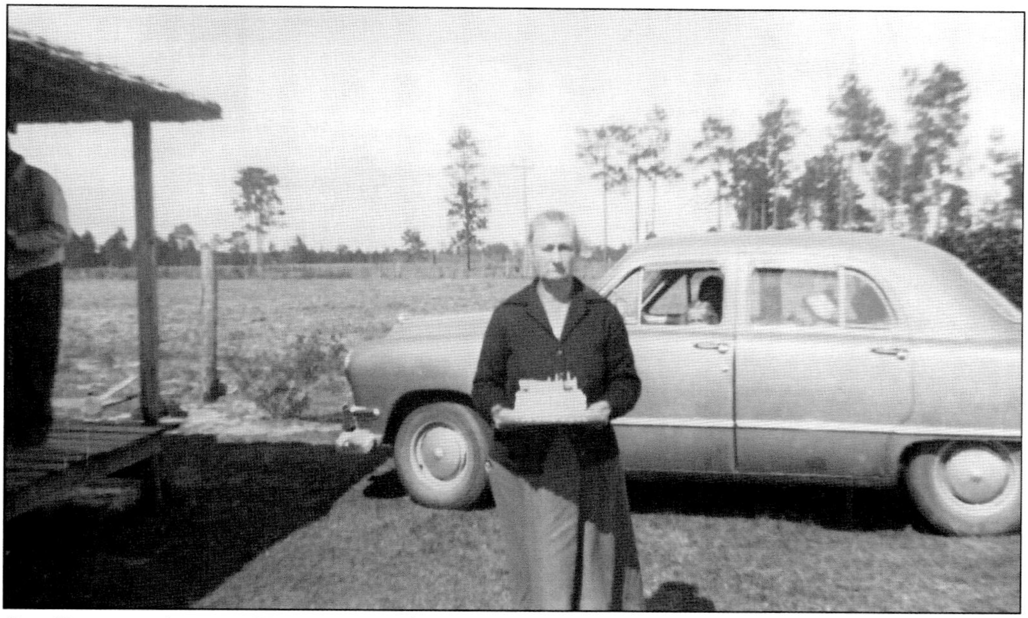

Otis Davis was born on Wetappo Creek, and Lovie McCall, in West Bay, Florida. Davis's parents were William Thomas and Shellie (Kemp) Davis of Wetappo Creek, and McCall's were Henry and Nettie McCall of Bay County. In this photograph, Shellie is celebrating her birthday with a cake in the Kemp community, west of town. (IDC.)

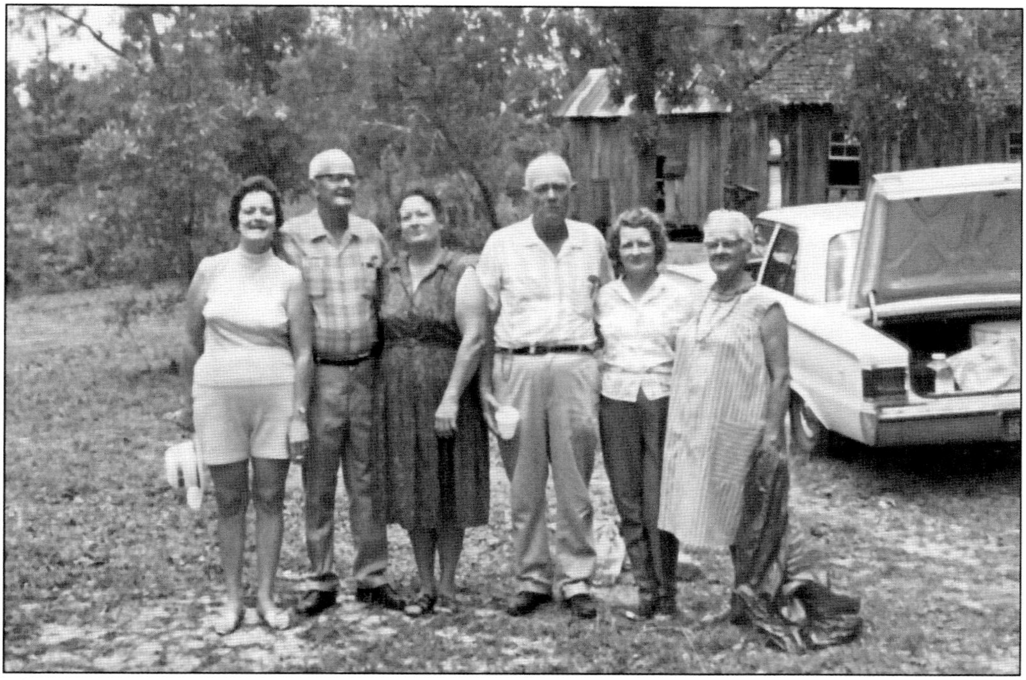

This is a 1960 Kemp family gathering at the home of Steve Gibbs, grandson of Vonnie Kemp Gibbs. The old home place was on Wetappo Creek and Kemp Cemetery Road. Almost all the brothers and sisters are present, except Essie (twin to Bessie), who lived in New York, and brother H. Dick Kemp. Pictured, from left to right, are Hazel (Kemp) Lister, Sam Kemp, Bessie (Kemp) Smith, Harvey Kemp, Versie (Kemp) Daniels, and Vonnie (Kemp) Gibbs. (NRG.)

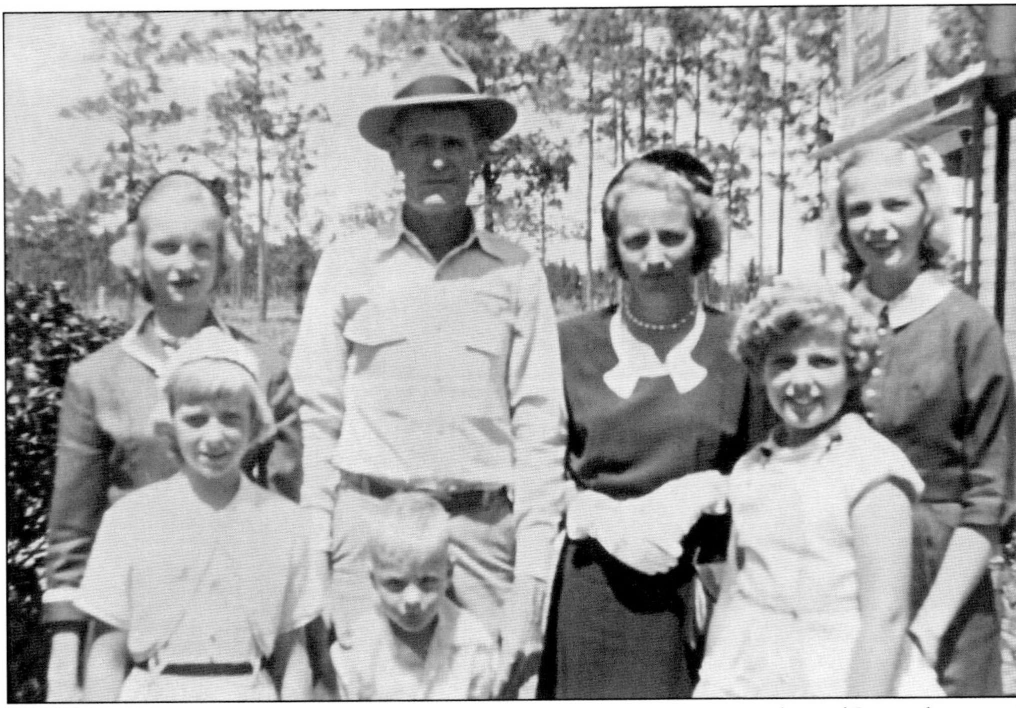

Otis and Lovie (McCall) Davis had a family of four girls—Iris, Doris, Judy, and Jacquelyn—and one son, Otis Jr. Besides operating a bait-and-tackle business, Davis also planted a large garden and sold fresh vegetables. At one time, he raised hogs and cattle, and he also drove the school bus until retiring from that job. The Davises lived there until their deaths—Otis in 1995, and Lovie in 2012. (IDC.)

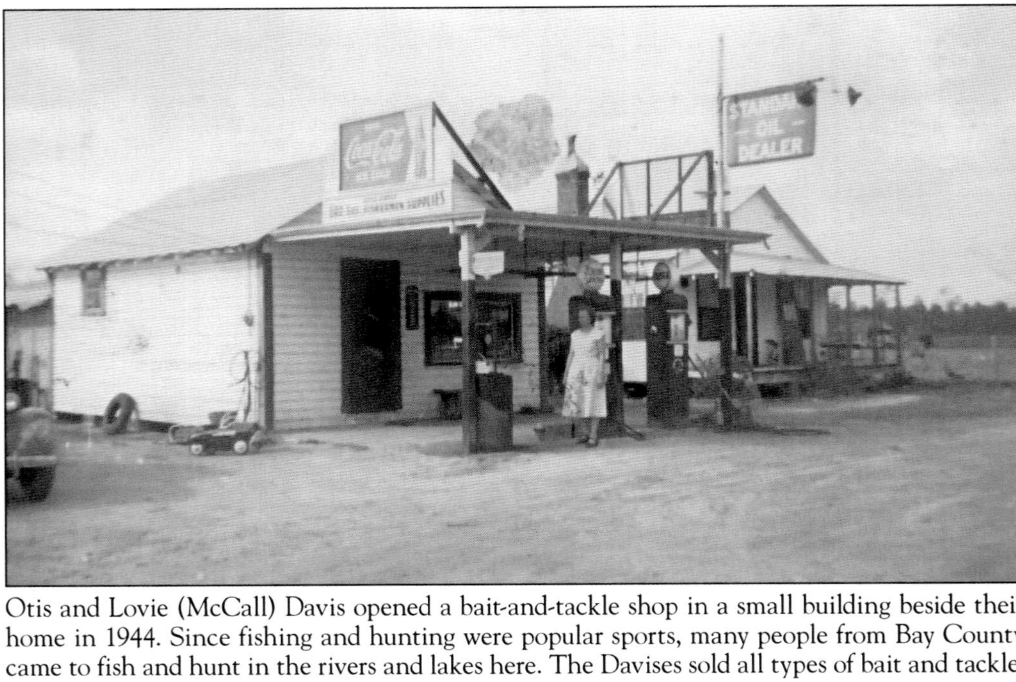

Otis and Lovie (McCall) Davis opened a bait-and-tackle shop in a small building beside their home in 1944. Since fishing and hunting were popular sports, many people from Bay County came to fish and hunt in the rivers and lakes here. The Davises sold all types of bait and tackle, ice, and fishing equipment to the sports fishermen. (IDC.)

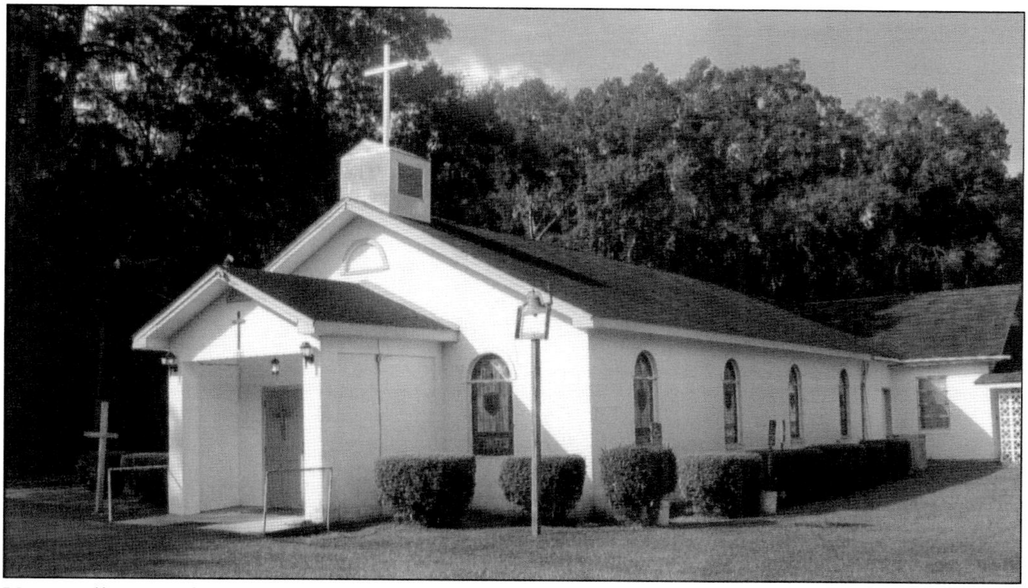

Honeyville United Methodist Church is four miles south of Wewahitchka. It began as a community church and later became the Honeyville School. The old wood-frame church was built around 1930. During that time, Reverend Martin became the first pastor, and the church became the Honeyville Methodist Protestant church. In the winter of 1950, the church burned. The community rebuilt the sanctuary as it presently stands today. (SAB and HDB.)

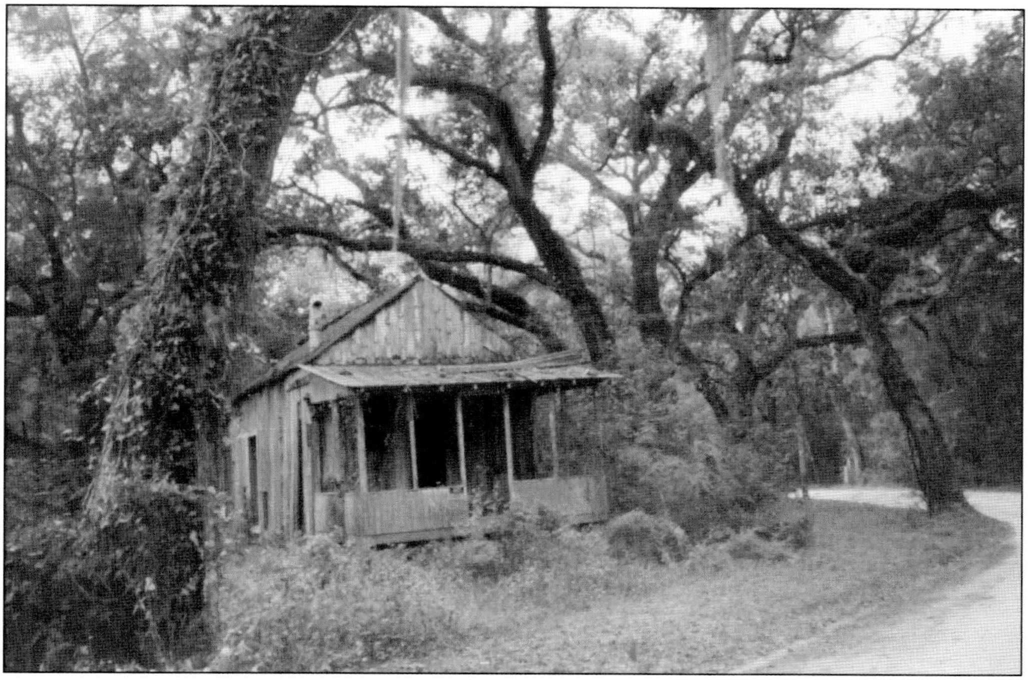

This old hunting camp was located on Howard Creek at Lower Landing. Owners were John Griffin, Charlie Norton, and Homer Cole. The original owner was a German man named Hintster who lived there in the late 1800s. This was also where Bay City operated one of its sawmills 100 years ago; it is torn down now. George Core (historian and county clerk of court) referred to it as the "Honey Rum House." (Author.)

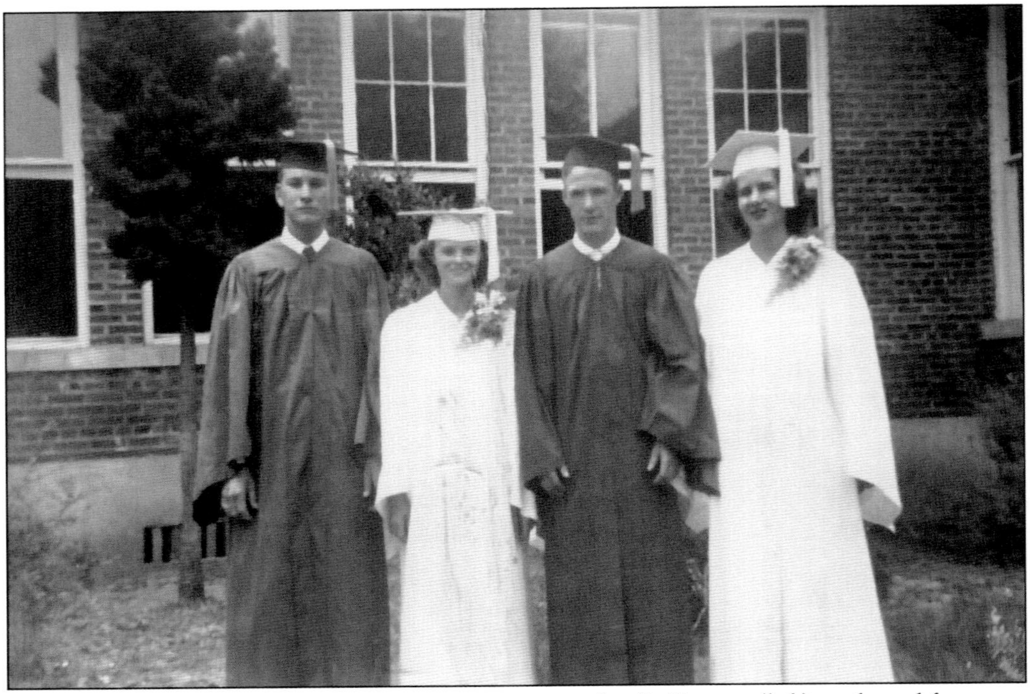

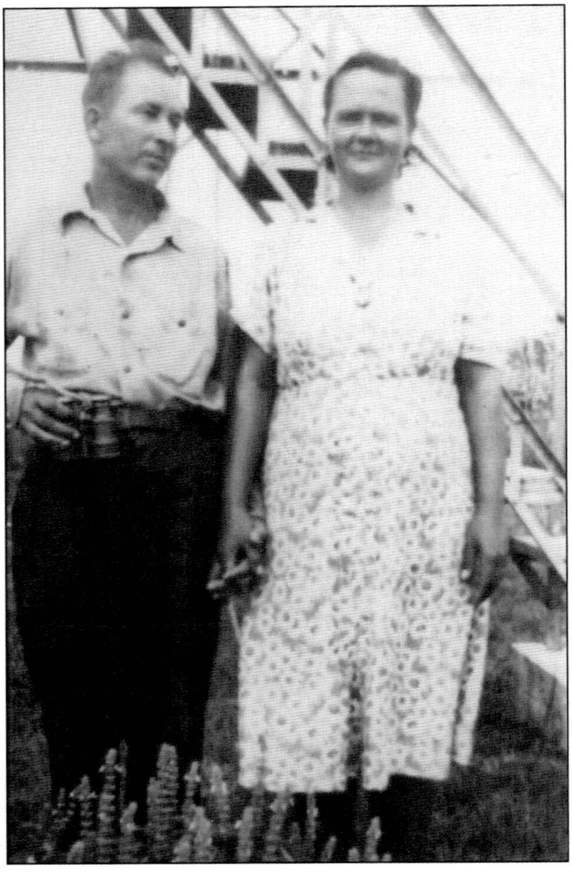

Joe R. Fortner (left) graduated from high school and joined the Army. He was stationed in Alaska, came back home, married Jean Whitfield, and worked at the paper mill in Port St. Joe. Betty Land (second from left) graduated and became a head nurse in Pensacola. Clyde Newsome (third from left) graduated and joined the Air Force, made captain, and was stationed in Russia. Vivian Anderson (right) graduated and taught English in the new high school. All four were 1950 graduates of Kinard High School. (FFW.)

Mary (Weeks) Pitts Rollins operated the Youngstown Fire Tower in 1944. She became the first woman in Bay County to operate a tower for the forestry service. Her husband, Jake, had the position in 1941, but started driving a transport truck. Mary, who was accustomed to assisting her husband in the tower, applied for the job and got it. During that time, the family lived nearby, and Mary worked the Smith tower at Frink. (Granny Rollins family.)

Lewis Griffin was born in Irwin County, Georgia, in 1830, the son of Benjamin and Sarah (Henderson) Griffin. He married Nancy Hendley in Irwin County on October 3, 1850. Nancy was the daughter of Elmore Hendley. Lewis was in Company E, 54th Georgia Infantry Regiment C.S.A. Rev. Lewis M. Griffin served the Cypress Creek Missionary Baptist Church intermittently for three years, but never as a regular pastor. The church was organized in 1910. (AHD.)

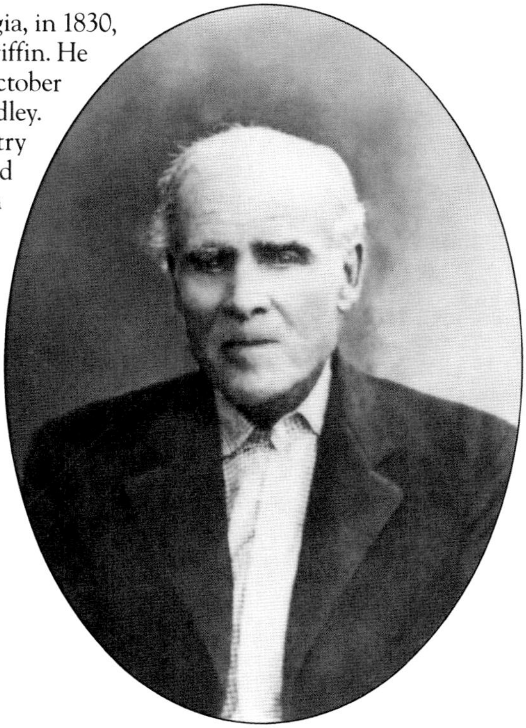

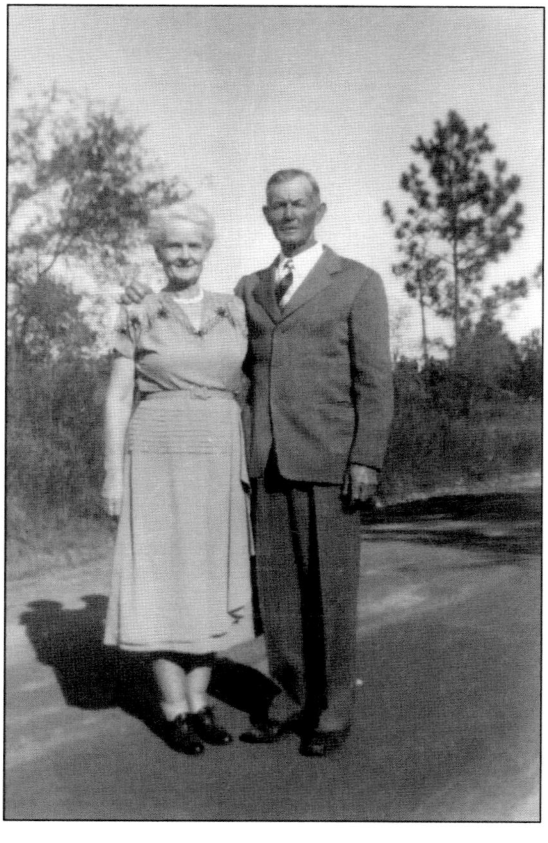

Robert Gibbs came here from Georgia, met and married Sarah Jane Daniels in 1909, and raised a family of six children in and around the Kinard area. He was a woods rider for the Neal Turpentine operation, as well as farmer. This photograph was taken in about 1952–1953. Sarah Jane was the daughter of John and Elizabeth Daniels. She was a natural herbalist and helped a Dr. Reeder of Blountstown on many occasions. (AHD.)

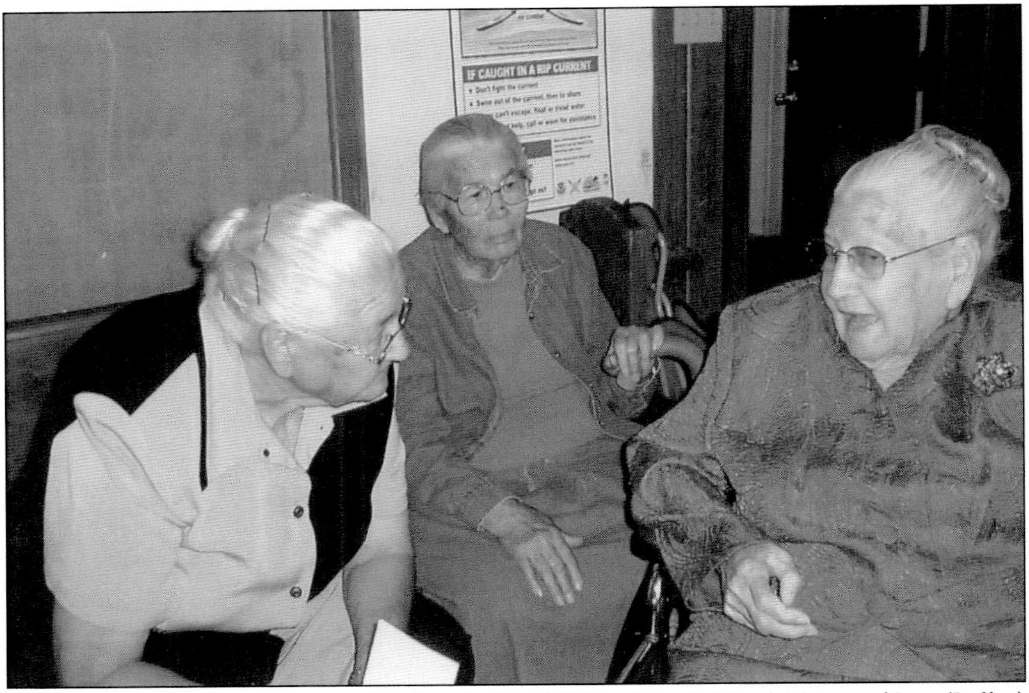

Pictured from left to right, cousins Thelma (Lolley) Walker, Maude (Pitts) Cain, and Inez (Lolley) Flowers catch up on family and life changes during the annual Kinard reunion held every May. This photograph was taken in 2005. (Author.)

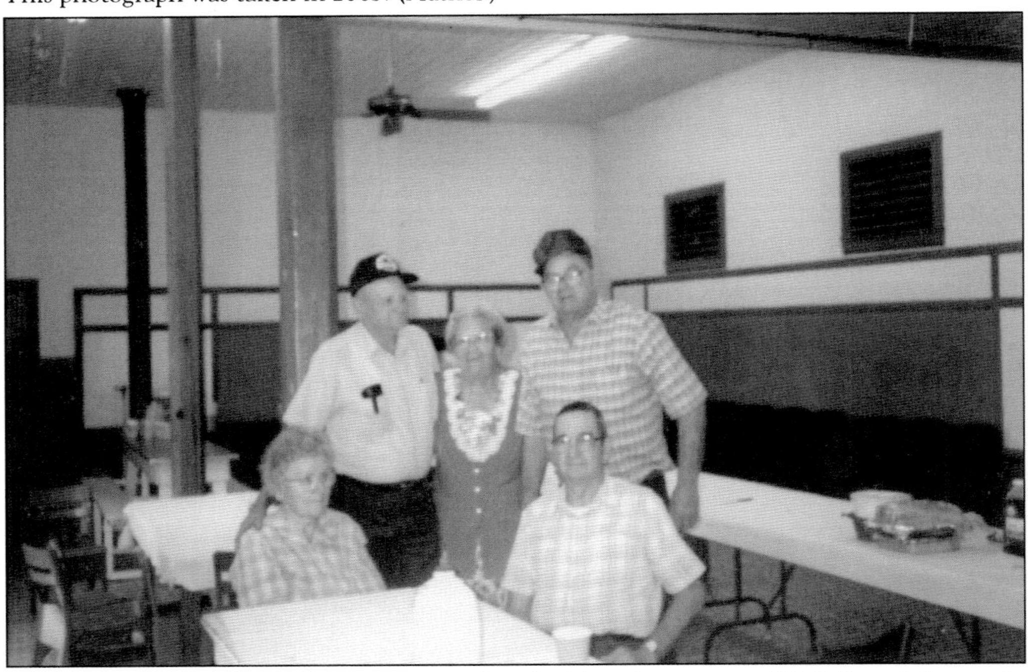

Pitts and Capps family members are pictured at the Kinard reunion in 2000. From left to right are (seated) Flossie (Pitts) Hand? and Loyd Pitts; (standing) Henry Capps?, Mildred (Capps) Alderman, and Mitchell Pitts. Mitchell, Loyd, and Flossie were the children of James Willis and Carlie (Capps) Pitts, all from the Calhoun County area. (Author.)

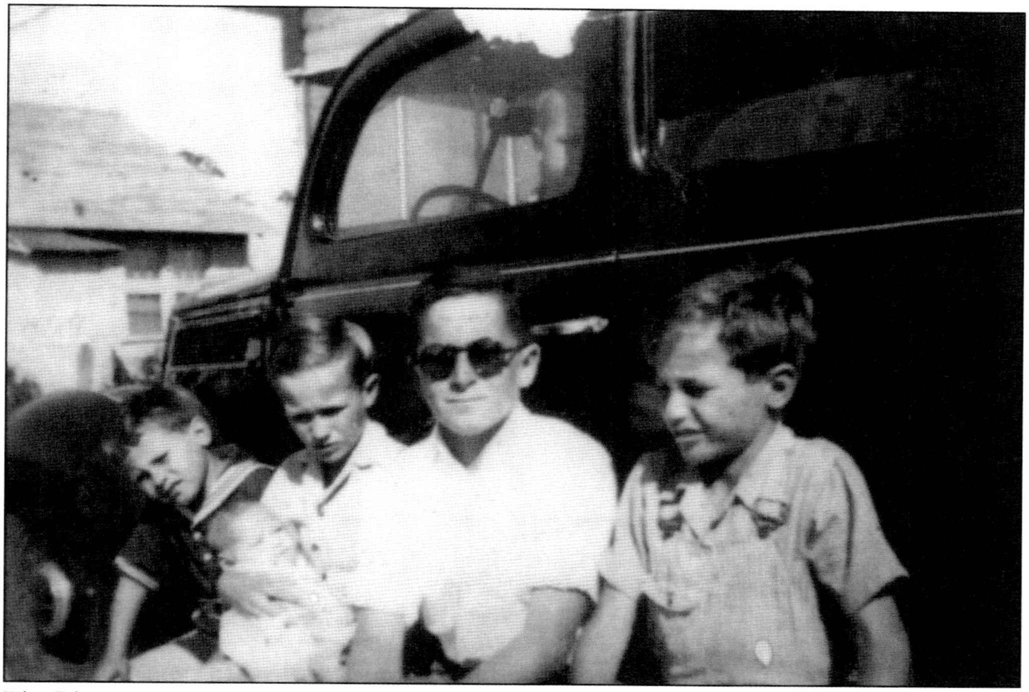

The Rhames family has been in this area for many years; the children were brought up during their early childhoods around the Overstreet and Wetappo Creek area. They first attended school in the schoolhouse at Overstreet. The children had to row a boat across the Wetappo Creek and walk about three miles through the woods to reach the school. The boys shown here sitting on a 1937 Ford are, from left to right, Tory, Lynwood, Amos, and Donald Jean Rhames. The baby is Carl, and in the window is Buck Rhames. (BR.)

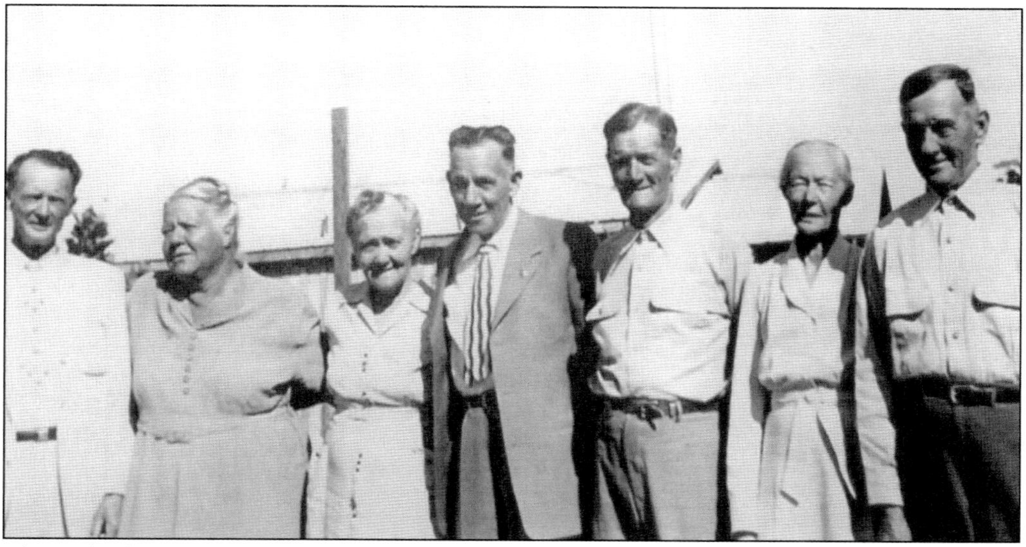

This is the family of Ira Ebenzer and Artemis (Anderson) Weeks. Pictured, from left to right, are Jeff, Essie French, Anna Woods, Kent, Jim, Jessie Armstrong, and Joe Weeks. Altogether, there were 12 children, but only 7 are pictured here. Those not shown are Mary, Rosser A., Ernest, John W., and Ebenzer Jr. Members of this family lived on in Calhoun and around the Gulf County area. (MWPR.)

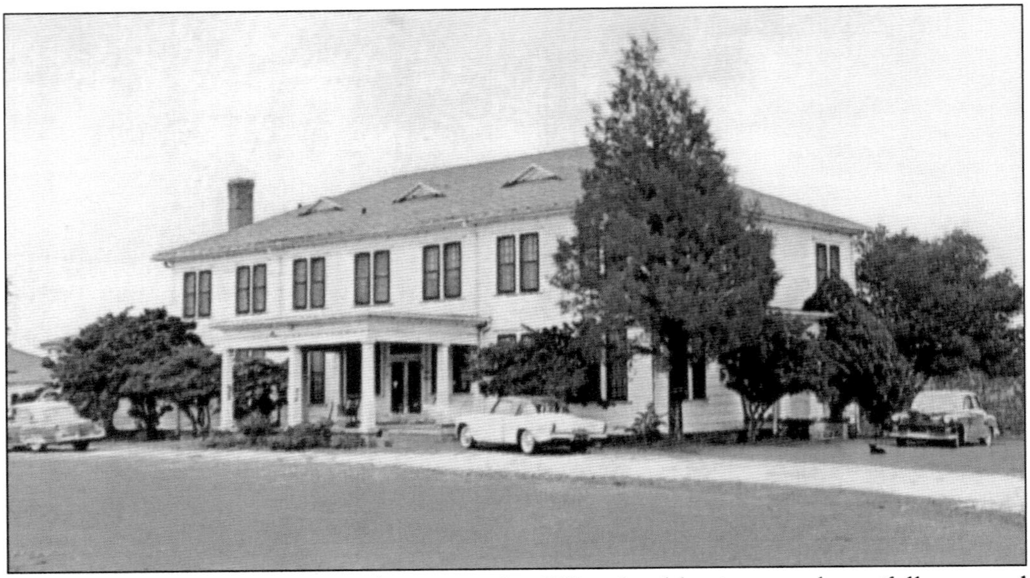

Covenant House, built in the mid-1920s north of Wewahitchka, is now a beautifully restored structure overlooking the Chipola River. Owners Mary Linda and Wibur Butts have turned this old building into a thing of beauty once more. The Covenant House has served as a crossroads in the lives of a number of people who needed a place to stay and heal their bodies, minds, and spirits. (WLIB.)

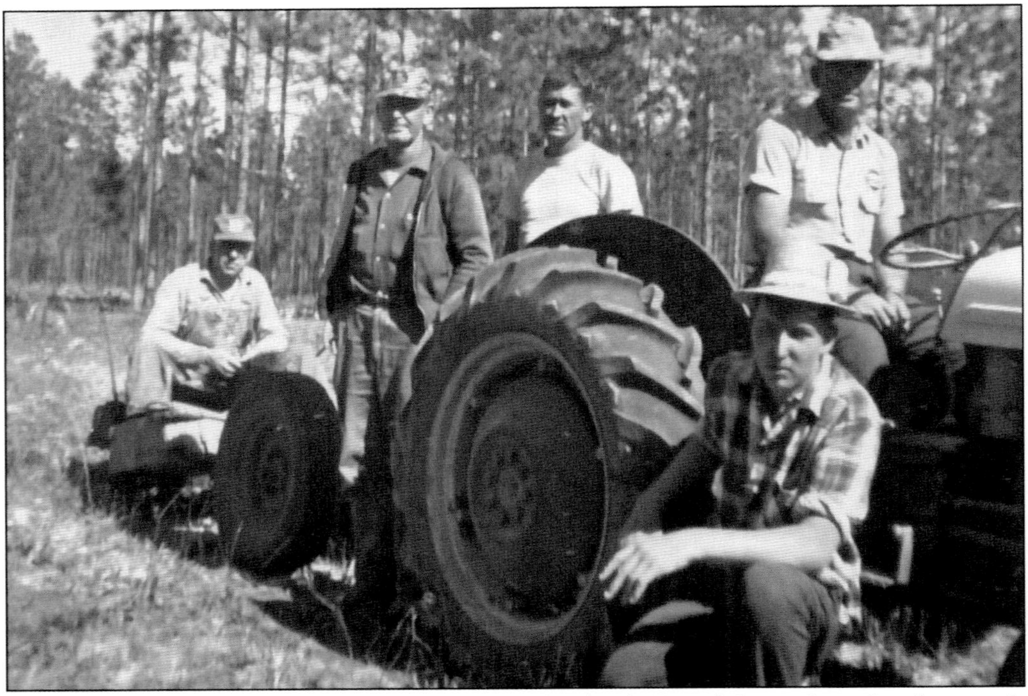

The Borders farm was located on Highway 386 at Early, Florida. From left to right in this photograph are Emory Robertson, Boyd, Bobby Lee, Haywood, and Lucky Borders. In 1965, Gil and Lynda (Borders) Shealey moved to this property, and they live there to this day. Lynda is the sixth generation on this land. (LBS.)

Nine

WEWA BEAUTIES

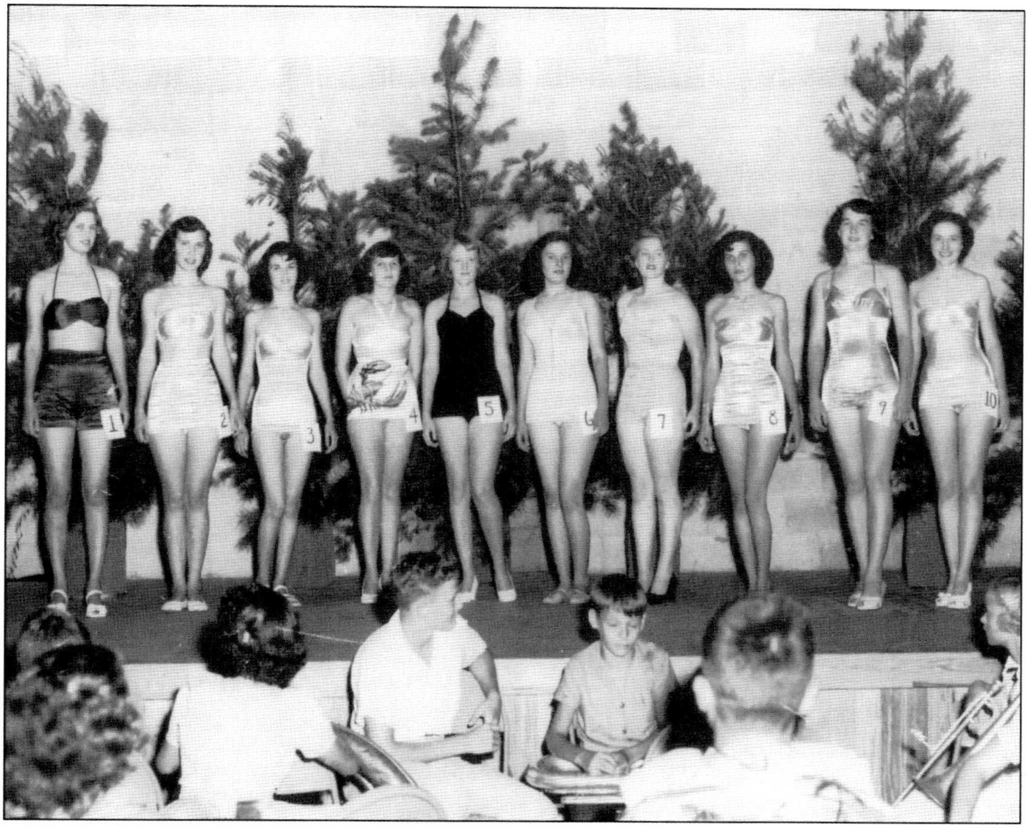

These Wewahitchka beauties are, from left to right, Carolyn Crutchfield, Peggy McGlon, Molly Joy Gay, Feraldine Hall, Geraldine Hall, Hazel Lamb, Vera Marie Gaskin, Lola Clem Hanlon, Myrle Summers, and June Hinton. The boys are Donald (left) and brother David (right) Taunton. The photograph was taken in about 1951 or 1952. (FHG.)

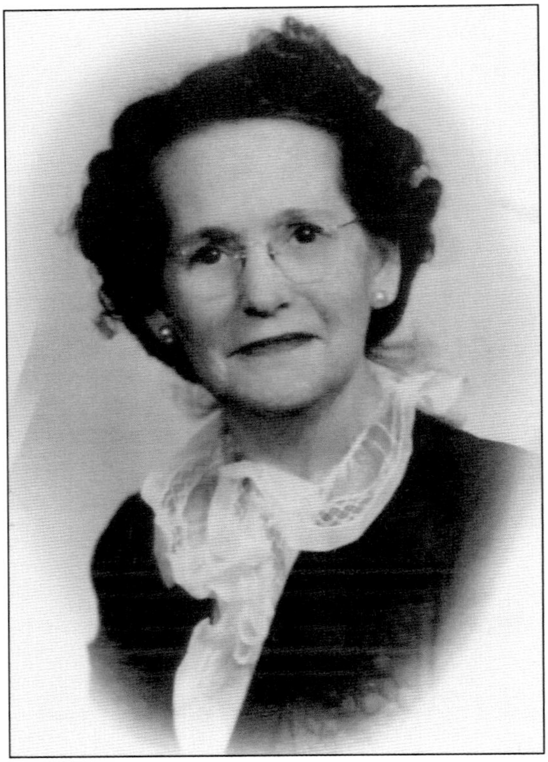

Annie Mae McMurria Connell, seen here in the early 1950s, was the wife of William Roy Connell. She was also the mother of one son, Alfred Jackson Connell, and three girls, Daisy Irene (now Brogdon), Ida Mae (now Lister), and Nell Louise (now Bandjough). Annie Mae was a longtime resident of Wewahitchka and died at the age of 92 in Blountstown. (BB.)

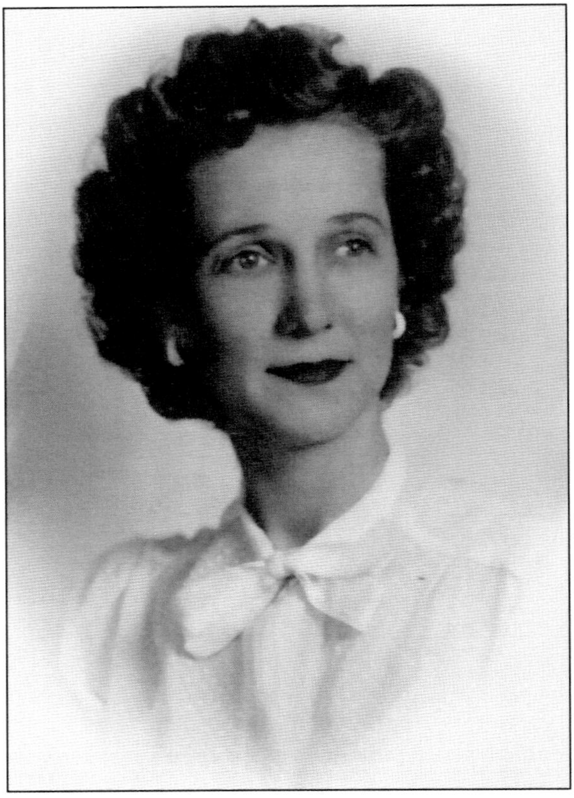

Ida Mae (Fleming-Lister) Connell, pictured in the 1940s, met and married Maxwell Woodrow Fleming Sr. while he was stationed at Tyndall Air Force Base in Panama City, Florida. They had one son, Maxwell W. Fleming Jr, who became the local dentist in Wewahitchka and passed away a few years ago. (BB.)

Nell Louise (Connell) Bandjough, youngest child of Annie Mae and William Roy Connell, graduated from Wewahitchka High School in 1936 at the age of 16 and went to secretarial school in Dothan, Alabama. Upon graduation, she was hired at the St. Joe Paper Mill as a secretary. She was working there when she met her future husband, Edward Bandjough, on a blind date arranged by one of her girlfriends. (BB.)

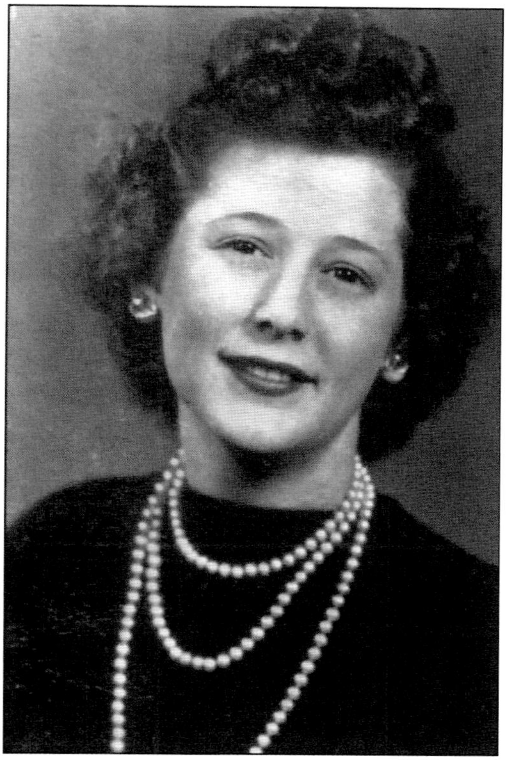

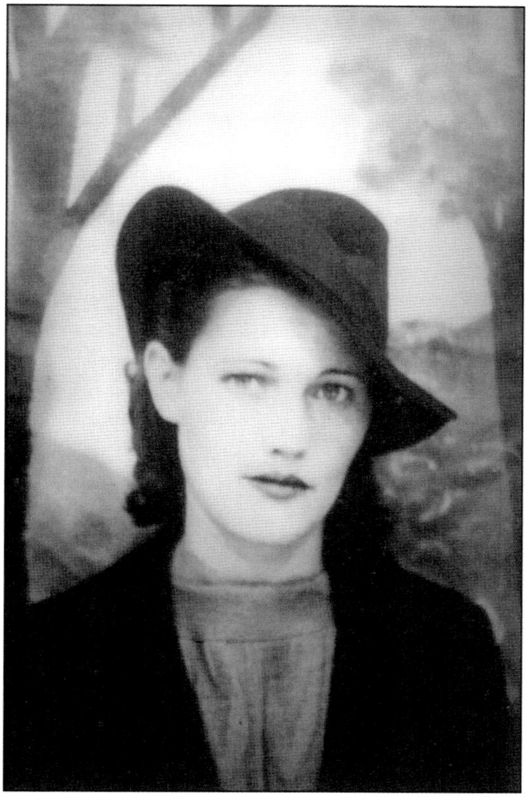

Ruth Bishop was the first nominee for the November 1999 "Wewa's Queen of the Century" article that David Taunton started for the *Gulf County Breeze*, Wewahitchka's locally owned and operated newspaper. At the time of this picture, Ruth was about 19 years old. She was born in North Carolina, and her family moved to Florida during World War I, where her father got a job in a shipyard. (JB and the *Gulf County Breeze*.)

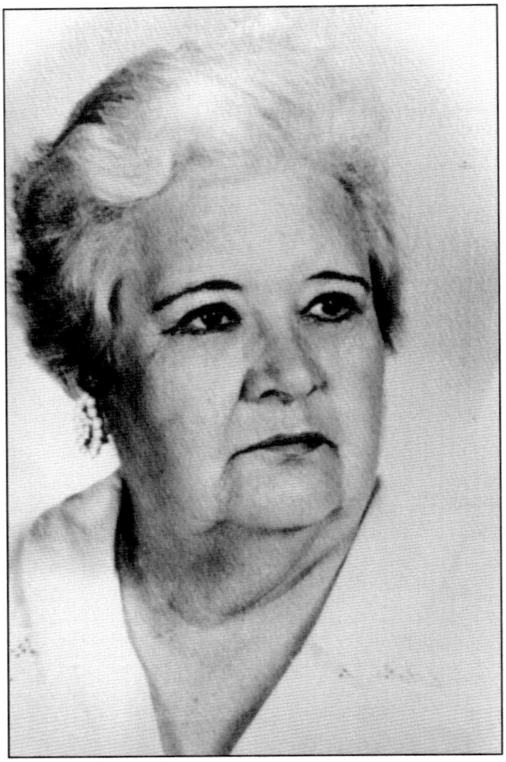

Irene Britt was Irene Briscoe until she married Sam Britt. She was a nurse, and she and Sam also operated a café in Wewahitchka. The Briscoe home was very large and faced Lake Alice. Irene was a member of the library board. This was in 1964 or 1965, when the Northwest Regional Library opened a branch in Wewahitchka. She worked long and hard to make the library what it is today. (WLIB.)

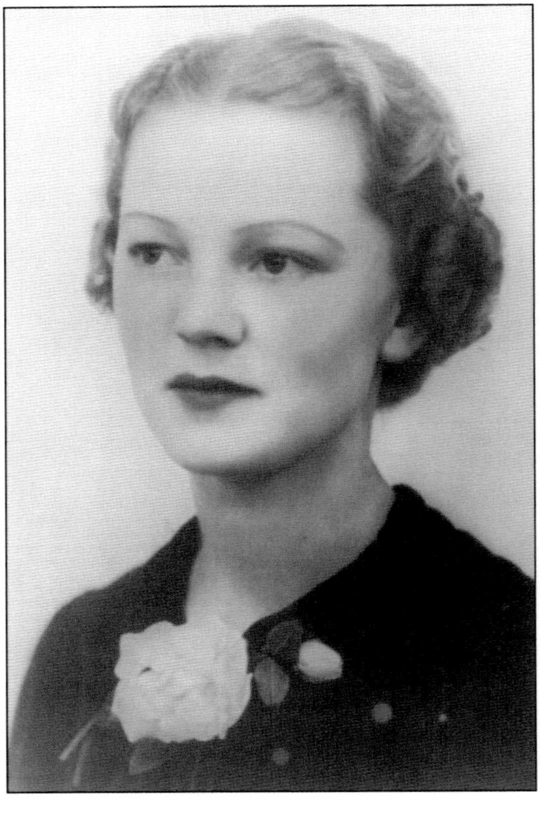

Marguerite (Byrd) Longshore was the daughter of Bramette (Farmer) and Tom Byrd. Marguerite and her sister Tweeta (Byrd) Gaskin were longtime residents of Wewahitchka, growing up around the Idlewood area. Marguerite was the mother of Jeannie (now Faulkner) and Carol Ann (now Childress). At the time of her death, she had been operating a store in Dalkieth. She passed away in September 1971 in the hospital in Port St. Joe. This photograph was taken around 1936. (CALC.)

Carmi Crutchfield was the youngest of a dozen children. When she was three, her mother died, leaving much for the children to do around the farm. Carmi and her sister grew up and married best friends; she married Walter Crutchfield, and her sister Stella married Buster Tillman. Carmi and Walter are the proud parents of two beautiful daughters; Carolyn Jean is in this photograph with her mother, and the other daughter, Mary Lou, is not pictured. (MG.)

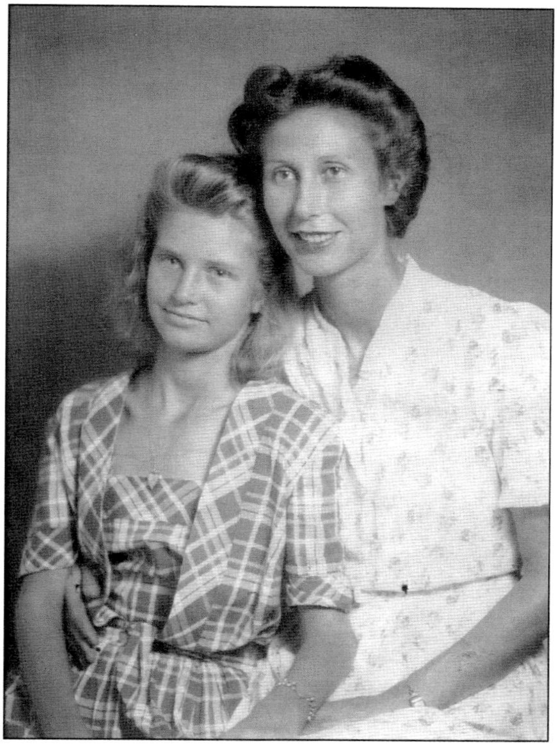

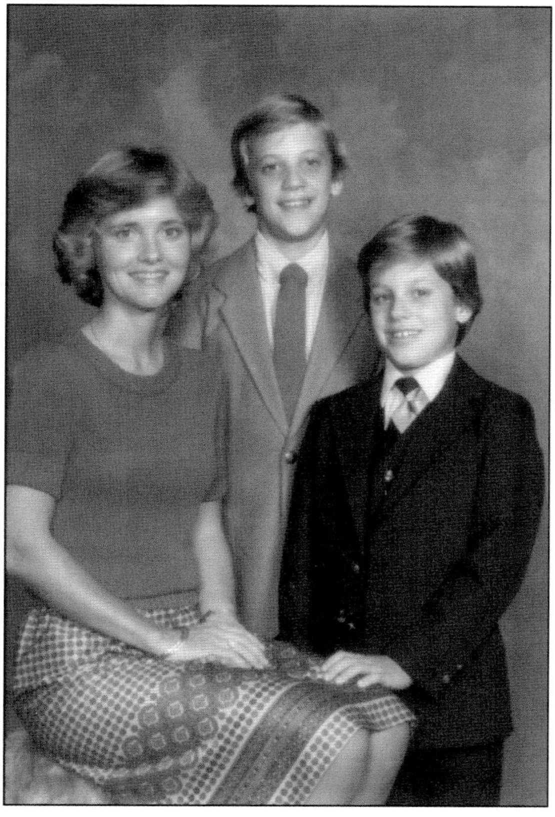

Barbara Britt Lister, shown here with her sons David (later Dr. Lister, DMD, left) and Daniel, was born to Frank and Kathleen Britt in 1951. Barbara was a beauty, but she was known to be even more beautiful inside. Her faith and her love of family and friends were beautiful to behold. Barbara was married to Bodie Lister for 46 years and thrived in her role as wife and mother. She passed away in 2014. (CBW.)

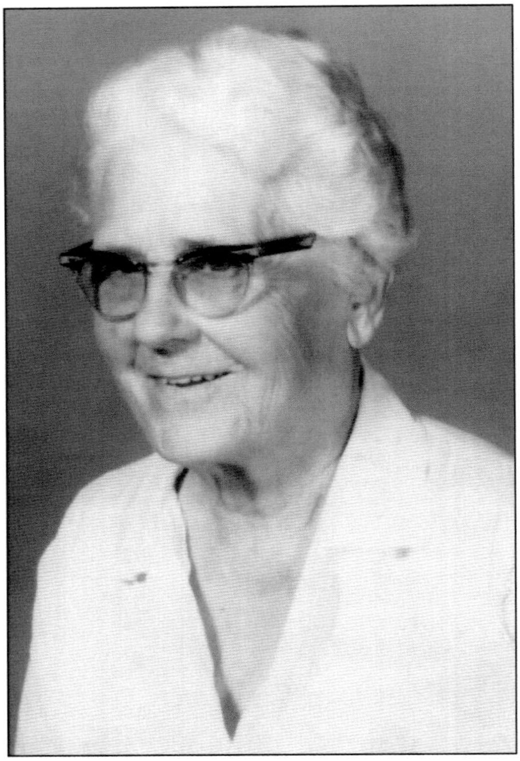

Everyone loved the cooking of Leitha (Meredith) Joines, a longtime resident of Wewahitchka and a retired school lunchroom lady. Joines, who died at the age of 82, was the mother of three daughters—Marie (now Costin), Nita (now Linton), and Amelia (now Busby)—and one son, Alfred. She also had 11 grandchildren and 12 great-grandchildren. (THL.)

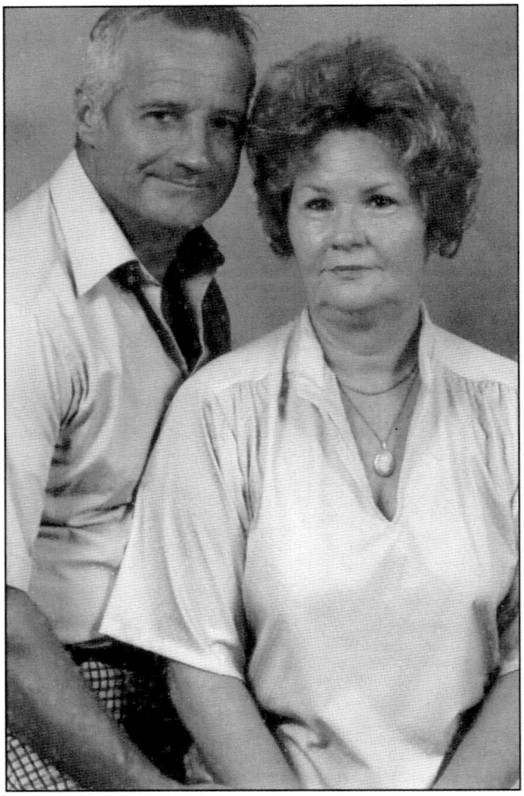

Joseph Louise (Gray) Larkins was the daughter of Daniel Joseph Gray and Maymie Ayers. Her paternal grandparents were Mary Hatcher, a full-blooded Creek Indian, and Levine Gray, who was Irish. Her maternal grandparents were Martha Jane Daniels and John David Ayers. Louise met Marvin "Buck" Larkins from Bristol, Florida, and they have 10 grandkids and 9 great-grandchildren. (WD.)

Doris Davis Lister is a real lady, sweet and kind with a very gentle soul. The youngest daughter of Ralph and Clemmie Davis, she moved with her family at the age of two (in about 1920) to Wewa, where her father was transferred as the mail carrier. In 1946, she married Floyd C. Lister, and today she still lives in the house that Floyd built for her on Lake Alice. (KLW.)

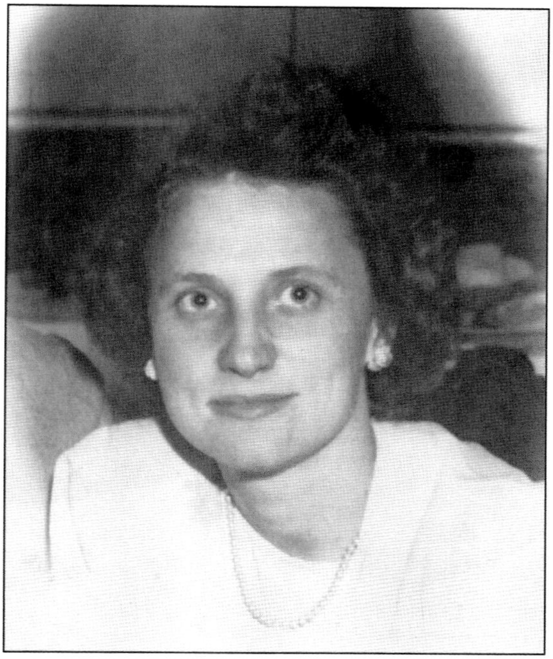

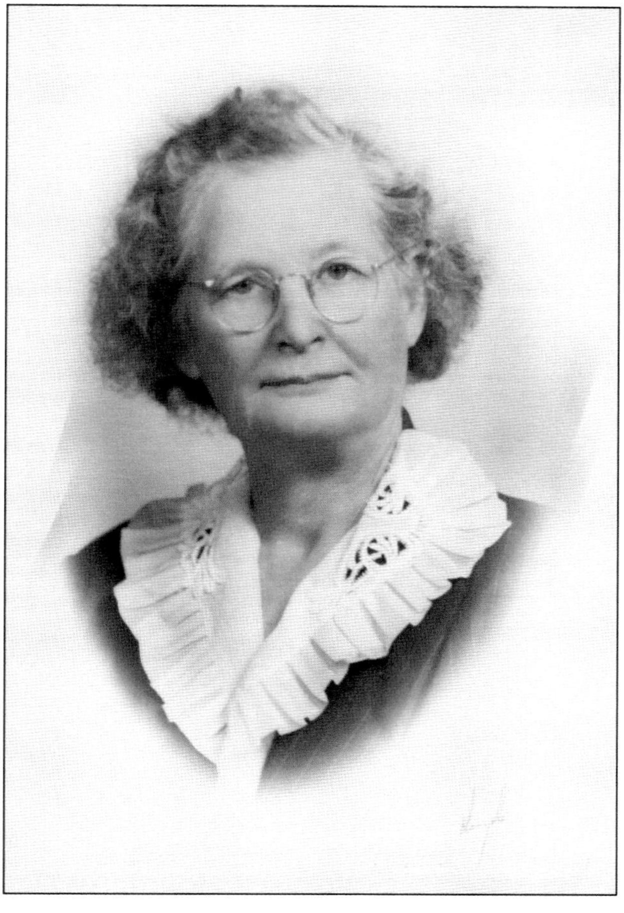

Mary Elizabeth (Gray) Lister was the wife of Henry C. Lister. She had one child with special needs, to whom she devoted her life, along with three sons, three daughters, eleven grandchildren, and one brother. She loved to fish—and did almost every day. (KLW.)

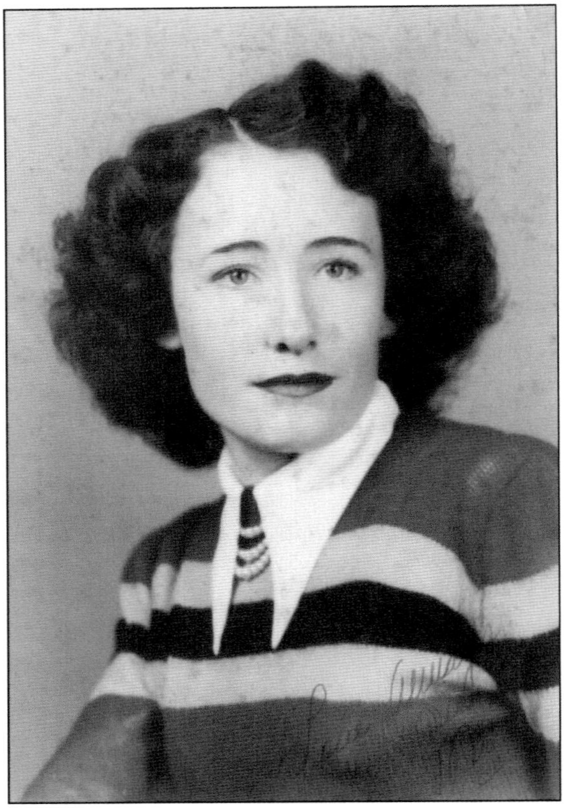

Mae Cunningham Murphy was born in the small town of Flag, Arkansas, to parents James and Ollie Cunningham. Mae met her future husband, Robert Murphy, in 1953 and moved to Florida. The pair came to Wewahitchka in 1956, and there, Mae's family was the focus of her life. Sadly, she passed away in 1998. Mae was truly a wonderful woman and blessed the lives of all who knew her. (RMP.)

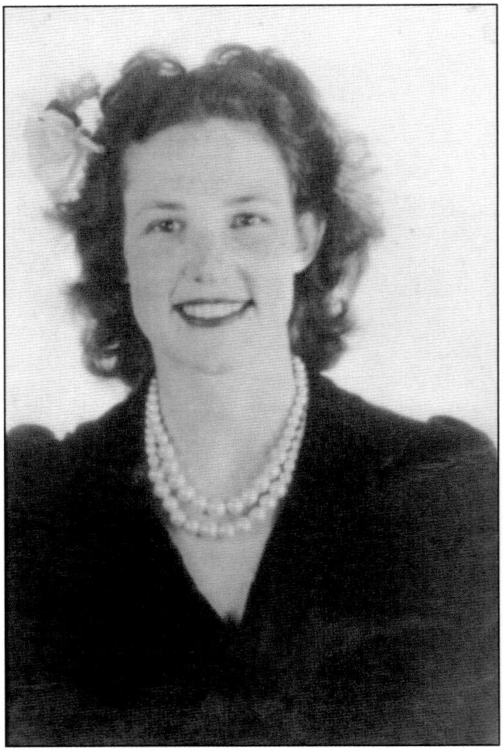

Minnie Ola McDaniel was the wife of Thomas McDaniel and the daughter of Ed C. and Emily Pridgeon. Minnie Ola was a very hardworking lady and a wonderful mother to Penny, Ward, Terry, Larkin, and Dixie. Everyone was always welcome at her house. She was beautiful, never met a stranger, and welcomed all, whether young, old, or in between. Friends and extended family were very important to her. She is pictured here around 1944. (PMM.)

Betty Jo (Batson) Rish grew up in Alabama. She met and married Bobby Rish while working for Southern Bell Telephone Company in 1950; two years later, they moved to Wewahitchka. By 1959, they had two girls and purchased property in Overstreet. Betty is so special because she is not only beautiful on the outside, but her beauty shines from within. The things she most values are her family and her more than 50 years of marriage. (DJRW.)

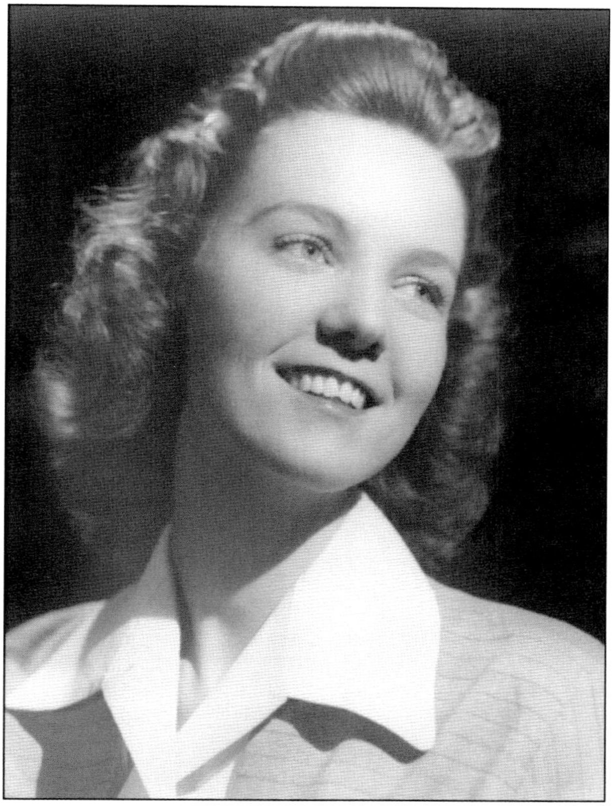

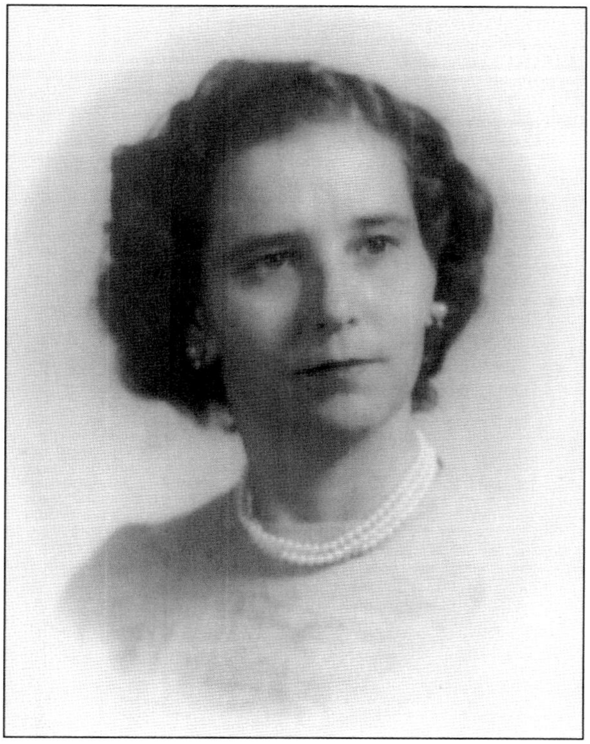

Dorothy Evelyn Martin Strength was the manager of Webb's 5 & 10 for many years. The store closed in 1966. She was known and loved by the community. She and Milton Strength married in 1954 at the Lake Alice Hotel. Milton and Dorothy reared three wonderful children—Johnny, Jimmy, and Sherry. (SSW.)

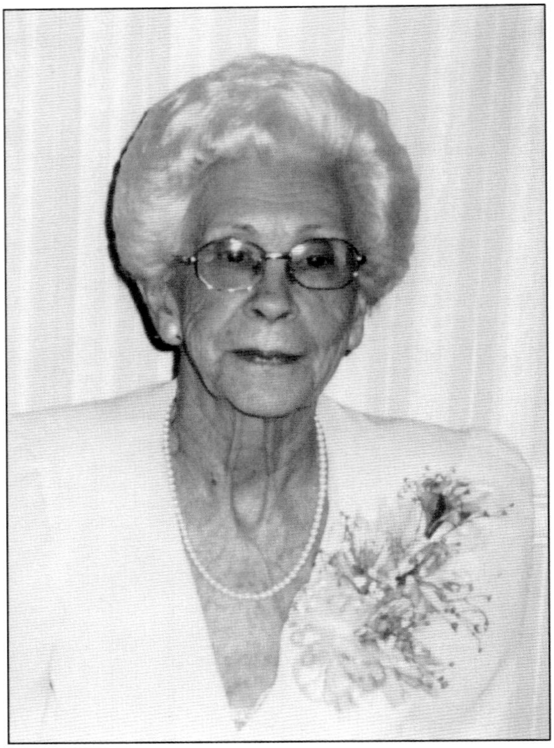

Stella (Birge) and husband Thomas "Buster" Tillman moved to Honeyville in about 1941. She was a faithful member of the Methodist church there. Stella was one of 12 children born to Thomas and Cecelia Birge in rural Holmes County during the Great Depression. She did a fantastic job raising five very successful Christian children. A fabulous and creative cook, she was a little lady with a big heart who had great Christian values. (KGT.)

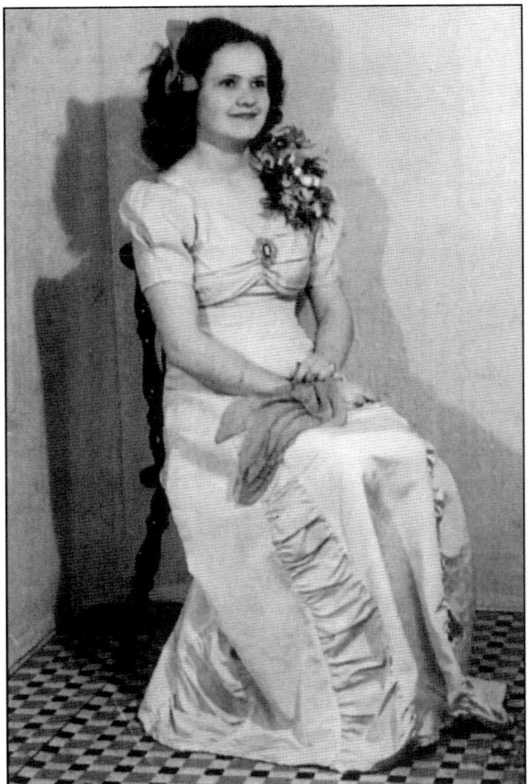

Gladys Inez (Walsh) Turner came from Washington County, Florida. She and Tommy Turner both worked in cotton mills in Alabama, where they met, and they were married in 1941. They moved to Wewahitchka and raised two boys. Gladys was known as a wonderful seamstress and was needed by all. Tommy worked for the local Gulf Coast Electric Co-Op before the Southport office was ever opened. (JJT.)

Nancy Artemis (Anderson) Weeks was the daughter of Willis Washington and Martha (Yon) Weeks. She married Ira Ebenzer Weeks in December 1880 in Alabama. They had 12 children; many married and their descendants live in the area today. Artemis is listed on the Eastern Creek Ancestor List, as is her brother Tom Anderson. She died in 1906, and her husband died in 1940. Both are buried in Jehu Cemetery in Wewahitchka. (MA.)

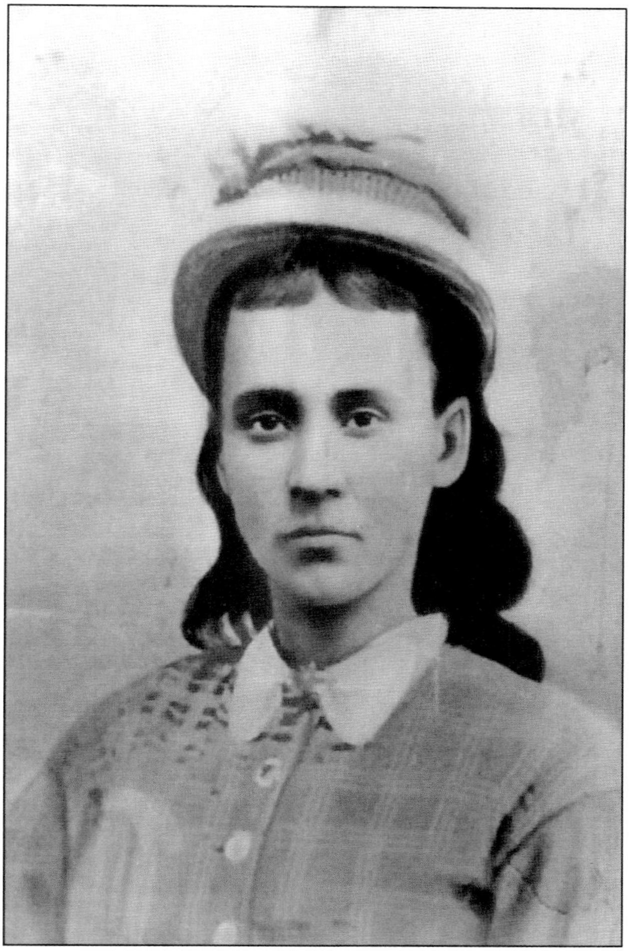

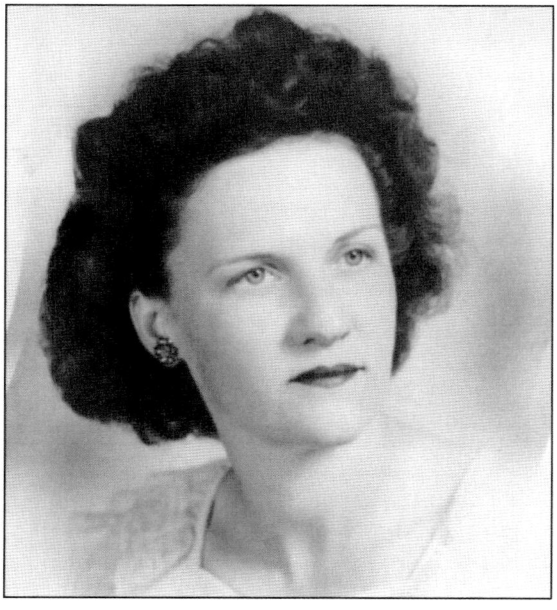

Burice (Davis) Gaskin Pridgeon was born in 1916 in DeFuniak Springs. She was the daughter of Ralph and Clemmie (Ford) Davis. Burice grew up to become a truly beautiful and charming young lady in Wewahitchka. This lovely mother had two girls—Betty Jo Garner and Kathay Tillman. Burice was the owner and operator of Burice's Beauty Shop. She had a humble Christian spirit, which showed in her love for her family. (KGT.)